D1241794

Work and Community

The Scott Bader Commonwealth and the Quest for a new Social Order

Fred H. Blum

Work and Community

The Scott Bader Commonwealth and the Quest for a new Social Order

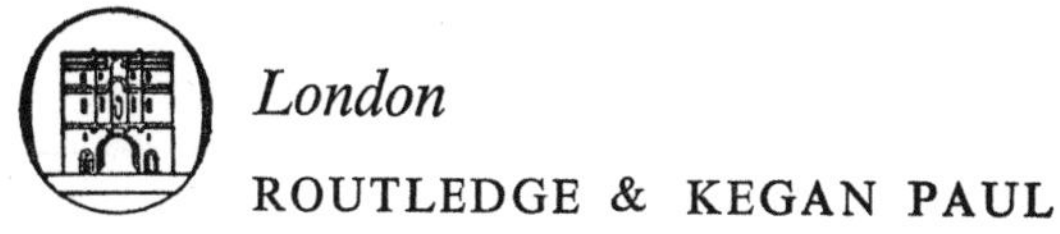

London
ROUTLEDGE & KEGAN PAUL

First published 1968
by Routledge & Kegan Paul Ltd
Broadway House, 68–74 Carter Lane
London, E.C.4

Printed in Great Britain
by Western Printing Services Ltd
Bristol

SBN 7100 6050 5

Contents

PART IV—THE COMMONWEALTH AND THE MEANING OF WORK

PART V—CONCLUSIONS

Acknowledgements

This book has been written as part of two interrelated projects: 'An Action-Research Project Dealing with the Significance of Religious Principles for the Industrial-Social Order' and 'New Modes of Participation in Work, a Cross-Cultural Study in Mental Health and the Organization of Work'.

The first project has been financed by a grant from the General Service Foundation in St. Paul, Minnesota and by funds given to the Social Order Committee of the Philadelphia Yearly Meeting of the Society of Friends. The Society of Friends received funds for this purpose from the Chace Fund in Philadelphia, the Hogle Foundation in Salt Lake City, and from individual contributions of a number of Philadelphia Quaker businessmen. I am particularly grateful to John M. Musser from the General Service Foundation for his interest and support and to David Richie and Robert D. Yarnall Jr. from the Friends Social Order Committee for their support and general sponsorship of the main project. I am also indebted to Dr. Loescher from the Chace Fund and to Lois and George Hogle for the interest they have shown. The second project has been financed by grants from the Research Foundation of the National Association for Mental Health in New York. I am particularly indebted to Dr. Malamud from the Research Foundation of the National Association for Mental Health and to Dr. Eberhard from the Institute of Mental Health in Bethesda for their understanding and help.

At Scott Bader where all the field work on which this book is based has been done, my colleague Roger Hadley and myself have found not only an open door but a friendly welcome and a personal trust which is rare in industry. Though I came from the very beginning on the understanding that I am free to publish what I want, responsible only to my own conscience, we had virtually a free hand on the premises of the firm and whatever information we have not obtained is due to our own shortcomings and to lack of time. My particular thanks go to Ernest

Bader, the Founder of the Scott Bader Commonwealth and Chairman of the Board of Directors, to his son, Godric Bader, Managing Director of the firm, and to Ted Nichols, the Secretary of the Commonwealth. We had virtually free access to their offices and had countless conversations with them. After we had submitted our basic findings, the Commonwealth also made a financial contribution to the main project, which has greatly helped us in carrying on and deepening our work.

We are greatly indebted to the people at Scott Bader who have given us generously of their time. A particular expression of gratitude is due to those who took part in interview-conversations lasting on average ten and sometimes up to twenty hours. Most of these interview-conversations took place in the evenings in the homes of the people. If an Englishman's home is his castle it is not a medieval castle surrounded by impenetrable walls but a place which has been readily shared with the stranger.

The field work on which most of the material in this book is based has been carried through jointly by Roger Hadley and myself. We first met when Roger Hadley, after completion of his degree at the London School of Economics, worked on the factory floor in one of the Philadelphia Quaker companies in which I undertook a study in 1956. Though the newly arrived worker did not fit into my 'sample', I interviewed him as a rare specimen of a British worker in an American factory. After completion of a post-graduate diploma in Industrial Sociology at Liverpool, Roger Hadley joined the work on the projects. I had begun the field work in 1959. Roger Hadley carried it on and completed most of the interview-conversations dealing with work and society besides working in the plant and doing a great deal of participant observation. He also did interviewing following a special schedule with a different group of people. In the autumn of 1961 I returned to the field, extending the interview-conversations to people's awareness of ultimate reality and probing additional dimensions of work and society. Group work which dated from 1960 to 1961 was also undertaken jointly by us.

The interpretation of the field material has been done quite independently by Roger Hadley and myself. Sharing a common concern for man's fate in modern societies we have different philosophical and, as I would say, theological views of life and hence different approaches as social scientists. This led to a quite unusual but very fruitful working relationship since we jointly use the 'data' collected by each of us. Roger Hadley, who is now a lecturer at the London School of Economics, is preparing his own study of Scott Bader as a separate publication.

I have greatly benefited from his own interpretations of the field material and from his observations, but I must assume full responsibility for the presentation of the material in this book and for the methods which I used in interpreting the material on which this book is based. Whenever important for an understanding of the results, I have compared my interpretations with his data.

In the preparation of this book I have also been greatly helped by my wife who helped in the interpretation of many questions and who did many of the cross-comparisons and innumerable checks on interview materials. Even my boys have done their little share by numbering interviews and transforming code sheets into beautifully coloured patterns.

Mrs. Peggy Smith typed the interviews with a supernatural ability to decipher my handwriting and Mrs. Rachel Ayre has typed the final manuscript. While I could not possibly mention the names of all those who have been helpful in different ways, I must mention the generous hospitality which Michael Rowntree extended to me while I was doing the field work at Wollaston.

FRED H. BLUM

This book is the first publication

of the

NEW ERA CENTRE

The Centre is concerned with the development of a new human consciousness and social order which has the whole man and hence the holy in man as its centre and circumference. The special focus of the Centre is on experiments to lead to a new understanding of the spiritual dimension in human life and its relationship to the present day problems of industrial man.

Introduction

I

We live at a time when cybernation is revolutionizing work and imposing upon us a fundamental re-evaluation of the problems of work. Opinions differ about the direction which this re-evaluation must take. Some people believe that cybernation will solve our major problems of work because it will eliminate monotonous and boring work while reducing 'necessary' working time to such proportions that leisure rather than work will be the central problem of tomorrow.

There is truth in such an attitude because the assembly-line of today and the problems which it poses are bound to disappear. But it is naïve to assume that we can replace Charlie Chaplin's portrayal of work in *Modern Times* by a film entitled *Paradise Regained* showing how cybernation once and for all has solved the problems of work.

The basic problems of work will remain (i) because work has a universal character and poses universal questions. Through work man partakes in the creative process and builds up cultures and civilizations. Work is a vital dimension of life—only by working does man become truly human. (ii) because the universal manifests itself throughout history in ever new forms. Indeed different times and cultures have 'defined' work in different ways and thus formulated problems typical of a given epoch in the history of man.

Cybernated technology is therefore best understood as an important manifestation of the evolution of human consciousness and the corresponding forms of social organization. To say this does not imply an acceptance of the naïve idea that technological developments determine the meaning of work and are an inescapable power determining man's fate. The basic values of a given social system—not technology as such—determine the meaning of work as well as the role of technology.

It is true that capitalism and certain forms of present-day socialism do indeed allow technology to be king. But this is a historically unique and not an unchangeable natural phenomenon of universal validity. The recognition of an evolutionary process much more complex than the simplistic evolutionary theories of the nineteenth century is, therefore, decisive for an understanding of our time.

II

In times when a social system is firmly rooted and functioning satisfactorily, a book concerned with problems of work could take the institutional framework of society for granted. But ours is not such a time. We live in an age of fundamental change and we are witnessing the dawn of new modes of human consciousness and of the corresponding forms of social organization. We live in an age in which a universal power is breaking through the crust of all established orders and creating the basis for the realization of new potentialities. At such times the experience of history does not limit any more the shape of things to come. Instead of looking back to learn from the past we must look in depth at the present to see the possibilities of tomorrow.

To be able to understand the problems of work at depth we must explore them in relation to the human as well as to the social order. The social order expresses the changing cultural definitions of work and the historically unique ways in which the problems of work present themselves. The human order expresses the human problems of work and 'contains' the universals which find divergent expression throughout history. Human universals are principles and forms of relationship which are not determined by a particular culture or historical epoch but which are shared by all men by virtue of being human.

The evolutionary process must be understood as a complex dynamic interrelationship between the social and the human order, as a process in which human universals find potentially an ever more articulate expression and in which ever new possibilities of development arise.[1] Suffice it to mention here that the

[1] In psychology the exploration of human universals has been part and parcel of the quest for trans-cultural standards of mental health. In political science

new conception implies a dynamic view of time and a clear distinction between the universal and the historical specific aspects of life. It also implies a new understanding of the relationship of facts and values. Not only the realized potentialities of yesterday must be considered as facts. The potentialities of today which are inseparable from values and which may or may not be realized in the future are also facts.[2]

III

A time in which the basic problems of work pose themselves in a radically new way makes much of traditional thought outmoded. In particular it makes the borderlines within the social sciences and between them, religion and theology obsolete. Instead of splitting life into fragments divorced from an underlying unity and wholeness we must deal with interrelated spheres of human experience in which man is involved in his totality. An integrative approach to man and society becomes, therefore, imperative. This book is an attempt to understand problems of work in such a perspective by relating a religious view of life to sociology and mental health.

To examine the problems of work in a religious perspective does not mean a sugar-coating of the harsh realities of industrial life with a sentimental piety. Nor does it mean to sanctify any particular—and hence historically unique—social order with

[2] Most social scientists still reason within theoretical models which are based on instantaneous time dimensions and do, therefore, not belong in the age of cybernation. Instead of having an understanding of the relativity of the social order seen in the light of universal principles and models of human relationship, they examine social institutions as data given at a moment of time. Hence we do not have an adequate theory of the development and dynamic evolution of society. An instantaneous time dimension reduces, furthermore, the concept of what 'is' or what is a 'fact' to the realized potentialities of yesterday. It excludes the potentialities which exist today and which may (or may not) unfold tomorrow.

---

it has been part of a renewed interest and re-valuation of the problem of natural law. In sociology, the interest in human universals has led to a deeper understanding of the dynamics of social change. In economics the problem of human universals is still hidden under the distinction of real and monetary terms.

the blessings of a universal eternal order. Quite the contrary: it means to penetrate to the depth of man and of the realities of life and to be able to see society as an evolving manifestation rooted in a universal ground of human experience. It means to grasp human life as a dynamic expression of Being and Becoming, to see man and life in their wholeness. Religion thus understood is an ultimate concern with Life, with the total human situation. There is an inner affinity between the whole and the holy since God always addresses the whole person.[3]

Wholeness is also an essential condition for mental health. In former times salvation and health were used interchangeably.[4] I am in no way proposing that we go back to this practice. I am opposed to an overhasty marriage between religion and mental health and we must be aware of the different dimensions of life to which they refer.[5] But we must also recognize their interrelatedness. In particular we must know that the Judeo-Christian understanding of man has been fully supported by recent developments in depth psychology. We are in the process of developing new standards of mental health which have variously been called 'democratic' or 'human' or 'non-violent'. They are democratic through their concern with the essential dignity of man; human because they deal with common human aspects of life; non-violent since all fragmentation of life does violence to man's development. The common characteristic of these standards is a concern with man's struggle for wholeness, for a balanced integrative development of his various potentialities and purposes within a creative relationship to a broadly conceived human community.

[3] The Old English word 'halig' is a derivative of the adjective 'heile', Old English 'hal' which means whole, hale. See *The Shorter Oxford English Dictionary*, Vol. I, p. 913. See also Chapter 14.

[4] See George F. MacLeod, *Only One Way Left*, Iona, p. 63.1.

[5] This poses intricate problems. The religious is a dimension in all spheres of life but it is in no way identical with any specific sphere. As an ultimate it has a quality which transcends all other spheres. But religion understood as an ultimate concern with the whole person must encompass a concern with the development of corresponding standards of mental health.

IV

The Scott Bader Commonwealth owes its existence to a deeply religious inspiration and is an attempt to realize these standards of mental health. It has wide significance because it deals with fundamental problems of work and is conceived as a model for a new social order. It directly challenges the existing society and the traditional forms of organizing industry.

The Commonwealth, established in 1951 and reorganized in 1963, is part of an as yet small movement to find new ways of organizing work. Some form of common ownership is the basis of this movement. New modes of participation in work are its essential expression.

This book deals with the significance of the Commonwealth for the development of a social order in which human values are central and whole people can grow. Neither the 'capitalist' countries of the West nor (as far as I know) the 'socialist' countries of the East have yet given adequate attention to the development of human potentialities. Both have comparable technological achievements but neither one has found a way to make man central in the organization of industry. The newly developing countries sometimes borrowing more from one, sometimes more from the other of these competing systems are too preoccupied with raising standards of living to give much thought to the meaning of work. The price which they will have to pay for industrialization which accepts a limited concept of technical efficiency is indicated in the human problems of the highly industrialized countries, and in their own difficulties to give a human meaning to the process of industrialization.

Whoever will make a real break-through by using modern technology within an organization which will foster men's development and make work part of a meaningful life will have found the key to the new order. Experiments at a smaller or greater extent are going on at various places. Yugoslavia is outstanding among 'socialist' countries, Great Britain among 'capitalist' countries.[6]

[6] I am counting Britain among capitalist countries in spite of the nationalization of basic industries. The dynamics of the British economy is

The Scott Bader Commonwealth must be seen in this perspective. Though being relatively small in size, it has the typical problems of industrial organization. It is large enough to offer a microscopic replica of the problems of our industrial civilization. Its experience with new ways of organizing work and new modes of participation is, therefore essential for all those concerned with the human problems of our time. No matter what aspect of life we are interested in, we must realize that in a rapidly industrializing world industry moulds the the basic attitudes of people. Our ability to realize the new potentialities inherent in the new stage of the development of human consciousness depends, therefore, upon our ability to reorganize industry.

What can we learn in this connection from the Scott Bader Commonwealth? What is its significance for the development of human potentialities? What problems arise as an attempt is made to make human values central in the organization of work? What guide-lines does this experience with new ways of participation give us in the quest for a new social order?

These are the fundamental questions with which this book is concerned.

We shall approach them by first giving the background information necessary to understand the experience of the first decade of the Commonwealth (from 1951 to 1963) in a wider perspective. We shall then explore the constitution of 1963 and examine the potentialities which it opens for a new understanding of the world of work. To be able to assess these potentialities and the problems of their realization we shall explore the basic influences determining the meaning of work. In this context we shall summarize the results of a study of people's experience of ultimate reality and of a secular society in so far as they are essential to grasp the fundamental problems of humanizing work. In a final section we shall draw the main conclusions as regards potentialities and realities, the new consciousness and social order.

---

determined by institutions and policies which have no peculiarly 'socialist' qualities. Essentially Britain is in the stage of welfare capitalism.

Part I

Background

Chapter 1

The Fellowship, the strike and the Commonwealth

I

In 1941, about two years after the beginning of World War II, a squadron of the German Air Force struck the industrial areas of London. 'The Blitz' had fraught new devastation. The factory of Scott Bader & Co. was destroyed. Within a month, the offices, located in the centre of the city, were also demolished. Foreseeing this possibility, Ernest Bader, founder and owner of the firm, had already located a place in the peaceful countryside of England. Shortly afterwards, factory, office and laboratories moved 70 miles north of London into a village called Wollaston.

Today a fast train from London will reach Wellingborough in a little over an hour. From there the road to Wollaston moves through gently rolling fields and meadows into the village where Scott Bader has made its home amidst many small shoe factories. Within about ten minutes we arrive at a beautifully designed and well-cultivated English manorial estate. As we enter through the main gate we see a solid, simple but well-proportioned seventeenth-century manor house now housing the offices of Scott Bader. To its left is the old coach house converted into laboratories. On our right we can see a striking modern building with a hyperparabolic roof and glass walls: the Commonwealth Hall. Its super-modern appearance blends well with the fourteenth-century spire of the church to the left. Immediately before us is a large circular lawn surrounded by flowers, shrubs and trees.

Another office building, located on the left side of the manor house, is first hidden from our view. It is a modern building, though more traditional than the Commonwealth Hall. Also hidden at first are the factory buildings which are behind a row of high trees bordering the lawn. As we walk by the Commonwealth Hall to the right we come to seven buildings housing five manufacturing plants, stores, a control laboratory and the works offices. Tanks containing raw materials and finished products are in the background and barrels with the finished product—liquid resin which is used for plastics—wait to be picked up near the factory gate.

World War II which made Scott Bader move to Wollaston was preceded by another historical event which marks the history of this firm: the great depression of the thirties. In 1929 on a famous black Friday the stock market crashed in New York. From there on the greatest depression in the history of Western industrialism spread like a series of irresistible waves all over the world. The 'law' of supply and demand seemed to have lost its equilibrating power. Prices fell. Production declined. People lost their jobs. In the United States 10 million people were unemployed when World War II started in Europe. In Great Britain about 3 million (over 20 per cent. of the insured work people) were what the British call 'redundant'. In Germany the Nazis were about to take over, riding high on the tides of hopelessness engendered by 6 million people unemployed—one in every three of those insured.

At the height of the depression, in 1932, Ernest Bader opened the factory in London which was to be destroyed a little less than ten years afterwards. A little more than ten years before having started the manufacturing, he had begun to sell the products of the Swiss and German chemical industries in Great Britain. In 1921 'Scott Bader & Co.' appeared for the first time as the name of a firm and as a duly registered company. Not too long before that time—just before World War I—Ernest Bader, born of Swiss peasant stock, had come to England. In 1920 he started a merchandising agency for celluloid. A year later, adding the maiden name of his wife to his own, 'Scott Bader & Co.' began its history.

II

In spite of its beautiful setting work at Scott Bader did at first not differ very much from that in other firms. Ernest Bader, a man with a very strong personality, had all the qualities typical of the individualist who could build up a flourishing business from scratch. The early part of his life could serve as a good illustration of Max Weber's *The Protestant Ethic and the Spirit of Capitalism*. In his business, as the 'entrepreneur', taking the risks and developing his ideas, he was 'the boss' in the traditional sense of the word. But he was a boss with a difference: underneath the Protestant Ethic which Max Weber described in his classic essay stirred another manifestation of spiritual power, the spirit of Christ as expressed in two important men: Leonhard Ragaz and Nicolai Berdayaev.

Leonhard Ragaz was a Swiss Christian Socialist for whom religion was 'not an opium but dynamite',[1] and Nicolai Berdayaev was an outstanding Christian existentialist to whom 'the spiritual world . . . is neither objective nor subjective but is pure activity and spiritual dynamics.'[2]

These undercurrents of spiritual affinity came to the surface when Ernest Bader started 'The Fellowship' in 1945, shortly after the end of the Second World War. The Fellowship as the name indicates emphasized fellowship and brotherhood. It was an organization open to all employees who accepted its principles and aims. It was based 'on the belief that the only sure approach to life is the Christian one, and that it applied not only to home life but also to working life, and to the organization of work'. The Fellowship hoped to give 'free play to the personalities of all our employees' and to provide opportunities for creative work. It aimed to give economic security so that 'members are to feel satisfied that in any circumstances in their lives, except that of gross misbehaviour, their material needs are provided for'. Regular meetings for worship were

[1] See Konrad Farner, *Fragen und Frager*, Christ and Marxist heute, Düsseldorf 1958, p. 41.

[2] See Nicolas Berdayaev, *The Destiny of Man*, London 1954, p. 9.

part of the Fellowship. Even a Fellowship hymn book was selected.[3]

As regards industrial relations, the Fellowship intended capital to 'become a trust in the hands of those who control it, and all decisions (to be) made with a view, not to monetary profit, but to their effect on the lives of the persons concerned'. It was hoped that such a 'radical change of approach' would substitute 'co-operation in a common aim, i.e. Christian service' for the existing conflict between capital and labour.[4]

It is not accidental that the fellowship arose when World War II had come to an end. Ernest Bader, deeply moved by the experience of the war, reflected about the praise given to the soldiers who gave their lives for freedom and he wondered whether war was necessary to allow people to render service. He became a convinced Quaker and pacifist and chose England as the country where he wanted to live rather than Switzerland partly because of the freedom it accorded to the conscientious objector. He was searching for a way to render service in peacetime and to open up to others the same possibility through finding a new way in industry. 'I wanted to show a true service to people in a way I could carry through in business' was his comment when asked why he started the Fellowship.

The Fellowship lasted less than two years. In 1947 it was terminated because it did not have the desired results. Ernest Bader, committed to experiment with new ways, searched for a better way to realize its fundamental ideas. He felt that it was necessary to change the actual organization of work which the Fellowship had touched only accidentally. He also felt a need to make it more 'acceptable' to the workers who resisted his pacifism and were, to put it mildly, lukewarm about attending worship services. They were sceptical in general and particularly about 'religion'. To them, 'religion' meant the church, and

[3] *The Fellowship Hymn-Book*, published for the National Adult School Union and the Brotherhood Movement, Inc., London 1933.

[4] The objectives of the Fellowship were summarized in eight points which included making 'our contribution as a body towards the establishment of a healthier society', the production of commodities of high quality, at a fair price.

traditional beliefs which had lost meaning for them. They were also sceptical about the somewhat 'disembodied spirit' which the Fellowship represented. They came to Scott Bader to work and—in spite of its pronouncements—the Fellowship changed little in the way in which they worked.[5] Their general suspicion of anything new reinforced these feelings.[6]

III

The interim period between the end of the Fellowship and the beginning of the Commonwealth saw a unique event in the history of Scott Bader: a strike in November 1948. As the only strike in the history of the firm, this was an unusual event. Also unusual were the major causes of the strike. First, a general sense of uneasiness resulting from dismissals. This is a 'natural' reason for a strike in a capitalistic society. The second factor, the expectation that some form of self-government would be given to the firm soon, is quite unusual. This expectation created some unrest and a desire to be self-reliant by standing up to the boss. The strike dramatizes, therefore, the first stage of the period of transition from an old world to a new world. Mistrust and animosity rooted in the capitalist organization of work were present. But there was already the germ of something new.

The strike showed that subsequent developments at Scott

[5] The difficulties of establishing many years later how people felt at the time of an event are tremendous. Even if people had a perfect memory, the experience of a past event is bound to be different today from when the event happened. Keeping these considerations in mind we may say that many people seem to have experienced the Fellowship as something well-meant but neither very congenial nor very important. Except for a small group of devotees it seemed to have aroused neither strong positive nor strong negative feelings among the majority of the people.

[6] Clear traces of suspicion could still be found over a decade after the foundation of the Commonwealth. Many people were not able to trust something good because they were so accustomed to something bad. Suspicion poses problems which must be met by anybody who pioneers something new in industry. In Austin, Minnesota, for example, when George A. Hormel introduced the annual guaranteed wage, the first reaction was 'Where is the catch?' 'What is he up to?' Suspicion is indeed one of the first strong emotions with which all those are faced who attempt to create something new in industry.

Bader were not built on some unusually fertile ground atypical of industry; quite to the contrary these developments were rooted in a soil typical of a hundred years of Western industrialism.[7] As we will see throughout this book, the Commonwealth dealt with basic problems of industry as they present themselves in Britain as well as in the United States.

There are indeed remarkable similarities between the problems arising on both sides of the ocean. Jay C. Hormel, for example, the president of the Hormel Company in Austin, Minnesota, though he never reorganized work as radically as did Ernest Bader, was an American industrialist who had greatness in his own right. He stood one day in front of striking workers who had taken over his plant and asked the National Guard to save his property. His response to this experience was the most significant annual wage plan in the United States.[8] Ernest Bader's response to the failure of the Fellowship and to the strike was—the Commonwealth. Like J. C. Hormel, he made his experience of failure the beginning of something new rather than merely the end of an epoch.

IV

Reflecting about the failure of the Fellowship, Ernest Bader 'came to the conclusion that the fault was really mine in so far as I had not acted on my own belief that those who constitute the essential element in a business should have equal status with the owner'. To achieve this he accepted the principle of common ownership and gave everybody a say in the conduct of the business. In 1951 he transferred 90 per cent. of his shares to a body called the Commonwealth.[9] What the Fellowship failed to do was accomplished: a radical break was made with the

[7] Without attempting to evaluate here how typical the people of the Commonwealth are as regards industrial Britain and Western industrialism we may say that there are many fundamental similarities of experience, though the people of the Commonwealth are moulded by the peculiarity of a specific region in England.

[8] See my book *Towards a Democratic Work Process, the Hormel-U.P.W.A. Experience*, Harper, New York, 1953.

[9] The 10 per cent. remaining in the hands of the Founder Members still exercised veto power. For further discussion of this question see Chapters 5 and 12.

traditional organization of work. From here on the work community as a whole rather than a few individuals benefited from the growth and development of the firm.[10]

Though the Commonwealth has undergone considerable development, the fundamental ideas and basic principles have not changed since its inception. Communal property is the ground on which a new system of democratic integration has been built. Divestment of the power held by those who traditionally controlled industry is complemented by the assumption of entirely new responsibilities by those who have so far played a subordinate role in the organization of work. These are the basic principles on which the Commonwealth is founded. Addressing themselves to industry in general, the founders of the Commonwealth called for a 'self-divestment of privilege and power on the part of the present employers and shareholders, and on the part of the employees the acceptance of their full share of responsibility for the policy, efficiency and general welfare of the undertaking'.[11]

In accordance with these twin principles the new organization of work makes those who have authority responsible to the whole work community and encourages active participation from every member of the community. Mutuality of control and responsibility animated by a spirit of respect for the individual person and care for one's neighbour are the watchwords of the new organization. The basic Commonwealth Memorandum states: 'By establishing Common-ownership in industry we mean such a fundamental reconstruction so that undertakings are communally owned and co-operatively run, and show that teamwork which is neither collectivism nor individualism, depending on leadership founded on approval rather than dictation within a framework of freedom of conscience and obedience to God'.[12]

10 In case of a sale of the firm all the money must be given for charitable purposes.

11 See *Memorandum and Articles of Association of the Scott Bader Commonwealth Limited, Incorporated,* the 1st day of June, 1951, p. II. From now on this document will be called '*Memorandum Commonwealth 1951*'.

12 See *Memorandum Commonwealth 1951*, pp. I and II.

The founders of the Commonwealth conceived the new kind of organization as part and parcel of a 'fundamental reconstruction', a move towards a 'peaceful society', an 'essential step towards a true Christian Industrial and Social Order'. They expressed the belief 'that we must obey the simple laws of Christianity in our daily lives, and present an alternative to a war-based capitalist economy on the one hand and to Communism on the other'.[13] The new industrial and social order envisaged is expected to establish new kinds of relationships to the outside world as well as within the firm. 'A socially responsible undertaking . . . is part of the whole national and international community, and as such it has responsibilities which extend far beyond its factory walls.'[14]

The Commonwealth attempts to broaden the meaning of work by making it a service to a broader community. Moreover, it aims to develop a new dynamic of social change. The traditional ways of change can best be understood within a range of opposites: in one extreme the only responsibility is given to the individual, and society is supposed to be transformed as individual people change. At the other extreme organizational change induced by the government is expected to bring about an improvement of individual character. The Commonwealth is based on a different conception: a group of individuals must take upon themselves the burden of change by changing their own outlook on work and life in the light of a vision of a new social order and thus help to bring about a radical transformation of society as a whole.

The new society conceived as a peaceful society requires (i) that war be abolished as a means of settling conflict between nations and (ii) that the social order of each nation be 'nonviolent' in the sense of striving towards justice.[15] 'In accordance

[13] *Ibid.* p. I.

[14] *Ibid.* p. I.

[15] The Founders stated: 'Since in our time the seeds of war go deeper into the life of the nations than ever before, and since not only the power politics of Governments, but also the profit-seeking of capitalists and the pressure for higher wages on the part of the employed are amongst the causes of war, we all need to walk humbly and to ponder over the problem of conducting our individual and corporate life in accordance with the demands of peace against

with the well-known testimony of the Quakers and other Christian Pacifist movements against war, we reaffirm that among the requirements of a peaceful society is included a reconstruction without participation in industrial strife and international war; and a refusal to take an active part in re-armament.'[16]

V

World War I, the Great Depression of the thirties, World War II, the quest for a New Way—these are the events which mark the history of Scott Bader and these are the events which mark the twentieth century.

Unique is only the fact that the Commonwealth was founded by Ernest Bader out of a deep religious conviction, an awareness that the ground of all being is love, and out of a search for community in a world of strife, isolation and destructive conflict. He had the rare courage and conviction to experiment with a new way in industry and has brought to life what many people in industry would like to bring. In doing so, he was guided by broad inspiration rather than specific directions. Essentially the idea of the Commonwealth had its roots in his own experiences and in his own spontaneous imagination. It was not a product of research and investigation but of an intuitive awareness of life. Indeed Ernest Bader is a man of an intuitive wisdom which puts to shame the learned knowledge of many people.

In saying this we have already transcended what is peculiar and unique in the origins of the Commonwealth since spontaneous imagination and intuitive wisdom are the work of the Spirit in us. This spirit is alive in Ernest Bader and underlies the

[16] See *Memorandum Commonwealth 1951*, p. II.

---

the current of a society war-based between Capitalism and Communism.' (See *Memorandum Commonwealth 1951*, p. I.). These sentences portray a society which has the seeds of destructive conflict embedded in every fibre of its being. Explicit reference is made to the problem of violence in the challenge to ask ourselves 'to what extent violence resides in the demands we make upon the earth's resources and the available new materials by reason of our self-indulgent existence'. (*Ibid*. p. I.) This query is complemented by a challenge to examine 'What is to be our personal contribution to the realization of peace.' (*Ibid*, p. II).

decisive act on which the Commonwealth is founded: the surrender of that power which capitalism gives to a few and denies to the many.

What historians call 'capitalism' is a complex economic system which has undergone constant changes and development during the past 100 years. It is, furthermore, a word loaded with emotional overtones of sympathy and antipathy, fear and expectation. For better or for worse, it sums up the most decisive forces shaping our century. The economic and political developments which led to the two world wars and the great depression are inseparable from the conflicts and achievements of capitalism and its unwanted offspring, communism. The Commonwealth, too, searching for a new way in industry, is inseparable from the human situation resulting from the social forces activated by capitalism. It is, therefore, imperative to see the Commonwealth as part of these historical forces.

Chapter 2

Capitalism and the Christian Social Testimony

I

Capitalism, like all social systems, is a historically unique attempt to solve the universal problems of work. Ultimately these are problems of interpersonal relationships because the work necessary to sustain a person is divided among a group of people. When we ask ourselves how many of the goods and services which we enjoy daily are the fruits of our own labour we get an idea of the widely divided and minutely differentiated work processes to which we owe our daily bread and general well-being. But whatever is divided in parts must be integrated to form a viable whole. The economic history of mankind could be written by describing different ways of differentiating the work tasks to be performed, and of integrating the divided parts into unified economic systems.

Exchange, markets and money are universal forms through which the process of differentiation and integration is mediated. They have found the most divergent expressions throughout history. In their successive manifestations we can discover a universal law of development. Just as every higher form in the organic life process implies more finely differentiated organisms —we need only compare a mammal with the one-celled *amoeba* —so higher forms in the evolution of work are more articulately differentiated and at least potentially they are integrated at higher levels.

At each stage in this evolutionary process a structure of values and of power arises. Power is used to make the decisions necessary to solve the universal problems of work. Values come into operation whenever choices between alternative means and goals are to be made in the decision-making process.

The power and value structures within which work takes place can best be understood as a framework within which people enter into mutual relationships. The process of differentiation and integration of work is but one aspect of a process in which ever new forms of human relationships are being developed.

The fundamental problems which this universal process poses are problems as to the kind of relationships between man and man which arise as the divided parts are brought together in a higher unity; problems as to the nature of the human bonds which are created as work becomes differentiated and integrated: problems of the moral bonds which unite men and the conflicts which separate them. Fundamental are problems of agreement, of ways of reaching decisions on the ethical standards necessary to determine who should do what work, receive what reward and how work should be done. Ultimately these are problems of how love and justice enter man's consciousness and outlook on life—to what extent and in which way they shape man's world view.

II

Every social system which has the power to mould the attitudes of generations of people has brought to life dormant potentialities. Capitalism was able to overcome the medieval world view because it freed the potentialities of a self-reliant individual and oriented his powers towards a transformation of the world. This break-through derived its ultimate power from a universal quest to render service to God. Only the acceptance of this central tenet of the medieval world-view made it originally possible to create the radically new world-view which culminated in capitalism. In saying this I do not espouse an 'idealistic' interpretation of history. I merely point to a major factor in the development of capitalism.

The basis on which the whole edifice of capitalism has been built is a consciousness of a harmonious natural order. This is the central meaning of Adam Smith's 'unseen hand' which brings order out of chaos of literally millions of unrelated actions of individuals. Adam Smith's 'unseen hand' is the hand of God as visualized by the eighteenth-century philosophers of the Heavenly City—a city which emerged from the same universal ground of Being as did the City of God of St. Augustine.

It is true that the philosophers of the heavenly city were men of the enlightenment to whom the medieval world appeared as the dark age. But the god of the enlightenment was reason, a universal holistic concept which meant wisdom, uniting thought and feeling. It expressed itself in self-interest whose original meaning was derived from the latin word *interesse* which means 'to be among', to share, to be related to each other. Self-interest was not an egocentric striving of the individual. It was a 'principle of unity' through which the individual was integrated into the harmonious laws of nature and society. When the philosophers of early capitalism elevated the principle of self-interest to the central ethical principle, they expressed faith in the possibility of realizing the heavenly city provided men were to follow what they truly shared with each other, what gave the deepest meaning and the highest purpose to their lives.[1]

The concept of balance which permeated capitalism is a universal expression of a harmonious order rooted in reason and self-interest. Granted that the balance sheet, a balanced budget and the balance of payments were historically unique expressions of balance. But only because of their universal roots could they gain such power over the minds of men and become the central criteria for economic policy.

Markets too are universal forms of organization. They are means to facilitate exchange. Capitalism developed them to such an extent that a capitalist economy has often been called a market economy. But markets as such are no more peculiar to capitalism than is money which has the universal function of serving as a means to facilitate exchange. Here again, capitalism has developed a universal function to a hitherto unknown extent and created a 'money economy'. Capitalism developed for the first time a consistent system of monetary accounting and thus enhanced the universal function of profits, namely to serve as indices whether a given task has been adequately performed, whether some surplus was 'left over and above' what

[1] See W. E. Lecky, *The Rise and Influence of Rationalism in Europe*, New York 1955, partic. pp. 222ff.

has been 'put in' to assure growth and development. Finally, the 'law' of supply and demand is a universal formulation of a basic adjustment mechanism bringing two forces into equilibrium—into balance.

The neo-classic temple as the architectural form for the stock exchange in New York's Wall Street and the City of London symbolizes the underlying concept of balance and the power of the universal on which the original edifice of capitalism was built. The neo-classical economists too have built their whole system of thought around the concept of equilibrium and balance. For them economics was the queen of the sciences and carried the sanction of absolute truth. It claimed to express the true laws of society which gave content and orientation to the principle of self-interest. In thus building a system of thought based on a universal truth the neo-classical economists have not only performed an impressive logical task. They have also turned the eyes of the faithful from those historically unique features of capitalism which are more problematic than its universal features—and which are essential for an understanding of capitalism as a decisive force in the history of man.

III

The historical uniqueness of capitalism may be expressed in five propositions: (i) the combination of formal freedom with a basic dualism in power and responsibility, (ii) the all-embracing nature of the market mechanism, (iii) the reduction of social relationships to the contractual freedom and the practically absolute sovereignty of the individual, (iv) the use of profits as an ultimate criterion to decide which human needs should be satisfied, and (v) the use of the balance of payment as an absolute reference point and of gold as an absolute yardstick.

The combination of formal freedom with a basic dualism in power and responsibility is one of the most decisive aspects of capitalism. Freedom was formal because the state determined only the framework within which people could act—particularly by the guarantee of private property and individual contracts. The state did not regulate the content and the purpose of action.

It neither determined prices nor wages, nor did it regulate markets. It determined only the formal rules of the game.

There is no doubt that formal freedom coincided in many ways with actual freedom and advanced the cause of freedom. But to realize fully the freedom given by capitalism a person had to own capital or be able to acquire it. For most people formal freedom was combined with an inequality of power and/or of money. Poor and rich were given equal rights to sleep under bridges. But not everybody was endowed with the same means though formally everybody had the same opportunity.

The inequality in power and money found its strongest expression in the sphere of work. Those who had power organized work and made the basic decision about work—inasmuch as the market permitted them to do so. Those who did not have power worked in a hierarchical and authoritarian organization or waited at the factory gates. Once asked why he did not hang up a sign 'No men wanted' when there was no need for more people, the owner of a factory said: 'We want the men inside to know that there are enough people waiting outside to take their jobs.' The fear thus instilled was considered an essential ingredient of the discipline of a factory.[2]

By speaking about 'the labour market' we have already referred to the second characteristic of capitalism, the all-embracing nature of the market ruled by competition. There have been markets for the products of work ever since men gave up barter. There have also been markets for land. And there have been markets for the purchase and sale of unfree people—of slaves. But only capitalism developed an all-embracing market system, including the services of formerly free people. Only capitalism applied the principle of competition to men, machines and nature alike, transforming all of them into commodities to be bought and sold.[3]

This was only possible because formal freedom of contract was combined with inequalities in power and money. A free

[2] It even played an important role in so-called scientific management. See p. 9. F. W. Taylor, *The Principles of Scientific Management* reproduced in *Scientific Management*, New York, 1947, p. 69.

[3] See Karl Polyani, *Origins of our Time, The Great Transformation*, London, 1945, esp. pp. 73ff.

person who has money-power does not sell his services on the labour market. He stays by himself or works in association with others. Such material freedom must be distinguished from contractual freedom. Material freedom presupposes that the *relationships* between people are subject to a code of ethics. Capitalism borrowed from the Judeo-Christian tradition a few principles, but on the whole these principles were limited to the behaviour of the individual who in principle was absolute sovereign. This was the third principle of capitalism: as long as no physical force was used anybody was free to enter into whatever contract he wanted or—was forced by circumstances. Justice was equated with the formal right of individuals to enter into contractual relations. The individual, reduced to the smallest possible denominator, was an absolute reference point of capitalism.

In theory 'the best of all possible worlds' was established. A free and perfect market was seen as the instrument to transform the self-interest of millions of independent individuals into the good for the whole community. In practice the freedom given with one hand was taken away with the other—on the market the 'law' of supply and demand was supreme and the individual was powerless. The lowest common denominator carried the day, be it the lowest possible conception of ethics or the cost of production which was lowest because all human values were excluded from it.

Costs arise whenever a person or a group of people take the responsibility for a human value. Cost accounting systems differ, therefore, in different social systems. In capitalism labour is a variable cost because a worker—unlike a machine—can be dismissed any time. Profits as seen from the point of view of the individual firm are only an indication that enough has been earned to develop those values for which the firm has taken responsibility. But if the state limits his budget to the minimum and leaves the ultimate responsibility to the individual, the possibility to make profits determines the way in which the resources of the whole economy are used, the direction in which it develops and the needs which it does or does not satisfy. This is the fourth characteristic of capitalism. Profits were not only universal indices of adequate performance of the task the individual firm set itself. Profits were also ultimate criteria determining whether human needs were to be satisfied or not. As a result the richest capitalist countries in the world had inadequate housing, education, health and culture.

Besides the individual, capitalism had another absolute reference point: gold or the value of money. The balance of payment was the overall focal point. Whenever there was disequilibrium, gold flowed automatically in or out of the country, dragging behind itself the whole price level of an economy and thus unleashing forces which restored a new balance throughout the economy. This fifth principle completes the historical uniqueness of capitalism.

To bring the balance of payment into equilibrium, to balance the budget by reducing communal responsibilities to a minimum and to keep close watch on the balance of payment and its offshoot—the profit and loss statement—this was the task of the actions of individuals and markets combined. The basic problems of work were thus solved through an intricate interplay of impersonal and personal forces in which the market usually had the last word.

This interplay of forces determined how much time and energy should be given to work, who should do what kind of work and how the fruits of labour should be distributed. How work should be performed was determined by a concept of productivity limited to technical-market chances. The only responsibility of the entrepreneur was to maximize the short-run yield of invested capital. Since people were formally free, investment in human beings or values did not pay. There was no responsibility for workers, only to shareholders in the case of joint stock companies. Social responsibilities—and hence costs—were eliminated as much as possible from the cost accounting system of the individual firm. The smoke of the factory may have sullied the town and poisoned people's lungs, rivers may have been polluted, but such social costs did not enter into the cost accounting system of the firm. Time spent to go to and from work, health, various factors making work part of a meaningful life—these were responsibilities given to the sovereign individual and not carried as costs by the individual firm.[4]

The by-products of such an organization of work were: the reduction of all products, people and of nature itself to marketable objects; capital accounting rather than merely monetary accounting became dominant and the principles of sound finance ruled over all human considerations; the transformation of all flesh, mind, heart and soul into prices and costs; the subordination of one group under another group thus making people means for the purposes of other people; the neglect of the ethics of interpersonal relationships and hence the separation of people from each other and from any humanly meaningful purpose—rule of impersonal market forces over all and of personal authority over most people; finally a division of labour without balance and consideration of human values.

Poverty amidst plenty, communal impoverishment and public squalor amidst private affluence resulted from such a situation. Being was transformed into saleable commodities and true Becoming was stunted.

IV

Capitalism as it exists today differs from the pure form outlined in the preceding sections. Unions have arisen a long time ago and the government had to legislate from the early beginnings of capitalism.

Trade Unions replaced the fiction of the freedom of the individual contract with the reality of collective bargaining. They exerted strong pressure to include some human responsibilities into the cost accounting system of the firm. Much if not most of the human concern in industry is due—directly or indirectly—to unions.

The government began its activities by setting minimum standards of safety, health and education. Eventually—after

[4] Any distinction between variable and fixed costs implies a time dimension. If we assume changes in productive capacity *all* costs are variable costs. In regard to this question see J. M. Clark, *Studies in the Economics of Overhead Costs*, Chicago 1933 and in particular K. William Kapp, *The Social Costs of Private Enterprise*, Cambridge 1950.

World War II—it developed a radical new concept—'the nation's budget'—expressing an entirely new concept of balance. This budget, like all budgets, was expressed in monetary terms. But it does not attempt to bring costs or expenditure and income or revenue into equilibrium. It attempts to bring the available resources—materials, machines, the labour force—into equilibrium with human needs. It thus substitutes 'resources accounting' for capital accounting.[5]

Trade Unions and the government joined forces to transform the original form of *laissez faire* capitalism into some kind of welfare capitalism. Practically all originally capitalist countries have a 'mixed economy' today: they mix elements of capitalism with corporate-bureaucratic or state-bureaucratic direction and/or with elements of socialism. But basic aspects of the power and value structure of capitalism are still intact. Even in Great Britain where large sectors of the economy have been nationalized, the hierarchical structure of the organization of work has been preserved. The spirit of capitalism, furthermore, continues to determine the basic criteria for the organization of work even in the welfare state. Technical-market chances determine the central concept of productivity—the god of capitalism to whom people give themselves with their whole mind, heart and soul. Much of the reform movement has contributed to allow capitalism to continue in some form rather than to transform it radically. This is why the Christian witness about the social order is still essentially concerned with capitalism.

V

From its very beginning, the rise of capitalism has been intimately connected with the rise of Protestantism. To understand this alliance we must focus attention on the universal aspects of capitalism and on the role which capitalism gives to the individual. There is an intimate connection between self-interest as a principle of unity and true self-expression and the Protestant idea of a vocation, or a personal calling which must be

[5] The concept of resource accounting was first used by Lord Beveridge in his book *Full Employment in a Free Society*, London 1944.

realized in work. As capitalism made the individual sovereign, Protestantism pioneered in making the man-God relationship a vertical relationship centred on the individual rather than the community. Protestantism was, furthermore, blended by the power of the universal conception underlying capitalism. Aided by classical and neo-classical economists a strong screen was erected between the 'satanic mills' where men's souls were ground to bits and the natural order of the market. The glow of the harmony of a marvellous market mechanism which brought millions of independent decisions of individuals into equilibrium was more powerful than the cry of the victims of the law of supply and demand. The latter, furthermore, was experienced as an unchangeable, natural, God-ordained reality.

Today when this universalism has spent its power we have difficulty in understanding how capitalism and Christianity could ever become allies. We also have difficulty in realizing the inner powers which were freed in man when Protestantism built the bridges between a religious devotion and activity in the world. When success in business, when the making of profits became symbols of favours in the eyes of God, the union of *The Protestant Ethic and the Spirit of Capitalism* opened the way to a new era.

We must beware of identifying the forces which created this new era with Protestantism. The Renaissance which created the prototype of the sovereign individual took place in Catholic Italy. The telescope which was an important instrument shaping the modern world view was invented by a Roman Catholic. Luther, furthermore, was as opposed to the rising market economy as was the Pope in Rome. But the Renaissance ideal of man was limited to the upper classes, Galileo recanted and Luther's ideals could not prevent capitalism from capturing the drive and power inherent in the Protestant ideal of the freedom of the individual, of a personal calling and of the justification of business activity in the eyes of God.

On the other hand, the idea of community was so deeply ingrained in the Judeo-Christian tradition that it could not be eradicated by the new emphasis on the individual. The historical uniqueness and reality of capitalism was, furthermore, so much in contrast with its ideal universal presuppositions that the spirit of Christ could not help coming into conflict with the disregard of human values inherent in the inequalities of power and the role given to markets and profits.

Capitalism was thus born in a twilight of Christian ethics. It denied at least as much Christian ethics as it espoused and was met with scepticism and rejection as well as acceptance and praise. The Protestant ethic suited so admirably the needs of the rising industrialists that we must doubt the purity of the inspiration of the Holy Ghost in forming the new Gospel of Wealth. The reaction was, therefore, a vehement one—but also a limited one. The Christian protest movement which arose in the nineteenth century made its impact but could not prevent the Protestant Church as a whole from remaining the silent partner if not the ally of capitalism until the middle of the twentieth century. This fact has become decisive for the fate of Christianity in Western industrial society.

It is true that the Roman Catholic Church has always lived in an uneasy co-existence with capitalism. The two world views are utterly irreconcilable. But during the period of the rise of capitalism Roman Catholicism was on the defensive. It was not in a position to impose its world view on capitalism and it could not prevent Catholics from becoming eventually indistinguishable from secularized Protestants in their basic attitude towards work.

VI

During the past thirty years a new Christian social testimony arose. The Roman Catholic witness dates back to the encyclical letter of Pope Leo XIII 'On Conditions of Labour—*Rerum Novarum*' issued in 1891. But only with Pope John XXIII does a new spirit come to full expression. The new Protestant witness had a forerunner in the 'Right Foundation of a True Social Order' worked out by British Quakers as a result of World War I.[6] In its best known form it has been summed up in terms of

[6] See 'The Right Foundation of a True Social Order' in *Christian Practice*, Being the Second Part of the Christian Discipline of The Religious Society

'the responsible society' at the Amsterdam meeting of the World Council of Churches in 1948 but its most penetrating formulations were made in the Oxford Conference of 1937. We shall, therefore, focus our attention on this Conference.[7]

Given the emphasis on the individual, the first and decisive step taken by the Oxford Conference was to call for a concern by the Church with the social order: 'Christianity becomes socially futile if it does not recognize that love must will justice and that the Christian is under an obligation to secure the best possible social and economic structure, insofar as such structure is determined by human decisions.' Oxford warned against indifference towards society because 'the ultimate and eternal destiny of human existence' transcends history. It also warned against identifying 'some particular social system with the will of God or to equate it with the kingdom of God'. The first error leads to 'indecisions in favour of the *status quo*'; the second imparts 'a dangerous religious sanction' to a specific social order.[8]

The Oxford Conference objected to unequal distribution of wealth, treating human labour as a commodity, the role played by the profit motive, and last but not least the absence of a spiritual centre, which leads to 'the progressive dissipation of the spiritual inheritance of Western life'. It summed up its

[7] See *The Churches Survey their Task*: *The Report of the Conference at Oxford, July 1937, on Church Community and State* edited by D. H. Oldham, London, Allen & Unwin, 1937, p. 1. This Report is from now on quoted as *Report*.

[8] *Ibid*. pp. 23 and 25. See also *Ecumenical Documents on Church and Society*, World Council of Churches, Geneva 1954, pp. 57–59. From now on quoted as *Documents*.

---

of Friends in Great Britain, London 1925, pp. 127–128; also extracts from '73rd Minute of London Yearly Meeting of Friends', held in London, 1917, p. 2; *Minutes of Conference on 'Industry for Service'* held at Devonshire House, London, November 24th to 27th, 1921, p. 7; 'The Seven Points of the Message from the Conference on "The Society of Friends and the Social Order" in October 1916 with explanatory notes', p. 7; 'Report on the Conference on Industry and the Social Order' held at Friends House in London, November 7th to 9th, 1958, prepared by the author for the Social Order Committee of the Philadelphia Yearly Meeting, pp. 1–65.

objections to capitalism in four areas in which 'the assumptions and operation of the economic order of the industrialized world affront the Christian understanding of the moral and spiritual nature of man'.[9]

(i) The enhancement of acquisitiveness. 'As long as industry is organized primarily not for the service of the community but with the object of producing a purely financial result for some of its members, it cannot be recognized as properly fulfilling its social purpose.'

(ii) Inequalities. 'Any social arrangement which outrages the dignity of man, by treating some men as ends and others as means, any institution which obscures the common humanity of men by emphasizing the external accidents of birth, or wealth, or social position, is *ipso facto* anti-Christian.'

(iii) Irresponsible possession of economic power. The Conference condemned 'the power wielded by a few individuals or groups who are not responsible to any organ of society' and who have 'some resemblance to a tyranny in the classical sense of that term, where rulers are not accountable for their actions to any superior authority representing the community over whom power is exercised'.

(iv) Frustration of the sense of Christian Vocation. Most workers 'are *directly* conscious of working for the profit of the employers (and for the sake of their wages) and only *indirectly* for any public good'; 'many workers must produce things which are useless or shoddy or destructive'. The problem of salesmanship was also examined in this context.[10]

Realizing that technical progress made it possible to remove 'the kind of poverty which is crippling to human personality' the Oxford Conference asked for a reduction of Christian thinking 'from charitable paternalism to the realization of more equal justice in the distribution of wealth'. It dealt in a forthright spirit with the problem of property. 'All property which represents social power stands in special need of moral scrutiny, since power to determine the life of others is the crucial point in any

[9] *Documents*, p. 61 and *Report*, p. 27; *Documents*, p. 66 and *Report*, p. 28.
[10] *Ibid.*, *Documents*, p. 67 and *Report*, p. 28; *Documents*, p. 68 and *Report*, p. 29; *Documents*, p. 69.

scheme of justice.' It also called for a realization of the idea of 'stewardship or trusteeship'.

The Oxford Conference stated that 'the working man, whether in field or factory, is entitled to a living wage, wholesome surroundings, and a recognized voice in the decisions which affect his welfare as a worker'. Last but not least it called for 'group experiments' as one of the three main ways of 'Action by Christians'. The Conference Report states that 'because some things cannot be changed without State action or international adjustment, the effective power of "two or three" men of conviction who make themselves into a Christian "cell" must not be underestimated'.[11]

The basic ideas of the Oxford Conference culminated in the demand for a 'responsible society' made by the World Council of Churches in 1948.

The key statement on the nature of the responsible society made in the Amsterdam report is as follows: 'Man is created and called to be a free being, responsible to God and his neighbour. Any tendencies in State and society depriving man of the possibility of acting responsibly are a denial of God's intention for man and His work of salvation. A responsible society is one where freedom is the freedom of men who acknowledge responsibility to justice and public order, and where those who hold political authority or economic power are responsible for its exercise to God and the people whose welfare is affected by it.' This statement is followed by a clear recognition of a point central to all religiously inspired social witness, namely that 'men must never be made a mere means for political or economic ends'. The Amsterdam report demanded a ' "No" to all that flouts the love of Christ, to every system, every programme and every person that treats any man as though he were an irresponsible thing or a means of profit'.[12]

The report was also forthright in recognizing that 'it is one

[11] *Documents*, p. 65; *Documents*, p. 79 and *Report*, p. 37; *Documents*, p. 77 and *Report*, p. 36; *Documents*, p. 77 and *Report*, p. 35; *Documents*, pp. 86, 87 and *Report*, pp. 44, 45.

[12] See *Statements of the World Council of Churches on Social Questions*, Geneva 1956, pp. 16, 19.

of the most fateful facts in modern history that often the working classes, including tenant farmers, came to believe that the churches were against them or indifferent to their plight'. The report discusses some of the reasons why this 'belief' may have arisen. 'Churches should not forget to what extent they themselves have contributed to the very evils which they are tempted to blame wholly on the secularization of society. While they have raised up many Christians who have taken the lead in movements of reform, and while many of them have come to see in a fresh way the relevance of their faith to the problems of society, and the imperative obligations thus laid upon them, they share responsibility for the contemporary disorder. Our churches have often given religious sanction to the special privileges of dominant classes, races and political groups, and so they have been obstacles to changes necessary in the interests of social justice and political freedom. They have concentrated on a purely spiritual or otherworldly or individualistic interpretation of their message and their responsibility.'[13]

It demanded that 'the Church should make clear that there are conflicts between Christianity and capitalism. The developments of capitalism vary from country to country and often the exploitation of the workers that was characteristic of early capitalism has been corrected in considerable measure by the influence of trade unions, social legislation and responsible management.' This acknowledgment of the evolution from *laissez faire* to welfare capitalism is followed by a recognition of the remaining conflicts between capitalism and Christianity: '(i) capitalism tends to subordinate what should be the primary task of any economy—the meeting of human needs—to the economic advantages of those who have most power over its institutions. (ii) It tends to produce serious inequalities. (iii) It has developed a practical form of materialism in Western nations in spite of their Christian background, for it has placed the greatest emphasis upon success in making money. (iv) It has also kept the people of capitalist countries subject to a kind of fate which has taken the form of such social catastrophes as mass unemployment.'[14]

[13] *Ibid*. p. 20 and pp. 17–18.

[14] *Ibid*. p. 21.

As regards property, Amsterdam stated that the Church cannot resolve the debate among those who advocate the socialization of the means of production and those who oppose it. 'In the light of the Christian understanding of man we must, however, say to the advocates of socialization that the institution of property is not the root of the corruption of human nature. We must equally say to the defenders of existing property relations that ownership is not an unconditional right; it must, therefore, be preserved, curtailed or distributed in accordance with the requirements of justice.'

The final call of Amsterdam is as follows: 'The Christian churches should reject the ideologies of both communism and *laissez faire* capitalism and should seek to draw men away from the false assumption that these extremes are the only alternatives. Each has made promises which it could not redeem. Communist ideology puts the emphasis upon economic justice and promises that freedom will follow automatically after the completion of the revolution. Capitalism puts the emphasis upon freedom, and promises that justice will follow as a by-product of free enterprise; that, too, is an ideology which has been proved false. It is the responsibility of Christians to seek new creative solutions which never allow either justice or freedom to destroy the other.'[15]

We find in this statement almost an echo of certain pronouncements of the Commonwealth, particularly the call for a 'third way' which offers a creative transformation of capitalism. The emphasis on responsibility and Amsterdam's insistence on the right 'to participate in the shaping of society' are also parallel. Amsterdam, furthermore, stated specifically the 'vital importance that society should have a rich variety of smaller forms of community'.[16]

VII

Compared with Protestantism which developed its social testimony in a dialogue with modern capitalism the roots of the Roman Catholic social witness are deep in the soil of medieval

[15] *Ibid.* p. 21.

[16] *Ibid.* p. 19.

Christianity. Natural law is the essence of the Roman Catholic view of man and society. The social order must be modelled according to a 'Divinely established' order as revealed to men in natural law. The divine order expresses itself in a moral order 'which is transcendent, absolute, universal and equally binding upon all'. It indicates 'the true hierarchy of values'.[17]

As far as industrial capitalism is concerned the Catholic tradition found a clear expression in the encyclical letter of Pope Leo XIII, *Rerum Novarum*, 'The Condition of Labour', which was issued in 1891. Forty years later, in 1931, Pope Pius XI published an encyclical letter *Quadragesimo Anno*, 'On Reconstructing the Social Order'. In 1961—thirty years after the publication of 'On Reconstructing the Social Order'—Pope John XXIII wrote his encyclical letter, *Mater et Magistra*, 'New Light on Social Problems', followed two years later by his encyclical *Pacem in Terris*, 'Peace on Earth'. In the following we shall mainly refer to these two encyclicals.

They consider the moral order as both transcendental and immanent: 'the world's Creator has stamped man's inmost being with an order revealed to man by his conscience; and his conscience insists on his preserving it'. The inner and the outer are interrelated: 'the order which prevails in human society is wholly incorporeal in nature. Its foundation is truth, and it must be brought into effect by justice. It needs to be animated and perfected by men's love for one another, and, while preserving freedom intact, it must make for an equilibrium in society which is increasingly more human in character.' In these words John XXIII sums up the Church's social doctrine: 'the light of which is Truth, Justice its objective, and Love its driving force'.[18]

Closely related to such a conception of the social order is an organic-communal conception of society and the understanding

[17] See Encyclical Letter of Pope John XXIII, *Mater et Magistra*, New Light on Social Problems, Revised Edition of the Catholic Truth Society, London 1963, Section 205, p. 53 and Section 176, p. 47. From now on quoted as *Mater et Magistra*. Page and section references are to the revised edition of 1963.

[18] Encyclical letter of Pope John XXIII *Pacem in Terris*, Peace on Earth, The Catholic Truth Society, London 1963, Section 5, p. 8 and Section 37, p. 18. *Mater et Magistra*, Section 226, p. 58.

of the social order as a body. In *Rerum Novarum* the organic-communal conception of society is still expressed with reference to Thomas Aquinas's idea of a Commonwealth: 'men communicate with one another in the setting up of a Commonwealth'. In *Mater et Magistra,* Pope John XXIII applied the organic-communal conception in a new way to the organization of work. 'Every effort must be made to ensure that the company is indeed a true community of persons, concerned about the needs, the activities and the standing of each of its members.' This statement sums up a long standing concern of the Roman Catholic Church for the dignity of man. John XXIII explicitly introduced the idea of 'the whole man' and said 'the common good is something which affects the needs of the whole man, body and soul'. He promulgated as a basic principle that 'individual human beings are the foundation, the cause and the end of every social institution'.[19]

The structure and organization of the individual firm is to be based on these principles: 'if we hold to a human and Christian concept of man and the family, we are bound to consider as an ideal that form of enterprise which is modelled on the basis of a community of persons working together for the advancement of their mutual interests in accordance with the principles of justice and Christian teaching.' More specifically the encyclical 'New Light on Social Problems' indicates that 'employees are justified in wishing to participate in the activity of the industrial concern for which they work'. 'The present

[19] Encyclical letter of Pope Leo XIII *Rerum Novarum*, The Condition of Labour, The Paulist Press, New York 1939, pp. 20 and 30. From now on quoted as *Rerum Novarum*. See also *Mater et Magistra*, Section 258, pp. 64, 65. The principle of subsidiary functions is also important in this respect. See *Mater et Magistra*, Section 53, p. 18, *Pacem in Terris* Section 140, p. 50, and *Quadragesimo Anno*, Section 80, p. 30. On the role of voluntary associations see *Rerum Novarum*, pp. 30, 31 and Encyclical letter of Pope Pius XI *Quadragesimo Anno*, 'On Reconstructing the Social Order', The National Catholic Welfare Conference, Washington, D.C., 1942, Section 30, p. 13, Sections 31 and 32, p. 14, Section 37, p. 15 and Section 91, p. 27. From now on quoted as *Quadragesimo Anno*. *Rerum Novarum*, pp. 13, 15, 16, 23, 25 and p. 34; also *Quadragesimo Anno*, Section 118, p. 42, see also Section 101, p. 36 and Section 139, p. 51. *Mater et Magistra*, Section 213, p. 55. *Pacem in Terris*, Section 57, p. 25. *Mater et Magistra*, Section 219, p. 56.

demand for workers to have a greater say in the conduct of the firm accords not only with man's nature, but also with recent progress in the economic, social and political spheres.'[20]

Property rights are clearly subordinated to work 'which as the immediate expression of a human personality must always be rated higher than the possession of external goods which of their very nature are merely instrumental'. Pope John XXIII insisted furthermore (as his predecessors did) 'on the extension of this right (to property) in practice to all classes of citizens' and recognized explicitly 'the lawfulness of State and public ownership of productive goods'.[21]

A final statement of John XXIII expresses the meaning of human dignity for the organization of the firm in these words: 'Justice is to be observed not only in the distribution of wealth, but also in regard to the conditions in which men are engaged in producing wealth. Every man has, of his very nature, a need to express himself in work and thereby to perfect his own being.'[22]

Catholicism was always sceptical of, if not outright opposed to economic liberalism—though even the Catholic social witness could not avoid the influence of liberal economic thought. But, on the whole, it consistently rejected the idea that 'the right ordering of economic life' could be left to free competition and equally consistently advocated a 'just wage' rather than a determination of wages by the forces of supply and demand originating in a capitalist market economy. Generally, the Church insisted that the economic order must be subject to the moral order and cannot be considered to be ruled by laws completely of its own.[23]

[20] *Mater et Magistra*, Section 142, pp. 39, 40. Section 91, p. 27 and Section 93, p. 28. See also Sections 31 and 32, p. 13, *Quadragesimo Anno*, Section 65, p. 26 and Section 81, p. 11; and *Rerum Novarum*, p. 12.

[21] *Mater et Magistra*, Section 107, p. 31. Section 113, p. 32 and Section 116, p. 33. Already in *Quadragesimo Anno*, Pope Pius XI acknowledged that 'certain kinds of property . . . ought to be reserved to the State', p. 40.

[22] *Pacem in Terris*, Section 48, p. 22.

[23] *Mater et Magistra*, Section 79, p. 11. In regard to the anti-liberal position of the Church, see *Quadragesimo Anno*, Section 14, p. 8; Section 27, p. 12; Section 30, p. 13 and Section 54, p. 23 in which the 'Manchesterian Liberals'

The Church never minced words about capitalism. In 'The Condition of Labour' Leo XIII said: 'the first concern of all is to save the poor workers from the cruelty of grasping speculators, who use human beings as mere instruments for making money.' He expressed sympathy with the workers who 'cannot but perceive that their grasping employers too often treat them with the greatest inhumanity and hardly care for them beyond the profit their labour brings.' In 'On Reconstructing the Social Order' Pius XI quoted this latter passage adding 'Property, that is "capital" has undoubtedly long been able to appropriate too much to itself.' He also noted that 'economic dictatorship' has replaced free competition, and he criticized 'the rulers of economic life abandoning the right road' stating that 'very many managements treated their workers more like mere tools with no concern at all for their souls, without even the least thought of spiritual things'. In his 'New Light on Social Problems' John XXIII wrote an epithet for the capitalist factory: 'for from the factory dead matter goes out improved, whereas men there are corrupted and degraded'.[24] One could hardly imagine a more shocking—and true—judgment on what some people consider the height of Western industrial development.

Significant in this connection is the understanding of violence as a power injurious to human growth and development. Already the encyclical on 'Reconstructing the Social Order' had condemned free competition as 'a headstrong power and a violent energy'. But only John XXIII's 'New Light on Social Problems' and his 'Peace on Earth' deal systematically with violence. 'For true Christians cannot help feeling obliged to

[24] See *Quadragesimo Anno*, Section 42, p. 17. See also *Mater et Magistra*, Section 205, p. 53 and *Pacem in Terris*, Sections 1 and 2, p. 7. *Rerum Novarum*, p. 25, 36. *Quadragesimo Anno*, Section 54, p. 22 and Section 135, p. 47.

are explicitly attacked. However, the discussion of unemployment in *Quadragesimo Anno* is based on classical-liberal economic thought on the relationship between the wage level and employment opportunities. *Quadragesimo Anno*, Section 74, pp. 28, 29. The present Pope Paul also attacked 'Manchester-type liberalism'. See *The Times*, June 9, 1964. See also *Quadragesimo. Anno*, Section 88, p. 33. *Rerum Novarum*, pp. 26, 27 and *Quadragesimo Anno*, Section 54, p. 22 and Section 88, p. 33.

improve their own temporal institutions and environment. They do all they can to prevent those institutions from doing violence to human dignity.' Most far-reaching is the following statement: 'A law which is at variance with reason is to that extent unjust and has no longer the rationale of law. It is rather an act of violence'. Here is a profound and radical conception of non-violence which makes it clear that we are at a new stage of development of man and society. 'We are confronted in this modern age with a form of society which is evolving on entirely new social and political lines'. This statement sums up a number of references to 'a progressive development of human society', the need for 'radically different principles to preserve peace' and 'the progress of human society'. 'Hence among the very serious obligations incumbent upon men of high principles, we must include the task of establishing new relationships in human society, under the mastery and guidance of truth, justice, charity and freedom.' [25]

A new task demands new modes of realization. In 'Peace on Earth' John XXIII asks for an 'integration of faith and action' and in 'New Light on Social Problems' he quotes the Jocist slogan 'look, judge, act'.[26] In this new way John XXIII admonished us to help in accomplishing the stupendous task 'to humanize and to christianize this modern civilization of ours'.

VIII

While the Christian social witness spoke up with an ever clearer and louder voice against the evils of capitalism, the Christian content of capitalism declined rapidly.

Success has ceased to have any connection with service to

[25] *Mater et Magistra*, Section 242, p. 61. *Quadragesimo Anno*, Section 88, p. 33. Pope Pius XI summed up his attack on the economic system of the nineteen-thirties as a violation of the right order. *Pacem in Terris*, Section 34, p. 16. See also *Mater et Magistra*, Section 179, p. 47. *Pacem in Terris*, Section 51, p. 23; Section 42, p. 19; Section 74, p. 31; Section 113, p. 42 and Section 166, p. 60. There is also a reference to 'stage of development' in Section 73, p. 31. See also Section 163, p. 59.

[26] *Ibid.*, Section 151, p. 54. See also *Mater et Magistra*, Section 236, p. 59. *Memorandum Commonwealth 1951*, Point 7 on p. II. See also Chapters 12–15.

God. People 'called' to a vocation have largely been replaced by jobholders for whom work is but a means to make money. Also gone are the real characters of the heyday of capitalism. Cynicism and apathy have replaced the fervour of a class struggle as well as the hope for a new order. There is no heavenly city of the twentieth-century welfare state. Glad hands have replaced the unseen hand without their activity being necessarily more aesthetic or ethically creative. The 'splendid misery' of the affluent society fills our pockets while emptying our hearts.

A fateful hour in the history of man has come. The spirit of capitalism, triumphant, has lost contact with its universal roots. It is, therefore, powerless to solve the basic human problems of work: how can human dignity and personal responsibility be restored in industry? How can work become part of a meaningful life rather than doing violence to the development of man? These questions are the key questions underlying the renewed Christian social witness. They are also the key to an understanding of the Scott Bader Commonwealth.

In its basic aspirations the Commonwealth is an experiment to realize the demands of the renewed Christian social witness. Based on a bold conception of common ownership it meets the fundamental demand that men be ends rather than means for the purposes of other men. It attempts to establish a community of work in which authority, responsibility and participation are interrelated. The Commonwealth is aiming to broaden the meaning of work. It envisages a new dynamics of social change and a non-violent social order based on justice.

These aspirations are like an echo of the call coming from Rome, Oxford and Amsterdam. Yet they were developed quite independently in the sense that Ernest Bader did not study the documents of Oxford and Amsterdam (the encyclical letters being published after the establishment of the Commonwealth). Yet in a deeper sense they are all expressions of a new spirit which is in the process of awakening everywhere and whose echo can be heard at the most varied places, some of them smaller in conception and thrust than the Commonwealth, but significant as attempts to move in the same direction. We shall better understand the significance of the Commonwealth by seeing it as part of a movement which has its early manifestations in the United States, in France, in Great Britain, and in Germany—to mention only a few examples of countries within the western industrial orbit.

Chapter 3

Precursors and contemporaries of the Commonwealth

I

All the attempts to develop new organizations of work have certain features in common: they want to overcome the gulf between those who have the power to organize work and those who have not. They want to equalize responsibilities by changing the structure of power and values. Since responsibilities find their clearest expression in the cost accounting system, new ways of dealing with profits and wages are sought. These endeavours may be summed up as a search for new modes of participation in work, new ways of preserving the dignity of men and making their working life part of a meaningful human existence.

In the United States one of the earliest attempts was made by the Columbia Conserve Company. This first experiment failed. We do not know enough about its development to learn from this first swallow of a new spring. The democratization scheme of the Leed and Northrop Company in Philadelphia was another early attempt to find new ways in industry. Three more lasting ventures will give us the first insights into the new organization of work: the Geo. A. Hormel & Co., the Nunn-Bush Share the Production Plan and the Lincoln Electric Company.

The Hormel Company, which has its main meat packing plant in Austin, Minnesota, is best known for its guaranteed annual wage plan. The basic idea of the plan is as simple as it is radical: no worker can be dismissed without a 52-week notice. The plan was initiated in 1933 at the nadir of the depression and about 6,000 workers have enjoyed the security it offers. It transformed wages from variable into overhead costs and thus made men equal to machines as regards the responsibility which 'the company' takes for them. Jay C. Hormel, a man of real vision who initiated the plan, used to tell a story which deserves to be widely known.

The idea of the Hormel Annual Wage Plan was born in an episode which occurred in the early 1920s.

Geo. A. Hormel & Company, grown since its start in 1891, had employed an efficiency expert. This man had pointed out the savings which would come by measuring the workmen's time by the tenth of the hour instead of by the half hour. This was a shock to Mr. Hormel when he recalled that his grandfather had started work by the year, his father by the month. Then came per hour, now per tenth.

Of course, the efficiency expert pointed out, office help should still be employed by the week or month or year, because they are 'company people'! Mr. Hormel wondered. The true cause and effect might be the other way round.

The unfairness of asking workmen to take the hazards of uncertain employment was brought out in an episode which occurred in 1929.

The Hormel Company had hit upon a brand-new product—a boom product—canned chicken. Wholesalers bought, retailers bought, housewives bought. The company doubled and quadrupled its production line; then went to three shifts. Then the boom busted. The housewife having the security of a chicken on her pantry shelf, kept it there.

The retailer and the wholesaler stopped buying, and Hormel laid off its extra help. Many went quietly on their way—all but one man. That man headed straight for the front office and said: 'You can't do this to me.'

'Can't do what to you?' asked Mr. Hormel.

'You can't turn me out in the street. You wouldn't turn a horse out in the street. You can't do it to me'.

'You can go back where you came from, can't you?' queried Mr. Hormel.

'No!' said the man. 'My town has 1,200 people. Before I got out of school, I was selling home-popped popcorn out of a basket. I finally got a little stand, selling peanuts, popcorn, chewing gum and pop. I just got to where I could count on $9.00 or $10.00 a week when you sent a man along who said you would pay me $20.00 a week to help you can your chicken. He didn't tell me you would only keep me a couple of months, just long enough to ruin my business, then turn me out in the street!'[1]

1 See my book *Towards a Democratic Work Process*. The Hormel-U.P.W.A.

This story sums up the basic ideas underlying the guaranteed annual wage. It also throws light on much of the industrial history of the West. An almost unbelievable disregard of human values recommended by an efficiency expert and accepted as a 'holy' maxim of 'scientific' management. In this case it led to the sudden realization by Mr. Hormel that there is something basically wrong. You really wouldn't do it to your horse, would you? So let's not do it in the cost accounting system of a civilized country!

Mr. Hormel carried this idea a step further by instituting a joint earnings plan. This plan is based on a conception of profits as a surplus which constitutes the joint earnings of the stockholders and workers. Such a conception in turn is based on a new vision of 'the business as a joint enterprise of the stockholders as one group and the employees as the other'. Workers are recognized as partners in the enterprise—a clear departure from the traditional organization of work.

Stockholders remain, however, the group with the last say. Mr. Hormel was aware of this and began to overcome this inequality by instituting a Business Improvement Committee. The Committee consisted of twelve people elected for a one-year period as follows: The first member was a divisional chairman of the union who chose a second member. The two chose a third person and so on. Every three months, three members retired and chose their successors before leaving the Committee. The Committee, autonomous in the election of its members, could discuss any problem connected with the product and with the production. It was independent of both company and union and constituted a new version of worker's control. Admittedly its scope of action was limited and the untimely death of Mr. Hormel brought it to an end instead of making it the beginning of a new development.

The Nunn-Bush Share-The-Production-Plan is another significant attempt to develop a partnership. The company, located in Milwaukee, produces shoes. The plan transforms wages into

---

Experience, Harper Brothers, New York 1953, pp. 14 and 15. A two-week notice can be given in case of cause.

income based on a certain percentage of the sales receipts. In addition workers receive a share of the 'residual income' at the end of the year. The basic conception of this plan is again of wide significance. A company statement says:

> It is the belief of the Nunn-Bush management that industry has no moral or social right to look upon Labor as a commodity—that competent management can offer no adequate excuse for purchasing Labor as it would purchase raw materials or supplies.
>
> Even if industry prefers not to believe the altruism that business is made for man, not man for business, it must, of practical necessity, consider the truism that no man can be expected to give his greatest skill or best loyalty to a job that discards him when trouble comes . . . we believe that the true status of Labor in industry is that of a partner, and that only when this is given practical expression can all those creative powers born of voluntary and willing co-operation replace the obstruction and frustration which characterizes so much of our Capitalistic Economy today. The initiative lies with Management . . . we deliberately surrendered our claim to dictate to our workers. This meant giving up many of the so-called 'sacred prerogatives' of Management: the right of arbitrary discharge, the arbitrary settlement of hours, holidays, layoffs, and rates of pay, and indeed everything which affects the workers' interests. Under our agreement with the Union all those questions became matters which could only be settled by joint agreement, failing which, arbitration.[2]

This is a pioneering statement demanding that labour instead of being a commodity, be a partner in an industrial undertaking.

A similar spirit and principles underlie the 'Incentive Management' plan of the Lincoln Electric Company. The plan originated with this question: 'why has work become something to avoid—something to do less of while being paid more for it?' To meet this question and to create a different attitude towards work an Incentive Management plan was worked out. The plan is based on five ideas:

(i) Belief in people: 'We must have a sincere belief in people. We must believe that people have abilities to do jobs much

[2] See Joseph L. Snider, *The Guarantee of Work and Wages*, Boston 1947, pp. 37–38.

bigger and greater than they are now doing; that they are not merely button pushers with no latent ability.'

(ii) Hard work: 'We hear a great deal about the "dignity of labor", but how many people really believe that hard work is dignified? Well, it is—where everybody is committed to it, and where there is truly no distinction made between management and labor. All labor must manage and all management must labor . . .'

(iii) Status of profits: 'Profit is not the primary objective for which a company is organized . . . it must be a by-product rather than a primary objective . . . The primary objective of any business must be one that makes sense to everyone connected with it . . .'

(iv) Individual responsibility: 'Every person . . . must be on the team *as an individual* not simply as a cog in a machine . . . Individuals have varying abilities and their work task should be paced according to these abilities, rather than through the arbitrary delineation of a job that is created through an organizational chart. . .'

(v) Fair recognition of contribution: '. . . when you have established a mutually acceptable common goal and have everybody working their best for that goal . . . everyone must be rewarded in proportion to what they contribute toward that goal. . .'[3]

The emphasis on the abilities and potentialities of a person, the insistence that 'all labor must manage and all management must labor', the demand for a new 'delineation of a job', the understanding of work as a human task—these are landmarks in the struggle for a new organization of work.

II

In Great Britain experiments in new ways of organizing work go back to Robert Owen who founded New Lanark in 1816 during the early days of the Industrial Revolution. Basing his ideas on a theory of environmental conditioning he attempted through education to 'accomplish with ease and certainty the supposed Herculean labour of forming a rational character in

[3] *Ibid.* pp. 22–25.

man',[4] G. D. H. Cole evaluated Owen's accomplishments in these words: 'At Lanark Owen paid better wages, worked shorter hours, and gave infinitely better conditions than most of his competitors. He abolished all 'pauper apprentice' labour . . . and refused to employ children at less than ten years of age when others were freely working them intolerably long hours at less than six years old. And yet he had no difficulty in making the factory pay, despite the large sums he was constantly spending on all manner of improvements and amenities. In short, he gave an astonishingly convincing demonstration of what later generations have called the 'economy of high wages', at a time when appalling under-payment and over-work were almost everywhere regarded as the indispensable conditions of commercial success.'[5]

Two movements link Robert Owen with our times: the co-operative movement and the socialist movement which has been under the influence of Christian ethics. Four examples of present-day Great Britain must suffice to illustrate the influence of these movements and the pioneering position which Great Britain has taken in the development of new modes of participation in work.

Best & Lloyd, under the guidance of Robert Best developed a participation scheme based on small groups. The company's products include lighting fixtures, balustrading, architectural metalwork and contract work of light engineering character. The company employs about 75 people.

The participation scheme consists of (i) a management board, (ii) a company news magazine, (iii) small group meetings of workers. Workers also share in profits.

The Management Board consists of three members elected by the foremen, the office and the other co-partners; as well as of four functional managers (sales, production, design and accounts). The Board may discuss everything except wages and salaries. Legally the Board of Directors is above the Management Board, and executive appointments are made in the

[4] See *A New View of Society* and other Writings by Robert Owen, Everyman's Library, London 1927, p. 41.
[5] *Ibid.*, p. x.

conventional way. Actually the Management Board functioned quite autonomously for many years. As Robert Best said: 'This is a private company. I am the proprietor and the Management Board is the effective governing Board of the company.' He felt that 'materially this method of administration will give you results better than an authoritarian structure . . .' Decisions of the Management Board must be unanimous. So far there has been agreement but sometimes outside advice has been sought.

The company News Magazine enables every member 'to keep fully in touch with what is going on'. The core of the whole scheme consists of small groups meeting about seven to eight times a year. Co-partners are free to discuss anything but actually most discussions have been about their work. A good deal of criticism, usually constructive, has been voiced at these meetings. There are no management representatives at these meetings.

This participation scheme is based on the recognition that workers need new vehicles for self-expression: 'Much has been written about the lack of satisfaction in the job of the ordinary industrial worker, and it has been ascribed to many factors, of which the most often quoted is the division of labour and specialization so that the satisfaction of making a finished article of high quality is denied. Less has been said about the effect of organization and hierarchies on the free will of the workman to make decisions about his own work. As organization grows, freedom of decision at all levels in an organization becomes less and less, until we reach the *reductio ad absurdum* of Charlie Chaplin's conveyor assembly line in the film *Modern Times* . . . It is much more frustrating to be prevented from making decisions about my own actions than to be prevented from making a finished article . . .'[6]

The experience of Best & Lloyd has shown the significance of small groups as an important channel for participation in work. In starting the free expression method Robert Best was much influenced by James Gillespie and his book *Free Expression in Industry*. As the method developed he realized that some of the

[6] See N. I. Bond-Williams, 'Informal Workers' Groups: An Interim Report on an Industrial Experiment,' *British Management Review*, Vol. II, No. 3.

principles had points in common with Quaker business meetings. Robert Best has also worked out a Participation Index to measure the extent of actual participation.[7]

The John Lewis Partnership has one of the most advanced participation schemes and is the largest among the co-partnership firms. In 1966 it comprised 16 department stores, four specialty shops, supermarkets and food shops with an annual turnover of over sixty million pounds. More than 17,000 people were working in the firm. The foundation for the Partnership was laid in 1914 when John Spedan Lewis, the son of a small shopkeeper, had taken over a derelict business and told the staff that if and when the business became profitable, they should have the profit. During the following decades an organization developed which became a far-reaching experiment in industrial democracy. The Partnership belongs to all those employed in it. It is based on an idea of sharing gain, knowledge and power. 'The broad aim of this experiment in industrial organization has been to provide the worker not merely with a better livelihood but with a better life; to admit him to a region where his voice can be heard, and his thoughts can count, and where he can have the satisfaction of feeling that every honest effort on his part contributes to a constructive idea.'[8]

The first impetus to the John Lewis Partnership arose when 'in a review of the annual accounts, Mr Spedan Lewis had noticed—or realized for the first time—that the income which he, his father and brother were jointly drawing from the business was substantially more than the whole of the pay-sheet put together. This fact, sinking into the mind of an ardent young man with a strong social conscience and keen critical abilities, left an impression that could not be effaced; and from that moment he began his persistent and life-long effort to devise a more equitable division of the rewards of industry.'

The organization of the John Lewis Partnership was

[7] See *An Index for Assessing 'Democratic Leadership', 'Participation' and 'Communications'*, B & L News, November 7, 1963.

[8] See the booklet 'About the John Lewis Partnership' issued by John Lewis and Company Ltd., Oxford Street, London, W.1, 1965. All other quotations in this section are from the same booklet.

completed in 1950 when a Constitution was accepted. The basic idea of the Constitution is to give to the members of the partnership security, freedom and justice. It aims to assure a reasonable, but limited, return on outside capital, to set a bottom for earnings adequate for decent living and a top for earnings of management. Inequality is to be reduced to the minimum compatible with efficiency and profits are to be distributed in proportion to pay. A generous sick leave and pension fund as well as provisions for amenities and social activities are provided. The need for expert knowledge and 'central wisdom' has been recognized but great emphasis is given to de-centralization of executive authority and management is made accountable to the Partners. Every member of the Partnership—which is open to all employees—has the opportunity to take an 'appropriate share in its policy and direction'. It aims to foster 'the greatest measure of democratic responsibility'.

To achieve these objectives a tripartite division of power between (i) the Chairman, (ii) a Central Board and (iii) a Central Council was carried through. The Chairman has the chief executive responsibility. The Central Board consists of the Chairman, the deputy Chairman, five partners appointed by the Chairman and five partners elected yearly by the Central Council. The Board operates the system of budgetary control and must consent to all major financial transactions. The Central Council is a body at least two thirds of whose members are elected by secret ballot. It, in turn, elects each year three Trustees of the Constitution and five members of the Central Board. The Central Council has its own fund amounting to approximately 1 per cent. of the total pay-sheet and has broad powers. It can hear any appeals, is free to discuss any matter of concern to the Partnership and can make any recommendations to Management. No alterations in the Constitution can be made without its approval. There are also local Councils which are similarly constituted as the Central Council.

To develop a strong sense of partnership and encourage participation, the Partnership has a weekly newspaper which publishes anonymous enquiries and criticism of any kind to which the management must reply. There are also Committees for Communication consisting of elected representatives which may meet the chairman or his personal representative about any question. The Partnership has developed many educational and cultural facilities, among them a Music Society, a Dramatic Society, a chess, a sailing and other sports clubs. It maintains a holiday camp and various residential clubs. Partners may buy tickets for operas, plays, concerts, etc., at half price.

Similar—but in some ways going beyond the John Lewis Partnership—are the new forms of organization of the 'Demintry' firms—'Demintry' standing for Democratic Integration in Industry.

The Basic Principles of Demintry are worth noting: 'Maintaining that the fundamental moral precepts taught by all great religions and philosophies form the only basis on which human society can be built in an interdependent world', Demintry advocates 'a creative economic order' based on 'sharing, co-operation and justice'. It demands that 'every undertaking should be carried on as a joint concern by all those working for it' and should have a clearly understood social purpose. For an undertaking to be 'socially healthy' every person must have an opportunity 'to develop his or her full capabilities and talents within the discipline of a shared purpose', the firm must control its size or decentralize so everybody can 'embrace it in his mind and imagination'. Besides acceptance of responsibility for the larger national and international community, Demintry insists on a 'clearly defined partnership . . . without any section having an exclusive right to ownership, control or profits. The form of ownership and control of the business must, therefore, make legal provisions for the whole body to express the principle of democratic integration and a sense of belonging by all its members.'[9]

Scott Bader is a member of Demintry and we will soon see how it attempts to realize these principles. Here we want to consider two other organizations implementing Demintry principles: Farmer Service and the Factories for Peace.

[9] Demintry, the Society for Democratic Integration in Industry, is registered at 12 Downside Crescent, Belsize Park, London, N.W.3. See *Basic Principles* of Demintry.

Farmer & Sons, a printing establishment founded in 1875 in London, was transformed in 1945 into a common ownership firm through the development of an organization called 'Farmerservice'. The basis of this transformation 'was the conviction of three people, responsible for this private company employing normally some forty or fifty people, that Christ's way is the only way which works well for everybody, and therefore leads into paths of peace'.

The fundamental principles on which Farmerservice is founded are contained in the Basis which may be summed up in three propositions:

(i) Acceptance by all of the authority of Right;
(ii) Equality of all those in the business;
(iii) Ownership of the business by the Community that works in it.[10]

'The Authority of Right' is rooted in the teaching of Jesus of Nazareth. 'Our concern is not merely to provide a possible alternative to the present order of society, still less to hold up before men a desirable though unattainable ideal. We proclaim the way of Jesus as the one practical policy for society—"The Way, the Truth, and the Life": His way alone does justice to the real character of human life . . .'

From this basic position, three demands follow: (a) that 'every human being without distinction of race, nation or class, possesses an intrinsic value. Human well-being must, therefore, be the supreme consideration in all political and economic questions'; (b) that 'the fruits of the earth, the skill of hand and brain must be devoted to the well-being of humanity as a whole' since they are 'God's gifts' and (c) that 'all man's activities must be directed towards the creation of a society in which full opportunity is offered for worthy fellowship with each other, and through each other, a living fellowship with God'.

Equality in business is considered to mean equality of opportunity and abolition of special privileges and power positions

[10] See *Christian Principles Practised in Industry*, A Record of seventeen years growth to Full Community Ownership; Printed and Published by Farmer & Sons Ltd., 295 Edgeware Road, London, W.2, 1962, p. 23. For further quotations see *ibid.*, pp. 11ff.

which are not rooted in people's knowledge, experience and abilities. Equality thus understood means transcendence of the employer-employee relationship through a divestment of power by those in privileged position and development of an organization based on common ownership. In this way it is expected that each person develops 'a sense of ownership and responsibility'. Profits become the common earnings of the community and the responsibility for policy is given to the community. This responsibility is exercised through a democratic machinery in which those in supervisory or leadership positions are appointed or elected.

The Basis contains a strong emphasis on a broad conception of democracy: 'Only a genuine democracy with vigorous life in itself can secure a full and free life to individuals. The best training ground for democratic citizens is to be found in the activity of small groups and local associations; without this the individual may find himself powerless in face of a great machine.'

In conformity with these principles an organization has been built up which offers manifold opportunities for participation.

The principle of equality of labour and capital finds its organizational expression in two kinds of shares: (a) ordinary shares which are held in common by all those working at Farmerservice who are at least 16 years of age and (b) preference shares which are owned by those who supplied the capital.

The Board of Directors consists of four people, two of them being elected by the preference shareholders and two by the ordinary shareholders. In case of equal votes, the matter is submitted to compulsory arbitration. It is the function of the Board to take the leadership in formulating the policy of the firm. But the ultimate authority lies with an annual general meeting at which policy recommendations are discussed and adopted.

While day-to-day decisions are made by the officers of the firm—the Managing Director, the Works Manager, etc.—there is also a Committee of Management appointed by the General Meeting which consists of the Secretary of the Community, a representative from each of the four departments, a representative of the women workers, and a representative of the preference shareholders. The Committee of Management takes a position intermediary between the Board of Directors and the day-to-day decision-making process. It may take up any questions which come up in connection with work, make policy recommendations to the Board or give instructions to those in charge of the day-to-day decision-making process.

The Management Committee also functions as an appeals committee which deals with any objections to dismissals or any act 'prejudicial to the spirit outlined in the Basis'. There is an independent arbitration procedure for appeals.

There is also a Departmental Committee in each department and there are Committees for social activities etc.

The main opportunities for participation are found in these Departmental Committees, the special purpose Committees, the General Meetings, the Management Committee and the Board of Directors.

All people at Farmer's are expected to be members of a union—the Printing Trades Alliance.

There is no clocking-in at Farmer's. In addition to sick-leave benefits and a modest pension plan, people working at Farmer's are entitled to 100 hours free-time in any period of three years over and above holidays and sick-leave. They do not have to give any special reason for taking time off under the 100-hour rule. This is a unique privilege .

The basic wage and salary scales are agreed upon at the General Annual Meeting. At present the basic wage rates are 10 per cent. above the going trade union rates. There are also special rates for outstanding service awards. These awards are made by the Managing Director and the Works Manager in consultation with the person immediately in charge of the work group. They are based on a graduated scale taking into consideration (i) quality of work, (ii) speed of production, (iii) readiness to take responsibility, (iv) interest in the firm, (v) interest in the system of Farmerservice and in carrying out the Basis of Farmerservice, (vi) readiness 'to put thought into instructions', (vii) 'willingness to help others', (viii) 'to be honest to put right something which is wrong', (ix) 'to be honest to improve something which is good', (x) 'to be honest with people rather than talk about them to others', (xi) interest in the Printing

Trades Alliance and (xii) other points concerning work rules, etc.

All people working at Farmer's call each other by their Christian names. In a country which is much more formal than the United States, this is a considerable departure from ordinary industrial practices.[11]

A final venture which must be mentioned here are the Factories for Peace. Their name is derived from their commitment to use profits not needed for their own development to further the cause of peace, to help under-developed countries and local community development. The first Factory for Peace, the Rowen Engineering Company, was founded in Scotland in 1963. The name was formed by using the initial and the last name of Robert Owen. The factory produces storage heaters and began work with two people. After three years already 25 people are working at Rowen Engineering. In 1966 a Welsh Factory for Peace was founded with considerable help from trade unions and the National Coal Board. Plans for further factories indicate the dynamics of this new movement.[12]

Tom McAlpine, a young Scottish engineer, has initiated the Factory for Peace movement. As a member of the Iona Community and a one-time member of the Labour Party, he stands in the tradition of British socialism and a Christian concern with man and society. Some of his ideas have been summed up in these words:

> 'He became convinced of the sterility and lack of genuine democracy in conventional party politics. He was greatly concerned about peace but felt that existing anti-war groups, although

[11] We have undertaken a careful study of the impact of the organization of work at Farmer Service as regards the basic attitudes towards work and problems of democratic participation. The primary focus of this study was on problems of mental health and the organization of industry. The relevant conclusions reported in this book have been carefully compared with the data of the Farmer study. The research design of the Farmer Service study was essentially the same as the research design underlying the study of Scott Bader.

[12] See the Statement *Factory for Peace* issued by the Rowen Engineering Co. Ltd., 78 Middlesex Street, Glasgow, S.1; see also Rod Prince, 'A Second Factory for Peace', *Peace News*, April 30, 1965; and *Rowen*, Factory for

doing an important job, were too negative and had failed to develop roots among the mass of the people for whom problems of international violence seemed remote and who had little tradition of active political participation. He felt that the peace movement should become involved in the creative solution of problems at all levels and should attempt to develop an understanding of non-violence in relation to everyday affairs. One could hardly expect democracy, responsibility and concern for others to thrive at the political level when the work group, which is such an important part of people's lives, is authoritarian and places great stress on individual competitiveness. In addition, there was the more mundane problem of finding sources of finance to further the cause of peace and for many other projects, in particular the setting up of similar factories in under-privileged nations.'

Tom McAlpine is convinced that the Factories for Peace have 'an important part to play in the non-violent revolution which is taking place in our social, industrial, religious and political affairs'. The factories themselves are organized on a radical democratic basis. The Rowen Engineering Company is owned by the Rowen Community, an organization which holds the shares of the company. After not more than three months all people working in the company become members of the community with equal voting rights. To make a genuine experiment the specific structure of the organization was left to those working in the company. The only condition was the establishment of an Advisory Council composed of representatives of organizations which have supported the project. The Iona Community, the Committee of 100, the Local Campaign for Nuclear Disarmament, War on Want are members of the Advisory Council. The Council has the right of veto if ever the personnel should try to sell the company for personal gain or make goods for war purposes. Apart from this the people working in the company are completely autonomous.

They constituted a General Council as 'the organ of management and control of the factory'. The Council consists of all

Peace, Donor's News Bulletin No. 4. See also Extract from Minutes of Annual General Meeting of the Rowen Engineering Co. Ltd. held on May 23, 1966.

members of the community and meets, as a rule, every two weeks. Chairmanship in the General Council is on a rotating basis. At its Annual General Meeting, directors, managers, foremen are elected by the membership. The meeting also determines wages. A systematic attempt has been made to reduce the usual worker-managers differential and no manager can be paid more than 1½ times the basic male rate on the factory floor.

Problems of the correct function of management in a system of co-operative control, of exercising authority democratically, of developing the knowledge necessary for responsible participation and of dealing with conflicts constructively are being constantly examined and subject to experimentation. The factory also intends to experiment with creative working patterns to avoid industrial boredom.

III

In France a movement similar to Demintry has realized some remarkable new forms of organization of work. The 'Communautés de Travail'—Work Communities—arose after World War II and have members all over France.[13]

The movement was initiated by Marcel Barbu, the owner of a watch-case factory at Valence, situated in the Dauphiné. During the occupation of France by the Nazis during World War II, Barbu began to think about new forms of organizing work. When asked to hand his list of employees to the Nazis he refused to do so and was eventually arrested and deported while other members joined the Maquis and fought in the mountains near Valence. When the war was over, Barbu was freed and began to build a new community of work. He

[13] *Les Communautés de Travail*. Bilan d'une expérience de Propriété et de gestion collectives, Entente Communautaire, 72 Cours de Vincennes, Paris, 1958; see also, Henri Desroche and Albert Meister, *Une Communauté de Travail de la Banlieue Parisienne*, Paris, 1954; For many detailed discussions see *Communauté*, Organe Bimestriel des Communautés de Travail, 72 Cours de Vincennes, Paris 12. See *Boimondau* 1941–1951, '10 Années d'Expérience communautaire', numéro spécial de la revue *Communauté*. All references in this section not otherwise indicated are from this publication, esp. pp. 15, 22, 145. See also *Communauté*, 20ᵉ année, No. 1–6 (1965) and 21ᵉ année, No. 1 (1966).

transformed his firm Boimondau—an abbreviation of BOIters MONtres DAUphine watch cases of the Dauphiné—into a communal undertaking.

The aim of the reorganization was a radical one: to create a new type of man. 'To create man, such is our aim. We did not simply have the ambition to create a powerful and balanced enterprise, our concern was to make watch cases to make men,'

The type of men which Boimondau wants to create are to be strong (*viril*), courageous and with a clear awareness of themselves (*une conscience claire*). They are to be 'men of character', who follow the maxim of Socrates 'know thyself'... 'free men... who can find the necessary social discipline... (and who can realize) the greatest freedom of spirit independent from any party or any organization'. They are also to be rooted in family life, cultivated, simple and peace-loving. They are 'to put into practice the old words expressed by the Nazarene: "Love each other!".'

The first step in building up a new organization of work within which such qualities could develop was a proposal by Marcel Barbu to the workers to meet periodically and to discuss the problems which come up each week. Out of these discussions the basic principles and a Constitution for the work community developed. A new view of society emerged.

Basic has been the recognition of the supremacy of the individual conscience and the desire to foster the development of whole persons. Community has been considered the natural expression of individuals who are interrelated with each other. 'The community is a grouping of men and not merely of interests and of things... Every fellow-worker must take a religious or philosophical position. He commits himself to cultivate his convictions... and, if he has chosen a religion, to practise it... The fellow-workers also commit themselves to observe the greatest possible tolerance and to respect sincerely the different belief or philosophical positions...' A community based on these principles was to allow men to be ends in themselves and not means for purposes of other men.

The Constitution states explicitly that 'the community of work engages the totality of man and envisages him from all points of view'. As a result work is defined broadly as an activity encompassing 'all human activities . . . a vocation . . . to develop and engage spirit, mind and body'. The community used farming to balance the work in the factory. It experimented, furthermore, with payments based on 'the human value' or 'the social value' rather than 'according to the professional value of the individual'. Though discontinued, these experiments remain significant.

Property is divided into two forms: community property and property owned by the fellow-workers. All means of production and everything that is used by all fellow-workers is community property. Individual property consists of the 'fruits of the labour' of the members of the community.

The ultimate power of the community rests in a General Assembly in which all fellow-workers have a vote. Formerly, decisions were made on the basis of unanimity, now on a majority basis. Whatever came up at the General Assembly had been previously discussed by the Basic Groups. The latter were the foundation of the new organization. They consisted of five or six families meeting in the house of a fellow-worker. They were organized in a Council of the Groupleaders. Now there are no more family activities and the communitarian movement is exclusively based on the work situation.

All executive functions are delegated to a General Manager who is elected for three years by the General Assembly. The General Manager can be recalled or be re-elected after the three years are over. He is 'helped, advised and controlled' by a General Council.

The General Assembly also elects a Tribunal with the function 'to regulate all the conflicts and differences arising in the community'. The Tribunal is composed of the General Manager, four fellow-workers, two members of the family of fellow-workers and two other people.

The community had to meet major competitive problems and discontinued many of the most daring innovations and experiments as already mentioned. Barbu himself left after some time. Yet Boimondau maintains its basic democratic constitution up to this day and the 'Community of work' movement has constantly developed new forms of organization. Recently it has developed an impressive programme of education, training and research.

As regards Germany we limit ourselves to mention the Zeiss Foundation established in 1896. The foundation aimed to give employees security and 'to fulfil higher social duties than personal proprietors would permanently guarantee towards the totality of co-workers in its employ . . .'. Beyond this the Foundation was concerned with the promotion of scientific research both inside and outside the firm and with the 'public good of the working population' of the local community.

The Foundation established a complex organizational structure which gave people certain rights of participation in the decision-making process while guarding the traditional autonomy of management.[14]

IV

The new ventures in organizing work reviewed in the preceding pages have many common features. They attempt to develop new forms of participation and partnership. They aim to create work communities within which the individual can develop fully. They recognize the value of the person and attempt to enhance individual self-expression through meaningful interpersonal relationships and a common purpose. They give to smaller groups an important role as instruments to relate people to each other and to foster the development of their potentialities. Ultimately these new ventures are groping for a new understanding of man and a new meaning of work.

The Scott Bader Commonwealth belongs to the Demintry firms which are pioneering new ways in Great Britain. It offers an excellent opportunity to examine the problems and the challenge posed by the most advanced of these firms. By examining its new organization of work and new modes of participation we shall get an understanding of the basic problems which all people in industry will be forced to deal with tomorrow unless they are wise enough to face them already today.

[14] See George Goyder, *The Responsible Company*, Oxford 1961, pp. 142ff.

Chapter 4

The People of the Commonwealth

I

Scott Bader has been a growing company since its beginning. In 1951 when the Commonwealth began, about 160 people worked there. Ten years later over 250. In 1965 more than 300 people were at Scott Bader.

When we began our research at Scott Bader in 1958 somewhat less than 200 people were working there. We selected two groups, one of them chosen to give the basic information necessary for an action-research project, the other chosen at random. With the thirty people in the first group we conducted interview-conversations averaging ten and lasting up to twenty hours. These conversations took place between 1958 and 1961. With the forty-odd people in the second group Roger Hadley had interviews of ninety minutes. We also participated in the working life of the community and worked with five groups of about ten people each for well over a year. This book is almost exclusively based on the intensive interview-conversations but major results have been compared to those gained from the group chosen at random and some of the experiences of our group work are included.[1]

Practically all of the 200-odd people who worked at Scott Bader in 1958 came from an area within a radius of four miles of Wollaston, a village with about 2,000 inhabitants, where the firm is located. Over one third lived in Wollaston; close to another third lived in Wellingborough, a town with about 30,000 inhabitants four miles from Wollaston. The remainder lived in the villages surrounding Wollaston. About 85 per cent. of the

[1] For details see Appendix on Method. Relevant data from random samples or significant differences of results between random and quota samples are indicated on pp. 373–375.

people working at Scott Bader were men, about 15 per cent. were women.[2]

With the exception of Wellingborough where many factories can be seen, the area has an agricultural appearance. Actually it is predominantly industrial but the typical industry—boots and shoes—is relatively small-scale and does not shape its environment.[3]

In Wollaston itself the boot and shoe industry is dominant. Close to one fourth of the people working at Scott Bader came from families where the father and sometimes the mother worked in this industry. A number of people from the factory have themselves previously worked in the shoe industry. This situation undoubtedly affected their experience of work.

Industrial relations in the boot and shoe industry have been good within a traditional framework. The actual work is extremely monotonous and is considered to have a detrimental effect on the people. Most tasks are on individual piece-rates and the operatives work continuously under pressure at high speed to make a bonus. Most of the workers are unionized though there is no union or closed shop in the industry. The union plays an important part in the day-to-day lives of the operatives since it negotiates all new piece rates with the employers.[4]

[2] To avoid identification we referred to all women workers as 'he'.

[3] In 1959, 4,500 or 26 per cent. of the insured people registered at Wellingborough worked in the boot and shoe industry. Only 450 people (2.5 per cent.) worked in agriculture. Distributive trades employed about 1,500 (8.5 per cent.); the iron and steel industry just over 1,000 (6.0 per cent.), construction 900 (5 per cent.) and plastics and plastic moulding about 850 (4.5 per cent.). The only other industries employing more than 500 people were food processing, clothing and railways. Information supplied to Roger Hadley by the Regional Office of the Ministry of Labour.

[4] In a general assessment of the industrial relations in the area, the Regional Office of the Ministry of Labour had this to say: 'Our general appraisal is that the area enjoys very satisfactory industrial relations. This may be ascribed in the main to the predominant industry being boot and shoe manufacturers. This industry has had over a long period an excellent record of satisfactory human relationships and in addition, has a well defined procedure for dealing with disputes at all levels.' (See letter from Regional Office of the Ministry of Labour to Mr. Roger Hadley.) There has not been a major strike since

II

The nature and conditions of work are quite different for the people working at Scott Bader. Their industrial history has been much shorter but also—until the Commonwealth was founded—less peaceful. The union, though fully recognized and even welcomed by management, has relatively low representation and plays no major role in the day-to-day working life. There is no piece work at Scott Bader and no need for the kind of continuous strenuous effort required in the boot and shoe industry.

The people of the Commonwealth work in the office, laboratory and factory. Accordingly, they dress in different ways. People in the office work in their ordinary clothes, in the laboratory in white coats and in the factory in green overalls. These concrete visual differences point to basic distinctions (and status identifications) but they also hide important differences.

In the office, tasks vary greatly. They cover a wide range from the overall co-ordinating activity of the Managing Director and the Chairman of the Board to the clerical work of people who type letters, copy figures, or dispatch letters. For the clerks there is a good deal of routine with a similar rhythm of work every day. They use pencil and paper or mechanical devices such as typewriters, calculating machines, etc., as primary instruments of their work. People who perform managerial tasks use their brains, their imagination and perhaps even their hearts

---

1895. In 1895 a comprehensive arbitration machinery was set up in the boot and shoe industry. A trade union leader at the Boot and Shoe Operatives' union conference in 1932 commented on work as follows: 'From meeting men in different parts of the country and trying to deduce what has been the effect of this new simplified machinery on the mind of our operatives, I have been forced to the conclusion that the tendency from a mental point of view is having a very profound effect on our members. In our efforts to try and stimulate the minds of our members, we are running counter to the system under which these members work.' See Alan Fox, *A History of the Union of Boot and Shoe Operatives*, Oxford 1958, p. 543. Negotiations are carried on by a full time official of the union and not by union representatives in the individual factories. A union shop means that all people working in certain occupational groups must belong to a union. A closed shop means that there is a union shop and that only union members may be hired by the employer. In Great Britain this distinction is not a customary one.

as primary instruments. In making this distinction we do not imply that the clerks do not use their brains and imagination. But the use of these capacities is indeterminate; in some cases they execute more the thoughts of others than their own.

The people in the laboratory use test tubes, gas burners, thermometers, and all kinds of oddly shaped glass-ware, as their instruments of work. Clad in white coats to protect their clothing, they use their brains, their imagination and hearts to degrees almost as variable as the chemicals which they mix in their tests and experiments. There are people who deal with complex theoretical problems related to the development of new products and there are people who perform relatively simple manual tasks. Some initiate ideas, others execute them. Experiments are largely carried out by laboratory assistants under the direction of a trained chemist. The assistants are mainly concerned with setting up the apparatus, carrying out the experiments, recording the results and keeping the equipment clean and in order. The equipment varies from simple retorts to complex instruments. There is a certain amount of repetition in the work done in the laboratories but there are constantly new problems.

The blue-collar workers would more appropriately be called the green-overalled people working in the factory. They use hoses to empty the incoming tankers, drive trucks to bring supplies to and from the store rooms, and they manipulate levers, open and close valves, observe indicators, push buttons and turn wheels. They are about equally divided between shift workers and day or general maintenance workers.

The manufacturing process takes place in semi-automatic reactors, condensers, etc. Most of the raw materials are pumped into the reactors in liquid form. Some are in powder form and have to be charged through hatches at the top of the reactors. Bags are lifted from the floor and their contents shovelled into the reactor. These powders may give off fumes and be extremely unpleasant to handle. They may oblige workers to wear protective masks. But this kind of labouring activity is relatively rare. A good deal of the work consists in watching the instrument board with its many indicators (since there is no automatic feed-back) and in handling the wheels, levers, etc. The finished product is filled into drums directly from the reactors. These drums are put on a scale, weighed, sealed and rolled away. Physical effort is limited to putting empty drums on the scale, rolling the filled drums away and assembling them for pick-up by trucks.

The degree to which levers, valves, wheels, trucks, etc. are people's primary instruments of work and the extent to which their brains, imagination and hearts are involved differ greatly. But in the factory the traditional separation of the brain and imagination from the hand and muscles is strongest.

Despite the differences in functions there are common elements between the people working in the office, the laboratory and the factory. Their work has an element of 'labouring' even if this is no longer strong enough to be widely felt. It also has an element of imaginative activity, of co-ordination and goal-orientation though it may not be strong enough to enter the basic image of work. Those who perform integrating managerial tasks and hence use primarily their brains and imagination have to overcome difficulties which only sustained application and efforts of a repetitive nature can master. Those whose tasks are most concretely related to the handling of machines and tools perform some integrative tasks of co-ordination or organization. Also shared is an element of 'working' activity in the sense of giving 'form' to a tangible object, a thing. But on the whole the nature of the product of Scott Bader is such that the form or thing-character of the product is little articulated.

III

In their educational background the people of the Commonwealth vary greatly.

In their origin and education the managerial group is quite typical of management in Britain. They come primarily from professional and independent business families and had a grammar or public school education. The group had an average age below 40.

The laboratory technicians are an even younger group. They

had the lowest average age—well under 30. All but one had a secondary school education. About half had been to grammar school and more than half continued their studies at night school. About half came from homes of manual workers, the other half from homes of clerical office workers, business and professional people.

The clerks also constituted a very young group. Most of the younger clerks were single or recently married women. Most of the women clerks work to their mid-twenties, leaving behind them an older group of predominantly male clerks. The clerks' educational background varied greatly, ranging from primary school to grammar school. About half came from homes of manual workers, about half from professional or independent business men's homes.

Most of the workers came from homes of manual workers. The large majority ended their education with primary school. In terms of average age they were the oldest group, with an average of over 40.[5]

The religious affiliations of the people of the Commonwealth are equally varied. About half of those who took part in the interview-conversations were members of the Church of England. Slightly over one third belonged to Free Churches, three were Roman Catholic and three considered themselves as agnostic or atheists. It is difficult to compare these figures to Church affiliation in Britain since there are no Census figures on religious affiliation and the comparability of available data suffers from differences of definition of membership. But there is strong evidence that the Free Churches were relatively more

[5] The British educational system provides for infant, primary or junior school from ages 5–11. Until recently practically all pupils had to take an examination at the age of 11 (the 11 plus) and were then divided into secondary modern (ages 11–15) or grammar (ages 11–18) schools. The latter prepare pupils for university entrance examinations. There are also Colleges of Further Education (ages 15–18) and Advanced Technical Colleges after the age of 18. The 11 plus examination is now in the process of being abolished and secondary modern and grammar schools are being combined in 'comprehensive schools'. All these are within the State system of education. There are also private schools, most of which are called in Great Britain 'public' or 'independent' schools.

strongly represented among the people interviewed than they are in Great Britain as a whole.[6]

Politically, the people of the Commonwealth leaned towards the Labour Party. In the general elections of 1959 about two thirds voted for the Labour Party, about one third for the Conservative Party. There was no candidate of the Liberal Party in the constituency. A large percentage—about twenty per cent. of all voters—would have preferred to vote for the Liberal Party if there had been a candidate. Compared with national figures which showed a Labour vote of 43·8 per cent., the people of the Commonwealth were relatively more inclined towards the Labour Party.

These differences are influenced by the large number of executives who voted for the Labour Party at Scott Bader. About 5 out of 6 senior managers voted for Labour. In the laboratory the ratio of Labour to Conservative votes was 2:3 in favour of the Conservatives and in the factory 2:1 in favour of Labour. The large Labour vote among management is untypical of Great Britain.[7]

[6] The last authoritative figures are those of the Census of 1851. Even then, there was no compulsion to answer the questions about religious affiliation. The official yearbooks and handbooks of various religious denominations are the only available sources. See: *British Political Facts 1900–1960*, by David Butler and Jennie Freeman, London 1963, p. 200. Comparisons are complicated by the fact that in 1956 the Church of England counted about 27 million baptized members, about 10 million confirmed members, about 3 million on the electoral rolls and a little over 2 million Easter communicants. See *Official Year-Book of the Church of England*, 1960, The Church Information Office of the Church Assembly, London, p. 314. The Baptist Church in the British Isles had about 318,000 members in 1960; the Congregational Church had in 1959 about 212,000 members in the United Kingdom; the Methodist Church had in December 1959 about 729,000 members in Great Britain and Ireland; the Presbyterian Church had in 1960 about 71,000 members in England; the Society of Friends had in 1963 about 21,100 members of the London Yearly Meeting. The estimated Roman Catholic population in Great Britain amounted in 1960 to about 4.8 million people. See *British Political Facts 1900–1960* for all denominations except for the Society of Friends for which data were obtained from Friends House in London.

[7] Data in this section are based on the random sample. For general data see D. E. Butler and E. Rose, *The British General Election of 1959*, London 1960, p. 226.

Part II

The First Decade of the Commonwealth 1951–1963

Chapter 5

The Commonwealth begins to reorganize work

I

When Ernest Bader decided in 1951 to start the Commonwealth after the failure of the Fellowship to bring the desired results he had a difficult task ahead of him. His own religious convictions were not shared by the vast majority of the people and his ideas about power and responsibility were met by many with lukewarmness and doubt if not outright cynicism.[1] 'What is "the old man" really up to?' What was really behind the search for new ways? What were the hidden motives? Why would any man give up money and power? These questions were asked at Scott Bader.

The idea of the Commonwealth also sparked off latent hopes and aspirations for a more human life in industry. For some the Commonwealth meant the new Jerusalem of industry. But the basic problem remained to build a new organization of work with people whose experience of life was moulded by an organization based on entirely different ideas of power and value. This problem raised some questions in Ernest Bader's mind. Were the people ready to take responsibility? What might happen if they would not use their power with discrimination and knowledge? Could they be given ultimate responsibility for a company which was in a tough competitive struggle?

These questions were not simply the result of personal doubts. There was a good deal of experience which justified them. The history of the British co-operative movement in particular showed the difficulty of combining a democratic organization of work with efficient management. But without efficient

[1] Over a decade after the Fellowship had come to an end a worker, speaking about the religious emphasis of the Fellowship, said: 'If Ernest Bader really expected us to follow these practices he might as well have fired all of us.' See also Chapter 1.

management no firm could survive. It is true Farmerservice had been operating with a common ownership scheme for several years before the Commonwealth was founded. But it operated in different circumstances. The John Lewis Partnership, the largest firm searching for new ways, had just accepted a Constitution which carefully safeguarded the right of management to make the ultimate decisions.

The first Constitution of the Commonwealth which was accepted in 1951 reflected this concern about the best possible management. The basic features of the Constitution were: acceptance of the principle of common ownership and recognition of the need to develop entirely new channels for participation, immediate divestment of the right to dispose of the profits, which, in conjunction with the principle of common ownership, assured the work community rather than any one person or group of the benefits of all future growth. Actual power was to be transferred gradually though a new structure of power was to be created immediately. The principle of a division of power in legislative, executive and judicial organs was to be followed in industry.

II

The main instrument to bring about these changes was the creation of a 'Scott Bader Commonwealth Limited', a charitable organization which exists as a legal entity independent of the 'Scott Bader Company Limited', an ordinary company. This dual legal structure is necessary under British company law. But the two organizations have been closely inter-related since the Commonwealth owned from its inception 90 per cent. of the shares of the Company. The remaining 10 per cent. remained from 1951 to 1963 in the hands of the Founder Members.

The 90 per cent. of the shares owned by the Commonwealth has been held corporately by the members of the Commonwealth. No individual member owns a share and no individual can personally benefit from a sale of shares. They are truly communal shares and if ever the company should be sold, the receipts must go for some charitable purpose.

Membership in the Commonwealth is open to anybody after a probationary period. Voting rights are related to membership in the Commonwealth, not to shareholding. Each member has one vote, not each representative of a piece of paper. Human beings count.

In 1951, when the Commonwealth was founded, any person over 21 years could apply for membership after six months of service with the company. In 1958 the waiting period was extended to two years. This rule was in force until the new Constitution was adopted in 1963. There also were—and still are—provisions for Associate membership for people under 21 years of age. Application for Associate membership is possible after six months of service. Associate members can participate in all Commonwealth activities without having the right to vote.[2]

Originally, members of the Commonwealth accepted a threefold obligation: (i) To give at least 8 hours voluntary service each year, (ii) not to enter into dual employment and (iii) to share losses as well as profits.

Voluntary service has been broadly defined as service 'on behalf of Commonwealth activities, assisting others in a good cause, and any other approved service to the Community in general.'

The dual employment clause has been felt to enable people 'to give of their best to the Commonwealth and their work . . . for the company. This applies to all but is of particular importance to those engaged in our experimental and manufacturing processes where the intricate machinery and inflammable nature of our materials, badly handled, could endanger the lives of us all, and cause thousands of pounds worth of damage.'[3]

The principle of sharing losses as well as profits has been considered a logical implication of 'the fundamental purpose of the Commonwealth to ensure security of employment and a stable income to all members.'

Members have never been required to agree with specific attitudes such as pacifism: 'The Commonwealth was founded

[2] See *Memorandum Commonwealth 1951*, Article 4, p. 7.

[3] See *New Life in Industry*, Handbook and Charter for the Staff of Scott Bader & Co. Ltd., Second Edition, July 1955, p. 54.

for the realization of the ideals of peace and principles of social justice which the Founders cherish. These are largely those of the Society of Friends and the Founders hope to awaken the interest of all their co-workers and encourage them to contribute their share to their realization. However there is no obligation whatever on the employees to endorse these specific ideas on peace and justice and membership is open to any employee of 21 years and over.'[4] But members have been 'expected to accept the principles on which the Commonwealth is founded'.[5] These principles, as laid down in the Memorandum and Articles of Association, call for a basic reorientation of people's attitudes and for a fundamental reconstruction of the social order based on the principles of common ownership.

When applying for membership, a person recognizing his or her 'responsibility as co-owners of Scott Bader & Co. Ltd., accepts the three specific conditions mentioned above and agrees to do everything in furthering the objectives of the Commonwealth'. Besides the right to participate and vote in all Commonwealth activities, the members of the Commonwealth have been entitled from the very beginning of the Commonwealth to six months' sick-leave with full pay for each year.

Membership in the Commonwealth does not imply a formal guarantee of employment but there is an informal understanding that members are not to be dismissed except for cause. To express this understanding members signed a certificate of mutual security.[6]

The main legislative body through which the members of the

[4] See the booklet *Scott Bader & Co. Ltd.*, 1955, p. 28.

[5] See *New Life in Industry*, *op. cit.*, p. 55.

[6] The '*Certificate of Mutual Security* through membership in the Scott Bader Commonwealth Ltd.' certifies that 'a duly appointed member of the Scott Bader Commonwealth and pursuant with existing Company Law as a legally recognized Co-Owner is entitled to the benefits, resources and assets of the Chemical Manufacturing business of Scott Bader & Co. Ltd. in accordance with the rules and regulations laid down in the Staff Handbook entitled 'New Life in Industry' and its Memorandum and Articles of Association. As an Industrial Self-governing Community Enterprise our members have bound themselves together in a solemn bond for mutual well-being and security against incapacity, unemployment and want, either during the time of active membership or subsequent old age retirement.'

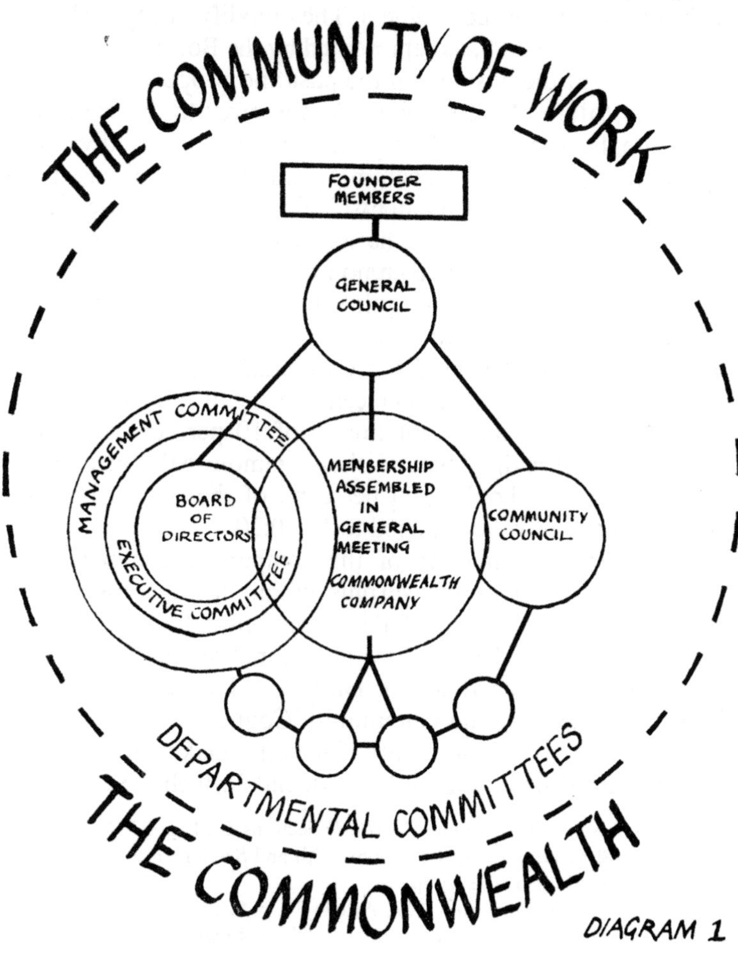
THE COMMONWEALTH 1951-1963
THE COMMUNITY OF WORK
FOUNDER MEMBERS
GENERAL COUNCIL
MANAGEMENT COMMITTEE
BOARD OF DIRECTORS
EXECUTIVE COMMITTEE
MEMBERSHIP ASSEMBLED IN GENERAL MEETING
COMMONWEALTH COMPANY
COMMUNITY COUNCIL
DEPARTMENTAL COMMITTEES
THE COMMONWEALTH

DIAGRAM 1

Commonwealth exercise their basic rights is the General Meeting. The circle in the centre of Diagram 1 symbolizing this organ is divided in two parts since the members assemble to do 'Company' as well as 'Commonwealth' business.[7] When doing company business the members of the Commonwealth deal with the conduct of the business. They modify or reject the way in which management, as represented by the Board of Directors, has conducted the business in the past and proposes to conduct it in the future. When doing Commonwealth business they distribute the money which they receive every year as 'dividends' for the shares they hold in common and they may discuss problems and conditions of membership in the Commonwealth.

The dividends are part of the surplus which they earned each year as the result of their common effort and which belongs to the community. The basic guidelines for its distribution are laid down in the Constitution. At first, in 1951, a minimum of 70 per cent. was to be used for 'consolidation, taxation and reserves', a maximum of 20 per cent. for 'staff bonus, including production bonus' and a maximum of 10 per cent. for 'gross dividends', that is dividends to the Commonwealth as a charitable organization holding 90 per cent. of the shares. In 1953, these percentages were changed to 60:20:20.[8]

The Board of Directors of the company recommends the actual distribution of the surplus within these constitutional limits to the membership of the Commonwealth assembled in General Meeting. The members then approve, modify or reject the suggestion of the Board of Directors. The elected organ of the Commonwealth, the Community Council of Management, briefly called the 'Community Council', makes recommendations for the distribution of the 'dividends' which the Common-

[7] See *Memorandum Commonwealth 1951*, Sections 5–21, pp. 7–10 in regard to the General Meeting of the Commonwealth and Sections 7–9 p. 2 in regard to General Meetings of the company.

[8] See *Memorandum Company 1951*, Article 39, p. 9. Actually these percentages are incorporated in the constitution of the company and not in that of the Commonwealth. This, however, is due to technical reasons. The inclusion of such a provision is certainly a result of the Commonwealth. It would have no meaning in an ordinary company since it could be changed any time through a simple majority vote of the shareholders.

wealth has received for charitable purposes.[9] Again, the General Meeting approves, modifies or rejects these proposals. The principle of common ownership was thus from the very beginning accompanied by a shift of actual power to dispose of the surplus earned.

To safeguard the development of the business during an experimental period, the 10 per cent. Founder Shares held by the Founder Members retained the following rights: (i) to appoint Directors; (ii) to veto any measure taken by any organ of the company or the Commonwealth if they felt that 'a clear breach of the principles upon which the company is intended to be managed' was involved; (iii) to require the Board of Directors to take any measure to restore the profit-making capacity of the company 'if at any time the auditors of the company shall certify that the business of the company is in their opinion being run at a loss'.[10]

Except for the appointment of Directors these rights were never exercised by the Founder Members while they existed between 1951 and 1963. The Founders emphasized, furthermore, repeatedly that these rights were temporary and that the ultimate goal was to abolish the Founder Shares—as in fact happened after a little over a decade. To move towards this goal new modes of participation were developed all through the firm.[11]

III

Besides participating in the legislative body the members of the Commonwealth participate in administrative and judicial organs.

[9] *Memorandum Commonwealth 1951*, Article 33, p. 14.

[10] See *Memorandum Company 1951*, Article 12, p. 3. The Founder Members also retained certain rights in regard to transfer of shares from other Founder Members. This, however, is not relevant in this connection. Actually the Founder Shares were in the hands of six Founder Members. But the distribution of shares and power among the Founder Members was such that in practice Ernest Bader could exercise the power of the Founder Shares.

[11] However during the first twelve years of the existence of the Commonwealth the Founder Member rights existed and must have influenced people's

The Community Council, already mentioned, is the main administrative organ of the Commonwealth. It consists of twelve people, nine being elected by secret ballot, two nominated by the Board of Directors, one member representing the local community is nominated by the Council and must be approved by the Board.[12]

The Community Council, as already mentioned, makes recommendations (i) for the distribution of the Commonwealth dividends, (ii) for the conduct of the members including rules for acceptance to membership. Each application for membership is decided on its own merit. The Community Council has, therefore, considerable power in interpreting the rules in regard to membership.

Another organ, the General Council, whose name and functions were changed later, had primarily a judicial function but also had some subsidiary non-judicial functions. It consisted of sixteen people, half of whom were elected by 'the staff' and the other half by 'management'. The Council dealt (i) 'with any disputes or questions affecting disciplinary action'. In this capacity its decisions were final. (ii) The General Council could also 'act as referee and give decisions on matters which are referred to it either by the individual employees, the departmental representatives, the management committee, the executive members of the Company or the Directors'.[13] (iii) Finally, the Council could take the initiative in discussing any matter of expenditure and finance and make recommendations to the Board of Directors for their decision.

IV

The general meetings, the Community Council and the General Council are the main new organs through which the people working at Scott Bader could participate in work and its organiz-

[12] See *Memorandum Commonwealth 1951*, pp. 10–16. Commonwealth membership is a prerequisite for serving on the Community Council.
[13] See *Memorandum Commonwealth 1951*, Article 31, pp. 7–8.

attitude towards work. Indeed it must have affected people's attitude towards the whole experiment and limited their experience of ownership.

ation. These organs were 'added' to a more or less traditional pyramidal structure of management. In this process the weight of the pyramid was loosened, a process which was carried a step further through the opening of new channels of participation within this structure.

To describe the structure of management is to describe the executive organs of Scott Bader. The main organ is the Board of Directors with a special feature: so-called Commonwealth Directors.

The Board—whose constitution was changed later—consisted of not more than nine Directors, not more than three of them being Founder Member Directors, not more than three ordinary Directors and not more than three Commonwealth Directors.[14] The ordinary Directors were appointed by the Founder Members. The Commonwealth Directors were elected by secret ballot from a list of not less than six members nominated by Commonwealth members and approved by the Board of Directors. In this way there was direct representation of the Commonwealth on the Board itself.

Around the Board of Directors has been since the beginning of the Commonwealth an Executive Committee consisting of the Board, the Secretary of the company and the chief department heads. Around the Executive Committee has been a Management Committee comprising the Executive, foremen, plant managers etc. The Management Committee has its own Chairman, Vice-Chairman and Secretary. The functions of the Management Committee have been '(i) to discuss appointments and dismissals of staff, general questions of wages and salaries, terms of employment and other schemes for the welfare of the company and its employees; and (ii) make recommendations to the executive members of the company and discuss all difficulties in the management of the company and in the relations between management and employees, with a view to fostering agreement and harmony in the internal relations of the company.'[15]

[14] *Ibid*, Article 14, p. 7. Actually, the number of Directors was never higher than 9 including the two Commonwealth Directors.

[15] *Memorandum Company 1951*, Article 24, pp. 5–6. As an administrative organ, the Management Commiteee proved of little significance.

While much of the Executive and Management committee is quite traditional in its conception, a first attempt has been made to allow more participation through the formation of departmental committees. The members of these committees consist 'of all the persons employed in each department of the company'. Their function is 'to represent the interests of the department in the internal organization of the company and to elect and advise the representatives of the department on the General Council'.[16]

V

The new organization of work which emerged from the formation of legislative, executive and judicial organs is illustrated in Diagram 1. The membership of the Commonwealth assembled in general meetings is at the centre of the work community. Its ultimate responsibility was balanced by the rights of the Founder Members (see top of Diagram 1). The Board of Directors—surrounded by the Executive Committee and the Management Committee—is represented to the left of the legislative; the Community Council to the right. The General Council, as the main judiciary organ, is represented above the legislative and executive organs.

Both the Board of Directors and the Community Council have executive and policy-making functions. When they perform the latter they may be considered as legislative committees. The significance of legislative committees is well known in the history of democratic institutions. They are decisive for the quality of the democratic process.

At the basis of the whole organization below the legislative and administrative organs on Diagram 1 are the departmental committees which may be considered as the basic groups for participation. Here we find the daily problems of work at the grass roots.

As we look at the way in which the various organs of the new

[16] See *Memorandum Company 1951*, Article 28, pp. 6 and 7. Membership in the General Council is not dependent upon membership in the Commonwealth.

organization of work were and to a considerable extent still are constituted we find that the members of the Commonwealth have the predominant influence in the general meetings and in the Community Council—they elect nine out of its twelve members. The General Council gave equal rights to management and staff. On the Board of Directors the Founder Members had the greatest power. They and their appointees constituted two thirds of the Board. The Commonwealth Directors were and still are a minority. The Founder Members also exercised veto rights.

The new organization began, therefore, as a mixed one. On the one hand was the traditional conception of a managerial hierarchy and power vested in the top. On the other hand there was a clear break-through of an entirely new conception which —for reasons to be discussed later—we have given a circular representation.[17] To indicate that we are dealing with a stage of transition we have drawn the outer circle symbolizing the community as a whole as a broken circle. We are dealing with a community in the making, a community which still has essential elements of a traditional hierarchy but which has already developed new ways of participation in work.

The beginnings are, therefore, in a twilight of the old and the new, of direction from above and participation based on common ownership and the recognition that each person has something to contribute according to his or her knowledge, experience and insight. To make such participation a reality and to assure the best management and democratic leadership is a problem which remained to be worked out. It required not only the implementation and further development of a new power structure. Power and values cannot be separated and a new structure of value was as imperative as a new structure of power.

Here too the Commonwealth began in a twilight, even more pronounced than in regard to its structure of power. The central value of the firm, a concept of productivity defined in terms of technical-market chances, was not changed. There was from the beginning an awareness of the need for new relationships

[17] See below Chapter 17.

between the people, for a growth from an egocentric adjustment to a mutuality of relationship through which both the person and the community could grow. There was also an awareness of the need to give new meaning to work by making it a service rather than merely a job and a commercial activity. There was also a desire to find a more just distribution of the fruits of the common labour. But besides the traditional concept of productivity there was the necessity to produce a competitive product. Since responsibility for values expresses itself in the cost accounting system of a firm, and costs must be competitive, certain limitations existed from the beginning.

How did the Commonwealth cope with the problems posed by its new structure of values and power? How are the institutional changes related to the basic objectives which it set itself and to the needs and aspirations experienced by the people?

Chapter 6

The transformation of wages and profits

I

Every organization of work must be understood as a historically specific attempt to solve universal problems. Hence every aspect of the organization of work has both a historically specific and a universal dimension.

Wages, for example, may be defined as the earnings or the income received for a labouring activity. In this sense everybody who does any work at all receives wages—whether he is the manager of a company or whether he services a machine, whether he is a capitalist, in a socialist or any other country. As soon as the economy has developed beyond a barter economy people receive wages in this universal sense of the word.

Wages, on the other hand, may be defined with reference to a particular wage system. In a capitalist society, for example, wages are earnings of wage-labour, that is of a worker who is dependent upon a capitalist, or to use the more neutral terms, of an 'employee' who is dependent upon an 'employer'. The historically unique aspects of such a relationship are (i) formal equality and freedom combined with inequality in money-power, (ii) private ownership of the means of production, (iii) sovereign rights of control attached to ownership and (iv) division of the community into those who have control and those who do not have control over the organization of work.

This historically specific definition of wages does not abolish the universal meaning of wages but it supersedes the universal definition to the extent to which the dynamics of the social system as well as the consciousness of the people are determined by the historically specific and not by the universal meaning.

A similar distinction is imperative as regards profits. The universal meaning of profits is that of a surplus available after current costs of production have been paid. In this universal sense profits are an accounting term which has validity whenever and wherever rational methods of cost accounting are used. The existence of profits in this sense indicates that a given task —defined by the specific responsibilities taken, that is costs incurred—has been satisfactorily performed.

The historically unique definition of profits under capitalism is quite different: here profits have a number of functions. They are the yardstick to decide whether a commodity should be produced or not. To the extent to which the individual firm has the ultimate decision, profits are also the yardstick for the way and the extent to which a country's resources are to be allocated and people's needs to be satisfied. Under capitalism profits are also a category of income, they are the reward of the owner-entrepreneurs or, as dividends, of the shareholders.

By creating the Commonwealth Ernest Bader rejected the capitalist definition of wages, profits and dividends and restored their universal function to the extent to which this is possible for an individual firm. He called capital 'a form of spirit'.[1] At first this seems an unreal way of speaking. But we understand the true meaning of such a conception as we recall that Max Weber referred to machines as *geronnener Geist*, as 'embodied spirit'.[2] The word spirit is taken here in the broad sense of a power which animates something, which gives it its peculiar form and function. Ernest Bader expressed in his designation of profits his quest for a universal spirit or reality. This is decisive for understanding the meaning of the new structure of power and values established by the Commonwealth.

II

From its very inception, the Commonwealth has changed the function and the meaning of profits. They have ceased to be a category of income which stands in opposition to 'wages'. The former owners, though retaining certain privileges of control,

[1] See *From Profit Sharing to Common Ownership* printed by the Scott Bader Commonwealth in January 1956.

[2] See Max Weber, *Gessammelte politische Schriften*, Munich 1921, p. 298.

divested themselves immediately of the right to dispose of the surplus over and above current expenditures for materials and current payments to all those who gave their services to Scott Bader.

Technically this surplus continued to be called 'net profits before appropriations'[3] but the money thus designated was no longer considered the earnings of capital but the earnings of the whole community of work. In this recognition common ownership finds its first concrete expression: the community has the responsibility to dispose of the surplus. As we have seen, the Constitution provides definite guidance for their disposal. During the time when we studied the Commonwealth a minimum of 60 per cent. was to be ploughed back for the development of the work facilities, a maximum of 20 per cent. for annual payments to the people working at Scott Bader ('staff bonus') and a maximum of 20 per cent. for charitable purposes ('gross dividends').[4] The total amount distributed to the staff cannot be higher than the total amount given for charitable purposes.

Actual distribution of funds for charitable purposes varied between zero and 10 per cent. between 1951 and 1963. Annual payments to the people working at Scott Bader varied between 5 per cent. and 10 per cent. Money ploughed back for the development of the work facilities fluctuated between 37 per cent. and 53 per cent. of the surplus.[5]

Since the surplus had a tendency to rise (though less strongly than sales) the actual amounts of money available for distribution were rising. During the first five years (1951–1955) the average yearly surplus amounted to £40,000. During the last five years (1959–1963) it amounted to close to £100,000. During the whole period 1951–1963 the total amount distributed for

[3] Net profits before appropriation were defined as profits 'before the deduction of income tax, profits tax and any other tax on the profits of the company, and before the deduction of any amount to be paid in staff bonus or dividends.' See *Memorandum Commonwealth 1951*, Article 39, p. 9.

[4] See *Memorandum Commonwealth 1951*, Article 39, p. 9.

[5] Until 1953 the percentages of funds distributed for charitable purposes and for annual payment to the personnel differed. From 1953 on these percentages were identical.

charitable purposes was over £60,000 (or over $150,000), for annual payments to the staff over £65,000 (or over $160,000), and the amount ploughed back (in addition to normal depreciation provisions) for development of the work facilities was approximately £390,000 (or over a million dollars).

The annual payments to people working at Scott Bader are made in addition to the money received at weekly or monthly intervals.[6] There are three important differences between these payments and staff bonus in the usual sense of the word. (i) The bonus at Scott Bader comes from what is acknowledged to be joint earnings of the community, from a common surplus. (ii) Its determination is in the hands of the Commonwealth. It is not given to employees by an employer out of so-called earnings of capital. (iii) The money given to the staff is part of a new evolving conception of just distribution of all earnings. For these reasons we speak about an annual distribution of common earnings rather than a bonus. During the year each person has 'current' earnings for current needs. At the end of the year, each person may have an additional 'annual' share in the common earnings.

As we have seen the members of the Commonwealth have the right to approve, modify or reject the recommendations made by the Board of Directors in regard to their annual share in earnings. From 1951 to 1963 they have not allocated to themselves more than a maximum of about a half the amount they were constitutionally entitled to distribute. Instead of giving to themselves 20 per cent. of the earnings they have at no time given themselves more than about 10 per cent. On the other hand they have allocated more than the amount constitutionally demanded for the development of the firm and the creation of new work facilities.[7]

[6] The executive and management are paid on a monthly basis. Everybody is encouraged to take payment on a monthly or fortnightly basis but many people prefer weekly payments.

[7] Between 1951 and 1963 the total amount allocated to 'consolidation and reserves' (excluding taxes) amounted to about £390,000. Of this amount about £200,000 was spent on additions to the physical equipment and creation of new work facilities, and £190,000 for increased working capital, mainly stocks (inventories) and debtors (accounts receivable).

III

In a traditionally organized firm demands for higher wages are often experienced as an encroachment upon profits which may endanger the ability of the firm to invest, expand and develop in a competitive struggle. In a common ownership firm the proper allocation of earnings between current expenditure and future development becomes a problem of just or proper allocation of earnings, it does not manifest itself as a conflict between management defending profits and workers wanting a bigger share of the cake.

The reasons for this are closely connected with the principle of common ownership and the right of the members of the Commonwealth to dispose of the surplus within the limits determined by the Constitution. These provisions abolish the dependence of wages upon privately owned capital. 'The new capital which is created by the business is thus removed from the sphere of private use and disposal.'[8] As a result a common interest of the people to develop new work opportunities for their own growth and development can develop. Though competitive needs continue to be important since a firm like Scott Bader cannot maintain its position in the chemical industry without new developments, the word interest as used here assumes again its original meaning of *interesse* which literally translated means 'to be between'. In a common ownership firm there is something activated that 'is between' people.

In traditionally organized firms demands for higher income are often motivated by reason unrelated to the need for higher incomes. A need for justice and/or unconscious wishes to cover up deeper dissatisfaction with work are often decisive. The existence of a framework within which justice is possible alters this situation radically. Decisions about the distribution of the earnings can be made through reasonable discussions of the actual situation on the basis of complementary and sometimes conflicting values in regard to the criteria used to deal with the situation. Conflict is not abolished but the new organization minimizes destructive conflicts. It fosters the development of

[8] See booklet *Scott Bader & Co. Ltd.*, 1955, p. 30.

criteria which may be democratically accepted, modified or rejected, and which form a basis for a just distribution of the common earnings.

I am speaking intentionally about a framework within which justice is possible and not about justice as an accomplished reality. The problems of realizing justice are so manifold that only a few comments pertaining to the major distributive shares can be made here.

IV

The justice of distribution of funds for charitable purposes can only be evaluated in terms of an overall appraisal of the respective responsibilities of individual people, of industrial firms, of the local, national and the international community.

The preamble to the Articles of Association states explicitly that the Commonwealth as a 'socially responsible undertaking . . . is part of the whole national and international community, and . . . has responsibilities which extend far beyond its factory walls'. The 'social obligations to the community' are '(i) to promote the health and welfare of persons who are or have been employed in the paint and plastics trades and their dependants by the establishment of clubs, health and recreational centres, hotels, rest and convalescent homes; (ii) to assist distressed and needy members of the staff of concerns engaged in the paint and plastics trades; (iii) to establish and support institutions whose objects (being wholly charitable) include the advancement of peace and education.'[9]

In 1952 the Community Council worked out guidelines for the use of the Commonwealth funds. Approximately one half of the funds were to be used for support of peace endeavours and the remainder was to be divided about equally between 'the support of employees of our organization that may be in need, and local good causes'. In 1956 the General Meeting modified these guidelines 'in order to provide for something of a more local nature in which our members could take pride and

[9] *Memorandum Commonwealth 1951*, p. 1. *Ibid.* Article 3, Sections B, C and D, pp. 1, 2.

active participation—such as the provision of a community centre in Wollaston'.[10]

Between 1951 and 1963 the Commonwealth contributed to the local community about £18,000 (or $50,000). A considerable part of this money was for a Village Hall. Old people's parcels, the local school and technical college, help to the blind and TB aftercare accounted for a good part of the donations. Funds given to the national community amounted to about £9,000 (or $25,000) and included contributions for cancer research, the Royal Life Boat Institution, the Pestalozzi children's village, the blind, spastics etc. For the international community about £17,000 (or $45,000) was donated and £15,000 (about $40,000) was promised for the Society for Training in Rural Industries and Village Enterprises.[11] Among international causes were various peace groups, race relations, world health, etc.

These contributions must not only be evaluated in pounds and shillings or dollars and cents. We must also consider that the members of the Commonwealth cannot add more money to their current earnings through annual disbursements than they give to other people. They render, furthermore, direct services to the community. From 1951 to 1963 they distributed a total of 10,000 parcels and 1,200 bags of firewood. They were mainly helping old people in a country where problems of old age are among the major social problems.[12]

V

The justice of the distribution of the annual earnings poses far-reaching problems. Initially the distribution was based on a formula combining the principle of equal distribution with distribution in relation to current earnings. Two principles

[10] *Minute Book*, First Annual General Meeting, Feb. 2, 1952, p. 3. *Ibid.*, Annual General Meeting 1963, pp. 21/22.

[11] Information given by Mr. Ted Nichols, Secretary of the Community Council.

[12] In 1962 over 17 per cent. of the total population of Great Britain were over 60 years of age. See *Annual Abstract of Statistics*, No. 100, H.M. Stationery Office, London, 1962, p. 12. The present old-age pensions are quite inadequate.

expressing different views of the relationship between work and remuneration, and hence about the nature and development of man, were thus combined.[13]

The distribution of current earnings is decisive for an understanding of the ideas of justice with which the Commonwealth experimented during its first decade. Three principles determine this distribution. (i) Basic rates must preserve the competitive position of the firm. (ii) The maximum ratio between the lowest and the highest earnings should be no more than about 1:6. (iii) Acceptance of the principle of sharing losses as well as profits with the understanding that 'should a need for economy arise, everyone will agree to a proportional reduction in their pay whereby those in higher positions would accept a larger percentage cut and the lowest paid be least affected'.[14]

As we have seen there has not been a formal guarantee of employment, but an informal understanding that members of the Commonwealth cannot be dismissed except for cause. Since they themselves make the decisions about earnings in times of crisis—as in ordinary times—they enjoy a relatively high degree of security. It is true that this principle of sharing to ensure security of all has so far not been put to a full scale test. But there was a period when the Board of Directors reduced its own earnings.[15] And there is little doubt that people are willing to put the common weal first as they already have shown in accepting a considerably lower annual distribution of earnings ('bonus') than they are entitled to by the Constitution.

There have repeatedly been pressures to increase the 1 : 6 ratio between the lowest and the highest earnings because of the need for highly qualified people who could earn much more elsewhere. So far a consistent attempt has been made to maintain this ratio by increasing the lowest earnings or by striving for a compromise solution with those who had considerably higher earnings elsewhere.

[13] The principles determining the distribution of the annual earnings were changed later. See below, Chapter 16, p. 212 and Chapter 17, p. 219.

[14] See booklet *Scott Bader & Co. Ltd.* 1955, p. 35.

[15] In 1954 the earnings of top management were reduced. Within a year they were restored to their previous level.

A comparison of the wage rates paid at Scott Bader and the going market rates in the chemical industry shows that the basic rates at Scott Bader are in the middle or upper range of the rates prevailing in the industry.[16] Comparable data for rates above the basic rates are more difficult to obtain. But the higher one gets, the lower are the earnings of people at Scott Bader in relation to comparable positions in the chemical industry. This is particularly true for people in key managerial positions.

However, an expanding company meets limits in attracting highly qualified people at considerably lower earnings. The maintenance of a 1:6 ratio poses, therefore, problems and the 'compressed' structure of current earnings has been subject to strains and stresses. At this point the world of industry as now organized impinges most strongly upon the internal structure of earnings and makes it difficult to create a structure which is radically different from the prevailing market structure.

Since the basic rates determine the bulk of the 'wage bill', Scott Bader cannot start from a basis much different from the going market rate thus relieving pressure on the 1:6 ratio or even reducing it.[17] Given these limitations the attempt of the Commonwealth to introduce principles of justice different from purely technical a-ethical market considerations deserves special emphasis.

VI

How has the people's experience of work been affected by the transformation of wages and profits and the attempt to develop principles of justice within a new distributive framework?

[16] Based on information given by Mr. Robert Edwards, the General Secretary of the Chemical Workers Union.

[17] A few figures will illustrate the limitations of freedom in the determination of the basic rates. In 1964 about 65 per cent. of the people of the Commonwealth with earnings up to £800 (or $2,250) account for about 45 per cent. of current earnings. If the earnings of these 65 per cent. were to be raised 10 per cent. the funds needed for higher earnings would increase by about 5 per cent. These calculations are based on the present structure of wages, that is on the existing differential between the earnings of different people. If there were a uniform remuneration, current earnings could be at a level of about £1,000 (or $2,800) per year.

The basic values of the people of the Commonwealth regarding the justice of distribution are, on the whole, still moulded by traditional ideas and values. Asked 'There are many ideas about what should be considered in deciding what income a person should have. Could you give me your ideas?' most people mentioned effort and going market rates rather than human needs or interpersonal relations. The overwhelming majority answered the question 'Do you think it would be a good idea if everybody had the same income?' in the negative.

Given this traditional outlook, the people of the Commonwealth are, on the whole, satisfied with the distribution of earnings. Asked 'How do you feel about the amount of pay you are getting now?' almost two thirds indicated in 1959 that they were satisfied, close to one third indicated satisfaction with qualifications while only a few people expressed dissatisfaction. A number of people indicated that they could get more money elsewhere but that they preferred to work at Scott Bader. These responses show good feelings though the strong incidence of qualifications among people working in the factory must be noted.[18]

When asked: 'How do you feel about the way profits are distributed?' the general feelings of the majority of the people were again positive. About half of them had some comments or suggestions. A considerable number felt that 'the bonus' should be paid equally. Two people wanted more profits distributed in 'bonus', two wanted more allocated to the plough-back. Two wanted the 'bonus' money used for other purposes and a number of people had suggestions for varying uses of the money given for charitable purposes.

These comments and suggestions indicate a wide variety of ideas which played their part in the years that followed. They do not qualify the conclusion that the traditional antagonism in regard to 'wages', 'profits' and 'dividends' has been overcome at Scott Bader. The removal of this antagonism takes a

[18] The criteria used by the people to measure satisfaction were: the kind of work done, the size of the firm, the kind of firm and the 'worth' of one's work as measured by the market.

sting out of the experience of work. It shifts attention from a struggle of two in principle opposed groups to a struggle for the realization of certain (sometimes perhaps conflicting) ideas within the community of work. Furthermore, it opens the door to reason since it makes possible considered argument and consideration of different points of view.

The creation of a new framework within which ideas about a just distribution of earning can be developed, tested and applied is a real accomplishment. Specific ideas as to what is just in distributing earnings will and should differ and change. What matters is the constant and explicit concern with justice. This concern gives to people's experience of work a new dimension.

The Commonwealth 'founded for the realization of the ideals of peace and principles of social justice which the Founders cherish',[19] is evolving an industrial organization in which the realization of principles of social justice is an explicit concern open to democratic discussion and communal decision. In this sense Scott Bader is an outstanding example of justice in an industrial society in which the word justice is rarely heard. The basis for the search for justice is a transformation of wages, profits and dividends from their historically unique definition under capitalism into a new communal form restoring their universal functions—as much as an individual firm can do. This transformation is the first basic change in the value structure within which work is taking place.

[19] See *Scott Bader & Co. Ltd.*, 1955, p. 28.

Chapter 7

Power, control and decision making

I

Changes in values and changes in power are interrelated. To realize values we need power and every conception of power implies a certain conception of the nature of man.

The term power is a universal category, it is not related to a specific social system. It is not even a sociological term. We speak about an electric power station, about the power of the spirit and about the power structure of a corporation. Power creates a field of forces which has movement, order and hence direction.

A specific system through which power is exercised is a control system. To organize work means to establish a system of control through which decisions affecting a group of people can be made.

Ownership is a legal category. The rights and responsibilities of ownership differ greatly, even within the same form of ownership. Common or communal ownership may therefore be the basis of diverse power structures and systems of control.

II

When the Commonwealth was formed in 1951 the principle of common ownership was clearly promulgated. But the veto rights of the ten per cent. Founder Shares left the ultimate control in the hands of the Founder Members. This situation created a transitional stage in which the Commonwealth was during the first decade of its existence. The new organization of work was also transitional because it combined two ultimately irreconcilable forms of power. On the one hand the hierarchical power symbolized by a pyramid with its narrow top and broad base and on the other hand power symbolized by interrelated circles where each person acting from his own centre, stands in a mutuality of relationship to other people.

Directors, middle management, foremen, chargehands formed a more or less hierarchical structure of power but at each stage of the hierarchy opportunities for democratic participation were established and a new conception of power was introduced.

This new conception was quickly appreciated by the people. 'Scott Bader is the best firm I have ever worked for or with'; 'The Commonwealth is a means of communication from the top to the factory floor which helps to bridge the old gap between management and workers. It gives added interest to the majority of workers. They are working more for themselves than for the old boss. Generally speaking it enables people to work *with* other people rather than *for* them.'

These responses mark a transition from an egocentric perspective to a communal orientation. The old ways of working *for* others are being replaced by the Commonwealth way of working *with* other people. The co-existence of two systems of control and two conceptions of power is well expressed by the references to working 'for or with' and 'top and factory floor'.

Asked 'Is there anybody who is above you?' a worker said: 'There is no employer there like in other factories, no one orders you about and yet you are responsible to those people.' He then explained that 'under the Commonwealth you're only answerable to one man' and referred to 'the black book' which contains the rules of conduct. He experienced himself as part of a hierarchical structure—there are 'plenty' of people above him, 'from a working point of view anyone from a plant manager up.' But he also felt that he is not ordered around because 'there is no employer there like in other factories.'

'We are working together . . . top and bottom' said another worker. He was still sceptical about 'them'. 'They are just thinking of themselves while never kind of improving general conditions of us' but expressed hope that 'we' feelings will eventually prevail: 'the distance between top and bottom will slowly disappear.'

The sense of having overcome the old employer-employee relationship was clearly expressed by a worker for whom the main advantage of the Commonwealth 'is the destruction of the (traditional) set-up we have discussed'. 'Better labour relations' and 'good human relations' were also mentioned. When asked what comes to his mind when using the words Scott Bader, a worker said: 'You're getting worse than the Gallup Poll now. Well, I don't know what to say. Just the name of the firm. I can't say the boss because there is no boss here.'

The changes in authority led to a more human way of dealing with problems coming up at work. When asked: 'What event in your life at work has given you the greatest satisfaction?' a person working in the laboratory talked about the way in which two workers who had persistently failed to live up to the working rules were dealt with. Instead of being dismissed, they were downgraded with reduction in pay, not as a punishment but because it was felt that they worked only about as well as a lower-graded man. 'This business over the two gentlemen who had this reduction in pay, it was my suggestion. I thought this was the only human way out of it. If those men had been in an ordinary firm they would have got the sack. Knowing the situation with unemployment they probably would not have got another job.'[1]

A number of people referred to the willingness to work through problems which arise instead of letting them develop into disruptive conflicts. 'We have taken disciplinary action with members of the Commonwealth, we come to decisions which in an ordinary establishment would probably have caused a strike. They have been taken without ill feelings.'[2] Or: 'I have seen things that could have caused serious situations in other industries, such as unfairness and wages. If we were in a bad spot we would all get together here in the Commonwealth Hall and EB (Ernest Bader) or Godric (Godric Bader) would say we are in trouble and we would all help.'

[1] This was said in response to the question: 'Do you see anything in the work you are doing now that would help people?'

[2] This was said in answer to the question: 'When you think about your place of work, what comes to your mind?'

To understand these feelings we shall now examine more in detail the opportunities for participation which existed during the first decade of the Commonwealth.

They were:

(1) Participation in discussions, putting forward of motions and voting in General Meetings.

(2) Becoming a candidate for election to various Committees, mainly the Community Council and the General Council.

(3) Becoming a candidate for election to the Board of Directors as a Commonwealth Director.

(4) Participation in Departmental Meetings.[3]

III

The Constitution provides for at least one General Meeting every year.[4] Every member of the Commonwealth is expected to participate and is entitled to a vote, usually by a show of hands but, if requested, by a poll. The General Meetings are divided into company and Commonwealth meetings.

The usual business of the General Meeting of the Company comprises a report by the Managing Director, dealing with business problems and developments and usually with plans for expansion. Any question pertaining to the conduct of the business and its future may be discussed. The surplus earned

[3] Among the people who participated in interview-conversations, four had been Commonwealth Directors at one time or another, eleven had been members of the Community Council while six had served on a Social and Educational Committee. All those who were members of the Commonwealth have taken part in some Commonwealth activity. Over two thirds mentioned meetings, and almost one half a social service. Social occasions were mentioned repeatedly while lectures were referred to only occasionally.

[4] All other general meetings are called extraordinary meetings. The latter may be called at the request of the Community Council or by the members under certain conditions. See Articles 5 and 6 of *Memorandum Commonwealth* 1951, p. 8. A meeting called by the membership must follow Sec. 132 of the Co Act. The Constitution demands that 14 resp. 21 days notice be given for meetings. See Section 7–10 of *Memorandum Commonwealth 1951*, p. 8. The Constitution also regulates the proceedings at general meetings, determines the quorum, chairmanship etc. See Articles 11–15 *Memorandum Commonwealth 1951*, p. 9.

by the community is announced and proposals are made for the distribution of the surplus between plough-back for expansion, funds for the Commonwealth and annual (bonus) distributions.[5] Only once was a motion made to reduce the amount of bonus proposed by the Director since part of the membership felt the company could use the money for expansion. However this motion to go below the Director's recommendations was not accepted.

Besides the General Meetings of the company, there are quarterly meetings at which reports of the various sections of the company are presented and discussed.

The General Meetings of the Company are usually followed by General Meetings of the Commonwealth.

The business at General Commonwealth Meetings consists of a report of the Secretary and of the Treasurer of the Community Council (the administrative organ of the Commonwealth) and of the recommendations for the use of the funds received as 'dividends'. The report of the Secretary deals mainly with the membership of the Commonwealth and a summary of the work of the Community Council during the year. The Treasurer reports on the accounts and balance sheet of the Commonwealth. Suggestions for allocation of the Commonwealth funds for charitable and educational purposes are the results of careful deliberations of the Community Council, to whom individual members have passed their ideas before the Annual General Meeting. Only once was a motion to change the proposed allocation of funds (by increasing one of the proposed contributions) carried in general meeting. There were other occasions when changes were suggested but not accepted.[6]

[5] According to the Constitution a General Annual Meeting and three General Quarterly meetings must be held every year. All General Meetings, other than Annual and Quarterly General Meetings, shall be called Extraordinary. See *Memorandum Commonwealth 1963*, Article 7, p. 13.

[6] At the 1960 Annual General Meeting a motion was made to increase the contribution to the Royal National Life Boat Institution from £50 to £200 (from about $140 to about $560). Other suggestions were made between 1960 and 1964 at General Annual Meetings but were not recorded in the Minutes. One suggestion proposed a contribution to the Frejus disaster fund. This

A snapshot picture of a General Meeting of the Commonwealth gives an idea of a more colourful occasion in the life of the Commonwealth.[7]

Chairs are arranged in a half circle around a long table. About seventy people are sitting in the Commonwealth Hall whose glass walls relate the inner space to outer nature and whose hyperparabolic roof brings height and depth into harmony. Behind the long table is a banner with the following slogan: 'We believe in overcoming evil with good. Service above self. General welfare, happiness—and no nonsense.' The Chairman gets up to make a brief speech and to read a passage from a book by Lewis Mumford. This is followed by a minute of silence. Then part of the preamble to the Constitution is read. Finally the chairman puts a clear analysis of the problems to be discussed before the assembled group. About twenty people raise questions or make comments. A lively interchange of questions and answers takes place before a vote is taken.

During the thirteen years from 1951 to 1963 there were twenty-six General Meetings of the Commonwealth preceded by twenty-six meetings of the company. In addition, since 1961, there were twelve quarterly meetings, a number of special extraordinary meetings as well as special meetings open to everybody working at Scott Bader (irrespective of membership in the Commonwealth). Attendance at meetings fluctuated considerably. However, there is no clear trend discernible.[8]

[7] The usual business of the AGM follows the pattern given below, in most of the meetings recorded between 1951–63: 1. Notice of the meetings. 2. Minutes of the previous meeting. 3. Treasurer's report and statement of account. 4. Readoption of auditors. 5. Secretary's report. 6. Announcement of results of election for the three vacancies in the Community Council. 7. Every three years, election in the meeting of the two Commonwealth Directors. 8. Recommendation on charitable donations by the Community Council. 9. Any other resolutions and discussion.

[8] For further data see *Minute Book* of the Commonwealth. Between 1951 and 1963 attendance varied between 35 per cent. of the members (Annual General Meeting of December 1960) to almost 90 per cent. (Extraordinary General Meeting October 1959).

suggestion was turned down on the grounds that amounts subscribed from other sources were already sufficient.

Participation in the meetings also varied greatly. At a number of meetings which we observed people with managerial responsibility or people from the laboratory participated more actively than factory and maintenance people. My conclusions about the quality of participation are very simiilar to those about national legislative bodies: namely that participation which goes beyond a 'yes' or 'no' vote or beyond rather elementary clarification of issues, needs a deeper knowledge than the kind of knowledge which can as a rule be obtained by participation in the assembly proceedings.[9]

Feelings about meetings differed greatly during the first decade of the Commonwealth. For most people it was a welcome opportunity to learn more about the company, to know what was going on. Extremes are indicated by a person who felt that there were 'not enough meetings' and another who felt 'that you got to go to meetings although you can't do nothing when you get there. I have seen meetings where it would have been better to chop wood.' More typical is the following evaluation: 'Having the opportunity of knowing how the firm is running, not being a cog in the wheel and knowing how it's going—you do get an idea of how the firm is working—quarterly meetings are very good.' He added: 'although it's very difficult to get people to stand up at quarterly meetings and say things, they do have the opportunity to say things.' There were a number of complaints that people don't attend meetings. Other people felt: 'To be able to talk together openly' and 'to take part in discussions on the company's future' were good aspects of the meetings.

During the past decade considerable changes have taken place in the meetings. The following comment on the quarterly meeting held in October 1963 illustrates the change:

[9] As a consultant to a Congressional Committee I had opportunity to observe the way in which specific legislation is prepared, the number of people who participate in the assembly debates on legislation and the extent of their knowledge in participating in debates etc. I have not made a systematic study of Congressional legislation along these lines but there is good reason for saying that the specific legislation which I did observe was representative in terms of the conclusions which I am drawing in this context.

> 'The key note of this Meeting was change—change in the form of the meeting itself and the changing situation so far as the company is concerned.
>
> The Managing Director's report is recorded in full as usual in a Management Circular. From this it will be seen that Mr. Godric (Bader) himself drew attention to the change in the form of meeting in that one section of our community would be high-lighted each time.
>
> At this stage I must confess that my thoughts rather wandered from what he was saying to the first Company meeting I attended at Wollaston. It was just about this time of year but ten years ago . . .
>
> The meeting was held in what is now our Fitters Shop but which was then the club room. The atmosphere was quite different and the number present considerably fewer. The reports given from the "top table" were very stiff and formal and were received by an audience just as stiff. In fact immediately after the Managing Director's report there was what is commonly referred to as a "deathly hush"! Questions were few and far between and it was difficult to judge whether the audience was bewildered, uninterested or even hostile! There was usually but one awkward customer who shall be nameless (it was not the writer!)
>
> How different was the presentation and reaction last Saturday. The reports were presented in a very interesting and understandable manner. In view of the wide scope of the reports everybody present must have heard something which related to their particular activity.'[10]

This report illustrates the changes in the quality of the meetings and indicates the constant attempts to improve opportunities for participation.

IV

Election to an office constitutes an important opportunity for participation. The Community Council, the General Council and the Board of Directors have elected officers.

The Community Council manages the affairs of the Commonwealth between annual meetings. It consists of twelve members, nine elected by the members of the Commonwealth,

[10] See *Fortnightly News*, October 13, 1963.

two nominated by the Directors and one nominated by the eleven other members to represent the interests of the local community.[11]

The nine elected members are chosen by secret ballot from a list of nominations by Commonwealth members. Each year one third of the elected members retire and new members are elected. The number of nominations for these three vacancies varied from five to twelve. Retiring members are not eligible for re-election until a year after their retirement. Members of the Community Council must be members of the Commonwealth or they must join the Commonwealth within a specified time.[12]

From its beginning in 1951 until 1963 thirty-four people served as elected representatives on the Community Council. A large majority of them were re-elected after having served their first term. About fifteen members of the Community Council came from the factory, about ten from the laboratory and almost ten from the office. Among those elected close to ten were workers, the same number were junior managers, somewhat less were technicians and only two to four were managers, executives or clerks. Ted Nichols has been Secretary of the Council throughout this period and W. A. Cross the Treasurer (until his retirement in 1965).

According to the statutes, the Community Council must meet at least four times every year. But it has met much more frequently. The number of meetings increased steadily and in 1963 the Community Council met almost every week instead of every three months.[13]

[11] The two members nominated by the Board are also removable by the Board; the community member is removable by the Council of Management. They are not subject to retirement by rotation. See Article 23 of *Memorandum Commonwealth 1951*, p. 11.

[12] For details see *Memorandum Commonwealth 1951*, Articles 34–39, p. 14, regulating length of office, filling of casual vacancies and removal of members. Until 1963 those elected to the Community Council have been members of the Commonwealth when elected for office.

[13] The council met 172 times from 1951–1959. This makes an average of 19 times per year. The number of meetings increased quite steeply from 3 meetings in 1951 and 1952 to 19 in 1953. The number of meetings remained in this region until 1957 when it increased to 25; in 1958 it increased to 27,

The Council elects its own chairman. Ernest Bader has been chairman every year since the beginning of the Commonwealth. Since 1961 meeting chairmen have been elected to conduct the meeting.

The Community Council may delegate any of its powers to Committees but has rarely exercised that right. Only one sub-Committee—the Social and Education Committee—was formally appointed.

The Community Council may deal with any problem affecting the Commonwealth. The Constitution specifically empowers the Community Council (i) to recommend to the members of the Commonwealth in general meeting bye-laws for the regulation of the conduct of members of the Commonwealth and (ii) 'to determine the charitable purposes to which the income of the Commonwealth shall be applied'.[14] Though the general meeting may change any of the recommendations made, the spade work is done in the Council. As indicated above virtually all the recommendations have been accepted.

During the first twelve years from 1951–1963 the Community Council dealt primarily with the use of Commonwealth funds for charitable and educational purposes and with membership. Education and information, public relations, social benefits, entertainment and voluntary work were other topics discussed.

Acceptance or rejection of people for membership in the Commonwealth is within the discretion of the Community Council. When the Commonwealth was founded in 1951 all those present at the meeting in Cambridge could become members by signing the register. Out of less than 165 eligible people 155 signed as members. After June 1951 an application for membership had to be made to the Community Council. In the following years membership declined as the number of people working at Scott Bader declined to 138 in 1954 in spite of increasing sales. As the number of people working at Scott Bader

[14] *Memorandum Commonwealth 1951*, Article 33 B, p. 14.

in 1959 to 34. The Council must keep minutes and its accounts must be audited. See *Memorandum Commonwealth 1951*, Articles 51 and 54, pp. 16 and 17.

increased again in 1954 membership in the Commonwealth also increased but in a smaller ratio than did the number of people working in the firm. In 1958 out of a total of a little over 200 people, 115 were members of the Commonwealth.[15]

From 1951 to 1963 the Community Council accepted 285 applications for membership and rejected 6. The reasons for the rejection were: (i) work not satisfactory, (ii) general conduct not in line with what is expected of Commonwealth members, (iii) insufficient interest in Commonwealth activities and non-attendance at meetings.'[16] Six members had their membership in the Commonwealth taken away. Of these three left and two were readmitted at a later date.

Election to the Community Council has been considered by most people an important avenue to participate in the

[15] At the beginning of the Commonwealth all full-time members of the firm were eligible for membership and at the first meeting of the Commonwealth at Cambridge in June 1951 there was a total of 155 members made up of 135 full members and 20 associates. Only about seven employees of the firm were not members at this time. Membership of the Commonwealth from 1951 to 1962 was as follows:

Year	*Commonwealth members*	*Total in firm*
1951 (June)	155 (135 full, 20 associates)	162
1952 (Feb.)	137 (119 full, 18 associates)	149
1953 (Jan.)	102 (91 full, 11 associates)	138
1953 (Nov.)	103 (94 full, 9 associates)	138
1954 (Nov.)	114 (109 full, 5 associates)	161
1955 (Dec.)	111 (108 full, 3 associates)	156
1956 (Nov.)		170
1957 (Nov.)	119 (116 full, 3 associates)	194
1958 (Dec.)	115 (113 full, 2 associates)	204
1959 (Dec.)	122 (119 full, 3 associates)	227
1960 (Dec.)	140 (134 full, 6 associates)	251
1961 (Dec.)	147 (143 full, 4 associates)	267
1962 (Dec.)	143	266

Two thirds of those who participated in interview-conversations were members. Most of the non-members were not yet eligible for membership because they had not been with Scott Bader for two years. Only two people who took part in the interview conversations were eligible for membership but had not joined.

[16] Information given by Mr. Ted Nichols, the Secretary of the Community Council.

government of the Commonwealth since the Council has 'members from all classes of the factory'. Or: 'I can become a member of the Commonwealth in two years if I have enough initiative and intelligence. I can help to run it by becoming a member of the Community Council . . .'[17]

Most people had a fairly clear idea about the functions of the Community Council. But there were a number of people who did not have an adequate understanding.[18]

The Community Council was seen as 'the governing body for the Commonwealth membership'; or as 'the voice of the executive of the Commonwealth'. Some people referred to it as 'the Board of Directors of the Commonwealth'. Others saw it as a general watch-dog.

A person mentioned discipline of membership as a function of the Community Council and spoke about a case in which the Directors referred a problem of slackening of discipline to the Council. 'The Community Council felt that this was a question where management had fallen down—if they had been slacking for a long time this was the fault of management. The Community Council pushed it back to the Board of Directors for a decision.' He added: 'The Community Council would watch the attitude of people after a management decision.' Another person referred to a situation in which a member of the Executive had attempted 'undemocratic things' which were discussed by the Council.

A final response illustrates the attitude of those who felt 'more or less ignorant' about the Community Council: 'I don't know anything about it. The only clue about that is what Jim said about it when he resigned. He said you can't understand half the things they talk about . . .'

V

During the first decade of the Commonwealth election to the General Council offered important opportunities for participation. The Council was meant to build bridges within the

[17] This was said in answer to the question 'What advantages and privileges do you get because you are a member of Scott Bader?'

[18] See Appendix on Method, p. 374.

traditional hierarchical structure, to modify this structure and help transform it into a communal one.[19]

The Council was composed of (i) eight members elected by the departmental committees, (ii) four members appointed by the Directors to represent themselves and the Executive and (iii) four members elected by those members of management who are not Directors or members of the Executive.[20]

The main functions of the Council were 'To discuss any question affecting the well-being of the company and its employees and to act as referee and give decisions on matters which are referred to it either by individual employees, the departmental representatives, the management committee, the executive members of the company or the directors.' Specifically, the Constitution charged the General Council to deal with disputes or questions affecting disciplinary action. The decisions of the Council on appeals from members were final. The General Council also had the right 'to discuss any matters of expenditure and finance and make recommendations to the Board of Directors for their decision'.[21]

The General Council was to meet once every alternate month. From 1951 to 1963, the Council met about seventy times, that is 5–6 times each year. About twenty people served as Chairman, Vice-Chairman, or as Secretary of the General Council; about seventy as elected or nominated members.[22]

[19] Technically speaking the General Council is part of the company and not of the Commonwealth. But it is part of the whole new organization initiated by the Commonwealth. See the booklet *Scott Bader 1955*, p. 23. The General Council is defined there as 'the link between the management at all three levels and the personnel'.

[20] Members of management are not eligible for this representation. See *Memorandum Commonwealth 1951*, Article 30, p. 7. All members of management formed a Management Committee analagous to the Departmental Committees. See *Ibid.*, Article 30, p. 7.

[21] *Ibid.*, Article 31, pp. 7 and 8. In exercising this function, the General Council takes an advisory role.

[22] The Constitution also provided for election of the Chairman, Vice-Chairman and Secretary of the Board, for calling of meetings, quorum at meetings etc. See *Ibid.*, Articles 32–35, p. 8. The General Council met 68 times in regular meetings and had 2 extraordinary meetings. 19 people served as officers, 14 of them were re-elected, some of them more than once. Among

The Council dealt with a wide range of problems. It was concerned with working conditions: holidays, sick pay, shift and night work, systems of wage payments, cloakroom accommodations, the canteen, car parking arrangements, safety equipment, ventilation, etc. The Council examined an appeal against a dismissal, a disciplinary action and a non-payment of sick leave. It also dealt with a charge of poor management. The Council took up a variety of questions such as the appointment of an editor for the house-organ, problems related to the pension scheme, to bonus payments and the question of a suggestion scheme. Problems of participation through the departmental and management committees were also explored. Among the more general topics discussed were sales policy and supplies for armaments.[23]

People's thoughts and feelings about the General Council varied greatly.

A person with managerial responsibility saw the General Council primarily as a grievance Committee. 'I was going to say it was a glorified joint consultation, but it's not. In some aspects it is but in others it is a sort of grand jury for any grievance or dispute anywhere at any level of the company'.

Another person with managerial responsibility made a sharp distinction between what the General Council was meant to be and what it actually has been. 'I would say that the General Council exists in two forms: as described in the Articles and as it functions. In the Articles it's enabled to discuss any matter affecting the welfare of the company including financial and also to act as a tribunal to settle disputes which cannot be settled through the normal channels. In fact it rarely gets disputes to settle. It's rarely asked to do its duty by its members. It's never asked to consider the financial side of the company.' Aware of his sweeping criticism he added: 'I qualify this by saying that the limitations boil down to that it can only act if it's

[23] See *Minute Book of the General Council*, Minute No. 187.

the people who took part in interview-conversations, 14 served on the General Council.

asked to act, and secondly, the dominance of Ernest Bader.'[24] It is true that the General Council did not discuss major financial problems though a number of the questions with which it dealt had significant financial implications.[25]

A person with clerical responsibility saw the General Council as an important instrument to run the Commonwealth. Similar was the experience of the Council by a person from the laboratory: 'The General Council is the final deciding committee consisting of equal numbers of management and workers to thrash out difficult problems that arise in a business organization'; others did not seem to know much about the Council. 'It is a body which represents workers in the firm', or 'the General Council consists of members elected by the workers to act as liaison between the workers and management and safeguard their general well-being.' Neither of these two statements reflects the actual situation.

Some people in the factory saw the General Council in quite broad terms: 'The General Council is a Committee consisting of representatives from every level—each one represents his own section and the Council can discuss any matters, yes anything. It can make decisions on certain matters. The General Committee is at the hub of everything else which matters. All sorts of things can be sifted and tension can be relieved.' Another person from the factory saw the General Council as 'part of the two communication systems, an elected body which can deal with any matter affecting the welfare of members.'

A number of workers spoke about the General Council as a body settling grievances: 'That's one from each plant plus the same from management side—in other words, its the spokesman from each plant. It is a case of grievances.' Or: 'The General Council looks after the department's interests. For instance,

[24] Ernest Bader was on the General Council from 1951–1963. It is noteworthy that the major complaint brought to the General Council involved the dismissal of a person by Ernest Bader. The General Council reinstated this person after careful deliberations. As regards the question of the 'dominance of Ernest Bader' see below p. 146.

[25] For example the question of delivery of goods for armaments. Minute No. 149, *Minute Book of the General Council.*

someone feels victimized for what he does, someone feels he is outside justice.'

Some of the people gave to the Council a rather minor place in the overall organization. 'The General Council is the Council where you air any grievances. They are the lowest ones. They pass it on to the Community Council and from there to the Directors.' Or: 'trivial matters are brought up by men who had a grievance. Matters not all that important, mostly it's for complaints.'

A person who served on both Community Council and the General Council felt that he got most out of the Community Council 'because there was not a great lot to do on the General Council. A good many times it was hardly worth while to go. A few meetings were good sessions like the session where the dismissal of the clerk was discussed It showed them that the General Council was a body that could do anything for the personnel who were really in trouble.' Another person expressed mixed feelings. 'Until this last time I said it is a waste of time and a bore, the same as everyone else, because there was nothing on the agenda. Now it has served a very useful purpose; it brought several things which needed to be done. It all depends who got on there . . .' This person expressed a widespread feeling: the General Council was not active enough but it did good work when it was active.

About a fifth of the people did not know what the General Council was really all about, and a few were very vague about the functions of the Council. People with clerical responsibilities knew least about the Council; the factory followed though lack of knowledge was less apparent there.[26]

VI

Election as a Commonwealth representative on the Board of Directors constitutes another important opportunity for participation.

According to the Constitution up to three Directors chosen by the Commonwealth may serve on the Board. These 'Com-

[26] See Appendix on Method, p. 374.

monwealth Directors' are elected from a list of not less than six members nominated by Commonwealth members and approved by the Board. Commonwealth Directors hold office for one year and are eligible for re-election.[27]

In an explanatory booklet the Commonwealth Directors are called 'worker directors' and the presence of these worker directors on the Board is considered 'a much more flexible arrangement than the appointment of labour representatives to the Board of Directors, as now practised in some countries.'[28]

From 1951 to 1963 a total of seven people served as Commonwealth Directors on the Board. One of them was elected three times, another four times. Not more than two Commonwealth Directors served at any one time. Three of the seven Commonwealth Directors came from the factory, three from the laboratory and one from the office. One person was a chargehand, the others were technicians or junior managers. None of them would ever have come close to the Board of Directors in an ordinary firm.

Speaking about the advantage of the Commonwealth one of the Commonwealth Directors said: 'I think you have the advantage of being able to serve on Committees which govern the working of the company. For my part I am on the Board. Commonwealth Director. I have achieved something by being on the Board, contributed something on behalf of the people, their well-being.'

VII

Departmental Committees were listed as the fourth opportunity for participation. In Diagram I we considered them the basis of the whole system of participation because they offer the opportunity for discussion in small groups and are closest to the day-to-day working problems.

At the beginning of the Commonwealth, Departmental Committees met regularly. However, after some time they began to

[27] See *Memorandum Commonwealth 1951*, Article 14, p. 4.
[28] See the booklet *Scott Bader, 1955*, p. 20.

meet less regularly and at the end of the first decade they had ceased to be real instruments for group discussions.[29]

In Chapter 16 we will examine the general significance of these developments. To understand the experience of the first decade we must raise a final question: Who really had the power to make the basic decision?

A comment made by a person with managerial responsibilities will help us to answer this question. He felt that 'most of the things which people talk about could be achieved whether there is a Commonwealth or not. I mean most of the steps taken so far towards a democratic organization . . . There are two methods of applying democratic integration. One applies to ultimate authority and control; the other applies to the ordinary participation in the decisions of the day-to-day business. The Commonwealth has not very much altered the ultimate authority. We move towards that. The authority has said that it does not wish to enjoy the fruits of that authority: the profits. But the authority still stands. It is not really affected by the Commonwealth set-up. The other section of the democratic aspect could be achieved without the Commonwealth—like in the X company, there is a kind of democracy. People are assisting in arriving at the right decisions throughout the pyramid. They also make people feel that their views are taken into consideration.'

It is undoubtedly true that the Commonwealth was 'on the move' towards a decisive change in ultimate authority or control but had not yet achieved its objectives. As long as the ten per cent. Founder Shares carried veto rights and much of the old pyramidal structure was left, the transfer of ultimate control and power to the community was incomplete. This was reflected in a wide range of opinions about the actual control exercised. Some people experienced a good measure of control. Others were sceptical.

A worker who felt that too much power for one man is a bad thing because he would be an 'uncrowned king' said: 'Mr. Bader is boss but there are the Commonwealth Directors and the Committees so that not just one man has all the say. There

[29] See Appendix on Method, p. 375.

is the General Council and the Community Council. Management is all shared out.' Another worker said: 'You got a right to share in the decision made in the firm, which you wouldn't in an ordinary firm.' A plant manager said, 'Responsibility has come over the years. This made my job easier . . . everybody has the opportunity to voice their own opinion—you have the opportunity to take part in management in varying degrees—you are given the opportunity to know about the business.' This view found an echo in the opinion of a worker: 'The Commonwealth is set up to enable everybody to participate in management. It has the necessary machinery for the discussion of all matters—including grievances.'

A sceptical voice was: 'I don't think the workers have any more control. I was on the Local Department Committee on the railway . . . it was much the same as far as conditions are concerned.'

There is no doubt that the final power of decision making remained with the Board of Directors on which the Founder Members had a dominant influence. But the Board had divested itself of the ultimate disciplinary power as well as of the right to dispose of the surplus. The General Council had the last word about all matters of discipline. This created a new situation which people began to experience as a sense of freedom.

A manager mentioned 'freedom of speech throughout the company from top to bottom'. A person from the laboratory said: 'You have a tremendous amount of freedom which you can abuse if you don't honour that freedom. You are not called upon continuously to account for what you are doing. You're not harrassed by petty things and people who don't know as much as you do. One of the privileges—for the people who don't clock in—we don't have too much trouble to go to the dentist or a funeral or something.'

This person contrasted the petty servility of a capitalistic factory with the new Commonwealth organization which gives a sense of openness and freedom. At this time—in 1959—people in the factory still clocked in every morning. This fact is reflected in their general attitudes. They mentioned 'The personal touch you feel by belonging to the Company', and the sense of 'all being treated the same—well', but none of the workers spoke about freedom as such.

People's feelings about power and control illustrates again the problems of a period of transition. Since the traditional structure within which discipline has been administered—'the pyramid'—had not been basically changed, there was a problem of making new wine in old bottles. The old sanctions have gone or were less effective while a new sense of freedom and responsibility was not yet clearly felt. This led to complaints that 'people go around in a slap-happy way—in a way that people can't do outside'. Actually there is no objective evidence that this posed any serious problems. The newly won freedom and control has not been misused.

It is true that technically speaking the actual transfer of control may have been possible without common ownership. But this would have created an inconsistency which would have precluded further development. Once we recognize that the fruits of the labour are the result of a common effort we must also accept common ownership of the means necessary to achieve these fruits. If these means were divisible between individuals, there would be no common fruits. Once the indivisibility of the means of production as well as a common effort and common fruits are recognized, common ownership is a logical implication. It simply means to recognize in outer form what has been understood as the inner meaning of working together.

This inner meaning is expressed in the attempt to develop a new organization of work based on a new understanding of power and responsibility. Each person was meant to have the same chance to develop his own powers and to contribute his or her knowledge and experience to a common work process. As tentative as the first attempts to realize this new conception may have been during the first decade, the Commonwealth created a new field of forces which in turn created a new atmosphere—as we will see as soon as we have gained an understanding of the role of the union in the new organization of work.

Chapter 8
The Union

I

In 1948, at the time of the strike, the Chemical Workers Union was recognized. Two and a half years afterwards, the Commonwealth came into being. This created a unique situation. The union was friendly towards the Commonwealth and the Commonwealth was friendly towards the union. But since the division into employers and employees ceased to be a primary dividing line, most of the usual functions of a trade union were discharged by the members of the Commonwealth. The union decided, therefore, on its own initiative, not to insist that all people eligible for membership join the union. In its publication *The Chemical Worker* the new Commonwealth scheme was written up in a leading article to encourage other companies to follow this example.[1]

However, the union has not taken much active part in the new organization of work. In 1951 four union meetings were held, in 1952 five. In 1953 only one—the last until a decade later when another meeting was held in 1963.[2] The annual convention of the Chemical Workers Union has been usually attended by one or two representatives from Scott Bader. Some of their Reports on these annual conventions were published in the house-organ of Scott Bader—*The Fortnightly News*. It carried reports on the 1962 and 1963 conventions. Reports were also published when members of the union attended weekend schools organized by the National Council of Labour Colleges.[3]

Membership in the union did not go beyond thirty-two

[1] See comments on 'Discussion Meeting—Wollaston Branch of the Chemical Workers' Union', *The Fortnightly News*, No. 171. July 1, 1966, pp. 6 and 7.

[2] Information given by Reginald Barrick who has been Secretary of the Union from 1953–1963.

[3] See *Fortnightly News*, No. 73, Friday June 22, 1962, p. 4.

people. The people who participated in the interview-conversations in 1959 form three groups: (i) union members—about one fourth of the people, (ii) those who were members but who had left the union—about one fourth, and (iii) those who never were members of a trade union—about half of the people who participated in the interview-conversations. All the people who were members of the union in 1959 worked in the factory or in maintenance departments. About a third of the people with managerial responsibility had some personal experience as members of trade unions whereas none of the people with clerical responsibilities and only one of the people connected with the laboratory were previously members of trade unions.

What were the reasons for membership in the union?

One of the members said 'it offers . . . not the feeling of security but a solicitor. Back of your mind you feel it may be needed.' For him, legal aid is the main advantage of belonging to a union. It also makes sure that 'the rights are not taken away' and this gives some added security. In spite of the denial that security plays a role the union is experienced as a safeguard in an insecure world. This worker felt that he 'should take a more active part' in union activities but wondered how to do it since there is 'no following' and 'really no need for a union in the set-up (the Commonwealth) as it is'. Asked: 'What comes to your mind when you say "I am a member of the Chemical Workers Union"?' he indicated that he is 'pretty vague'. He had a feeling that the union somehow play an important role as a movement. But this feeling remained inarticulate. He spoke about the Commonwealth as an example for the union without establishing any vital connection with the Commonwealth and the trade union movement. 'For other people being a member was important because unions 'fight for better conditions for the working man' but 'we achieved things they are still struggling for'.

Another person who gave very similar reasons for being a member of the Chemical Workers Union felt that 'there are definitely some benefits that Scott Bader is giving their workers thanks to the union . . . once shift workers when sick got only day pay; thanks to a change in the union, Bader's changed'. He also mentioned that when computing overtime 'at one time every day was counted on its own. For the first two hours you got time and a quarter, after that time and a half—now all overtime is time and a half except Sunday which is double time'.

A third person said 'The original idea of the union was to protect you if you were sacked. Also the reason I am in was if I was hurt in an accident—they fight your case. But we're already paid above the union rates so it doesn't help there.' He felt that the union gives 'no advantages over anyone else because it's not a closed shop. It helps if you go to another job.' At the back of his mind is a remembrance of difficult times and an awareness of an insecure world. In such a world a little extra protection could be useful.

'Well, actually we all joined', said one of the members, 'because the fellow who used to run the union was a boilerman and he was a great friend of mine. But being in the union before I didn't want to be out of it. I always remember someone wrote: "No matter how good a boss you work for, you always want your safeguards. Your boss may change."' His fears are understandable since he had a rather wide experience of the insecurities and vicissitudes of work.

A final response is from a worker who felt that 'In an ordinary factory where you'd be liable to be victimized the union would stand by you. At Scott Bader, they don't take much interest in it.' He joined because 'no one knew what the firm was like. Now people wouldn't join.' Having joined he remained faithful to the union though he sees no real point in it in a firm in which you are not victimized. Asked about the advantages of unions, he said: 'It depends what you want to pay in for. You can pay in for sick pay or old age. There's no advantage in Scott Bader for itself. If I was starting at Scott Bader I wouldn't join myself. Now it's all peaceful.'

The union members who spoke to us so far have all been members of the Chemical Workers Union. They joined the union when it was first formed or when they came to work at Scott Bader and were not familiar with the conditions of work. The union does not give much meaning to their work. Essentially it stands for the security of legal protection and satisfies a more or less articulate need for security in an insecure world.

II

Two of the people who were members of trade unions in 1959 maintained their membership in other unions instead of transferring it to the Chemical Workers Union. One of them kept up his membership because of the sick benefits. He has no strong feelings about unions and joined originally because at that time it was the thing to do. The other is very deeply involved in trade union matters and still goes regularly to their meetings. Unions, for him, mean a desire for unity and mutual security. Since wages and working conditions in general 'are determined by employers and trade unions, it's only right you should contribute your share.' He has a strong ethical awareness of trade unions which are concerned 'with the emancipation of the working class.' These convictions make him also a firm supporter of the Commonwealth.

Those people who were formerly members of trade unions but gave up their membership continue to feel, on the whole, friendly towards unions. All of them are working in the factory. 'They are a good thing—until everyone does the same as we are doing . . . capitalists would take advantage of the workers if they have anyone to work for them. As regards us I don't think we need them because we can decide the wages. We can say when they go up and, if necessary, go down. . . . After all, we own the place. It looks to me that if all firms were run on the same lines, then the union need not exist. We are owners. If we want changes, we have the annual and the quarterly meetings. Problems are discussed around the table. We get paid according to the way the firm is running though a good many won't agree. They are strong trade union members and say it is impossible to do it. In the Boot and Shoe trade union we were frightened to death. When the boss wanted to sack you, the union could not do anything.'

The twin ideas that unions are a good thing in industry in general but not necessary at Scott Bader came up repeatedly.

For some it was mixed with disappointment about unions in general. A few workers felt that if they would join the union at Scott Bader, this might indicate that they are 'not quite sure' about the Commonwealth, that they lack trust in it: 'I think you betray your friends. You mistrust the person who employs you.' Such an attitude is based on a vision of unions as opposing the employer rather than helping to build a better world: 'If you got to have industrialists you got to have trade unions . . . if you have greedy people you got to do something about it . . . the more greedy capitalists . . . the more you need unions.'

Among the people working in the laboratory only one person was previously a member of a trade union. He welcomed unions bcause 'they're trying to break down this barrier between the employer and employee . . .' but he expressed doubt whether they are really concerned with the basic problems of work, with the meaning which work has in the life of the people. Among people with managerial responsibility, two people had previous union membership. One of them was very sceptical about unions whom he considered 'a bolshy mob, a communist lot'. He accused unions of 'merely using their power to get a rise in wages which is unrelated to rise in production, or when sending people to Coventry'. Another person felt trade unions were a good thing 'because they give a chance for people to identify themselves with a group larger than their immediate circle'.

Friendly attitudes towards trade unions were not limited to those people among management who had previous membership in trade unions. Generally speaking, the attitude of people with managerial responsibility tended to be the more favourable towards union, the greater their managerial responsibilities were.

'It's a good thing we have union members here. I would hope that the union members here would leak backwards to the union the kind of things we're doing here so that union members demand it.' For him, unions are a 'community of people, a means for spreading certain ideas—an expression of solidarity on certain principles'.

Others were more sceptical, accepting unions as a necessary

thing but being more impressed by the sectional interests represented by the unions rather than seeing them as a movement to bring about a better world. But few denied the significance of unions in counteracting 'the power of the vested interests in the country . . . '

People working in the laboratory who did not have any previous membership in trade unions were often ambiguous or expressed outright negative attitudes towards union. Some of them are upset about strikes. Others felt that unions in general were too powerful. 'In this country unions run riot, strike over silly things. In that respect I am afraid I have not much time for unions. If you face up to what normal people expect of them I would agree. As far as Scott Bader is concerned there is no real need for a union. People get a fair crack at the whip.'

The two people working in the factory who have never been members of unions were not much more favourably inclined towards trade unions than were those people in the laboratory who never were members. They expressed fear of strikes or of the possibility that unions may upset the balance of power: 'they are trying to become the boss instead of doing more or less the job they set out to do . . . to get a fair deal for the workers . . . It's becoming too political I think . . .' He also expressed fears that 'they might upset the economy if they press their claims too much . . .'

Among people with clerical responsibility, nobody had any previous membership in unions. Their attitude towards trade unions was a rather mixed one. 'To be perfectly honest, I really don't know. I suppose in a way they must be a good thing, thinking back, lots of advances wouldn't have been made if the men hadn't had the unions behind them . .' Another person indicated that 'office staff aren't in trade unions generally . . . John doesn't belong to a trade union but they always get the same things as the trade unions without going to strike . . .'

III

The summary picture shows clearly the impact of the work situation and of people's actual experience with trade unions on their attitudes towards unions. The pattern of awareness has certain unexpected features. The aloofness among the clerical staff and the ambiguous feelings of people working in the laboratory are not unusual. But the positive attitude among people with managerial responsibilities is striking. People in management have, furthermore, a tendency to see trade unions in broad terms as a possible vehicle for social change. Among workers this vision is relatively less frequent.

The general theme which recurs in all groups is: unions are, on the whole, a good thing but at Scott Bader they are not really needed. Only a relatively small number of workers feel that the union gives useful legal help and enhances security. A subsidiary theme is that unions in general are a good thing provided they stick to their job and are concerned with working conditions without indulging too much in strikes or trying to rock the boat of a precarious prosperity in an insecure world. A third theme, not too clearly articulated, is scepticism about unions because they are not concerned with the fundamental problems of work.

Only exceptionally were trade unions experienced as a rival to the Commonwealth—and then only in the sense of dual loyalties expressing lack of trust. The general feeling—accepted by the Chemical Workers Union itself since it does not insist that eligible members join the union—is that the Commonwealth has superseded the union as far as the organization of work is concerned. The protective function of the union and its role of giving workers a say-so has been largely taken over by the Commonwealth which has at least in principle—that is in beginning and in power—overcome the traditional division between 'employers' and 'employees'. Trade unions which consider their prime function to operate within the traditional framework have lost their place in the Commonwealth. Only a trade union movement concerned with the basic human problems of work and aiming to bring about a new social order continues to have an important role to play in the Commonwealth as we will see later.

If we have not much to say about unions in discussing the new organization of work the cause lies in the limited way in which unions define their primary task as much as in the new ways shown by the Commonwealth. Unions which allow capitalism to define their central tasks and which form countervailing power blocs within the power and value structures of capitalism have no significant role to play in a Commonwealth situation. Membership in the Commonwealth becomes then a substitute for union membership—as a basis for the actual participation in the working life. This is the case at Scott Bader for the majority of the people.

The problems which this situation poses and the new relationship to the trade union movement which the Commonwealth is attempting to develop will be discussed later. Suffice it to say that in the new Constitution the President of the Chemical Workers Union—who is also a member of Parliament for the Labour Party—has accepted an important function as a trustee of the Commonwealth. Before exploring these later developments we must understand the immediate impact of the new value and power structure of the Commonwealth.

Chapter 9

The main advantages of the Commonwealth

I

The general impression of many a visitor to Scott Bader is that the atmosphere is friendly and relaxed, that it is, on the whole, a very good atmosphere. There is a sense of informality if not freedom in being met and meeting people. What accounts for this? What are the changes which the Commonwealth has brought about in the life of the people?

In this chapter we will deal with the most striking impact of the Commonwealth. Security, participation, the new form of ownership and the opportunity to render services indicate the four main themes with which we shall deal. Only later will we penetrate more deeply into the impact of the Commonwealth on people's experience of their work.

II

Protection against the threat of unemployment and sickness was the first major achievement of the Commonwealth. Security was mentioned most frequently in response to a number of questions about the advantages of the Commonwealth and about two thirds of the people listed either security or sick leave or both among its three main advantages.[1] A

[1] In answer to the question 'What are the advantages of the Commonwealth?' a total of 57 items were listed. Security and sick leave were mentioned 21 times, participation 14 times, social service 4 times and ownership twice. General advantages were mentioned 57 times. In answer to the question 'What advantages and privileges do you get because you are a member of Scott Bader?' 41 items were listed. Among these various aspects of the Commonwealth were mentioned 24 times. Personal privileges such as security, sick leave etc. were mentioned 14 times; participation in the work process 5 times, social service 3 times; others twice. Other aspects of the Common-

manager said: 'There is less fear in this firm of what the future holds, less fear of arbitrary dismissal. This is important. It leads to a more contented working population.' This opinion found its echo from people in the laboratory: 'Security is a very big thing'; 'One feels secure within it. As long as you're doing your best, you're not likely to be thrown out'; or 'A man knows he has got money whether he's good or not.' A person from the factory said: 'There is that sense of security—although there is no such thing as security in this world.'

Similar voices were heard from the factory in response to the question: 'What advantages and privileges do you get because you are a member of Scott Bader?' 'You get the feeling of security.' Another person asked: 'You mean material things, not self-satisfaction?' To the comment 'anything', he responded with the following list of advantages: 'Self-satisfaction, security, six months sick-leave. You don't get the sack, even when there is redundancy. This is high on the list.' 'You are the last one to be finished' and 'You can't be sacked' has been said again and again.

The combination of security with sick-leave is frequent. A worker said: 'Well, the advantages are such that you feel secure, which you are, of course. In sickness you're looked after.' Another: 'I still think unless you do something very wrong you are assured of your job. If you are sick you're assured of being looked after for six months. You are still invited to the Commonwealth functions.'

Like security, sick-leave was mentioned by people from the office, the laboratory and the factory, but most often by people from the factory. Usually sick-leave benefits were related to other advantages such as security. Combinations not yet mentioned were: 'No short-time working; sickness scheme—pension scheme. You are insured twenty-four hours a day.' Here is a reference to the quite novel fact that in our society one can get insurance against almost anything. In an age of insecurity this is of particular importance.

---

wealth mentioned were: the general atmosphere, human aspects, etc.: 10 times; company goals: once; others: 6 times.

Asked ‘What are the advantages and disadvantages of the Commonwealth?’ a person from the laboratory said: ‘How many times have I been asked this! Advantages. It gives a man a sense of belonging and security.’ Among people in the factory a sense of belonging was mentioned most frequently. ‘You belong.’ ‘You belong to something instead of just working there.’

All the people who mentioned sick-leave by itself worked in the factory: ‘Sick pay. You can go out with a clear conscience that your family will be looked after.’ ‘The first thing is six month’s sick pay’. Almost apologetic is this answer: ‘I don’t like to say—the main advantage is looked upon as the sick pay. It can’t be overlooked. . . . Pity it doesn’t come automatically after two years whether you’re a member or not.’ He felt that the Commonwealth should stand for something ‘better’ than sick leave—that is a material advantage—an attitude about which we shall have more to say later. He may also have felt somewhat uneasy about the significance of sick-leave as an advantage derived from Commonwealth membership. Asked what the Commonwealth means, one person said: ‘If they are members? Six months’ sick pay.’ Laughing, he added, ‘If they told the truth, the majority would say that. Of course, they all make up various excuses for joining, such as wanting to help the community.’

The answers to the question, ‘Do you feel secure in your job?’ confirm that the Commonwealth had substantial success in giving security of employment. The large majority of people indicated that they do feel secure. A number of people expressed reservations about the ability of Scott Bader to maintain secure work opportunities in times of crisis. A manager said: ‘One’s job is secure and there is no risk of redundancy. . . . Whether it works in practice I doubt, the thing has never been tested.’

III

Do the available facts support these reservations? Do the feelings of security reflect the reality of a secure world? To throw some light on these questions, a few basic aspects of the economic situation of Scott Bader, the chemical industry and the British economy must be mentioned.

Scott Bader has been an expanding firm during all the years of the Commonwealth.[2] During these years, from 1951–1962, the chemical industry expanded more rapidly than did industrial production as a whole. The industry could, therefore, absorb downward pressures more easily.[3] The British economy as a whole has been subject to fluctuations but maintained an upward trend. Unemployment fluctuated between a minimum of about 215,000 people in 1951 and a maximum of about 475,000 in 1958.[4] Except for the war years there has always been unemployment during the past thirty years. The area in which Scott Bader is located though it had a rate below the national average has suffered from greater fluctuations in unemployment than the country as a whole—with a minimum of fifteen people in 1951 and a maximum of 250 in 1958. During the thirties unemployment was particularly heavy in the area amounting to over 2,000 people in 1932 out of about 18,000 insured people.[5]

Though it may not look very much on paper if expressed as a percentage of the total working population, the continued existence of unemployment is a major factor making for insecurity.[6] This was clearly noticeable when unemployment in

[2] The ratio of its net profits to total pay roll varied between about 15 per cent. and 110 per cent. This means that profits constituted a minimum of 15 per cent. and a maximum of 110 per cent. of the total pay roll.

[3] The index of industrial production increased from 117.2 in 1951 (1948=100) to 138.4 in 1957. From 1958 to 1962 it increased from 100 to 115.0 The corresponding figures for chemicals were: 1951–1957 increase from 134.8 to 192.4. 1958–1962 increase from 100 to 128.0. See Central Statistical Office *Annual Abstract of Statistics*, No. 95/1958/p. 128 and No. 100/1963/p. 128.

[4] See Central Statistical Office, *Annual Abstract of Statistics*, No. 95/1958/p. 112; No. 99/1962/p. 103; No. 100/1963/p. 116.

[5] We owe this information to the North Midland Regional Office of the Ministry of Labour. The Regional Controller has gone to great trouble to get these data. We acknowledge with gratitude his letter of March 20, 1961, addressed to Mr. Roger Hadley.

[6] In 1954 the total working population amounted to a little over 24 million people. Unemployment during that year amounted to about 260,000 or a little over 1 per cent. of the total working population. See Central Statistical Office, *Annual Abstract of Statistics*, No. 99/1962/p. 103.

the area rose during 1962. People would comment on it and express concern about the situation.

It must also be recognized that Scott Bader is a relatively small firm among the giants of the chemical industry.[7] It has to maintain itself and to grow in a highly competitive market in an atmosphere of insecurity. This atmosphere affects all people to a greater or smaller extent. The reservations about the security achieved must be understood in this light. The Commonwealth forms a bulwark against this general insecurity and through the Commonwealth a high degree of security has in fact been achieved.

While the security of employment is a bulwark against the unpredictability of the economy, sick pay is a protection against the ever present insecurities inherent in man's creatureliness. We are all subject to sickness and disease. In Britain people do not have to worry about paying medical bills. The National Health Service gives the security of almost free medical care. But the welfare provisions for paying the grocery bills, the rent and other necessary expenses while the breadwinner is unable to work are inadequate as compared to the full maintenance of income assured at Scott Bader. The ordinary firm's salaried employees enjoy such protection since their income is usually not discontinued when they are ill. The Commonwealth gives the same security to all human beings.

IV

Next to security, participation was the second most frequently mentioned advantage of the Commonwealth. It was mentioned by about half of the people.

A person with managerial responsibilities simply listed 'a chance of taking an active part in the way things are done'. A clerical worker said: 'I should say that the advantages are that you do have a say in matters and I should think it's good for the people to have a hand in governing the place they work in.' A voice from the laboratory: 'taking things as a whole, the

[7] The Imperial Chemical Industries had in 1962 a turnover of over 570 million pounds and in 1963 a turnover of over 620 million pounds.

best thing is better understanding—from one end to the other. Previously if it wasn't done through the works manager, there was no hope in getting anything done down there.'

After having spoken of a sense of security and belonging, another person from the laboratory mentioned the fact that you 'can participate more than in a more normal firm.' A very similar thought was expressed by a worker who experienced 'a freedom of expression that you don't get in a normal firm.' These references to 'normal firms' show that people still take the standards of the existing order as the norms of behaviour.

Many people working in the factory were quite brief in mentioning opportunities for participation. One person spoke about 'the say' which goes with being a shareholder; another combined ' a right to say whatever he thinks' with 'greater responsibility'. A third said, with some hesitation, 'You get a vote don't you?' Similar are the following responses: 'the best advantage is that you have a say in the company'; 'everybody can have a voice in management'.

Besides mentioning participation in response to the question 'What are the advantages of the Commonwealth?' people referred to participation repeatedly when answering such questions about Scott Bader as 'Does being a member make you feel you are a partner in doing an important job?' and 'What advantages and privileges do you get because you are a member of Scott Bader?' Even more frequently—by about a fifth of the people—was participation mentioned in answer to the question 'If a friend were to ask you "What is the Commonwealth?" what would you reply? '

People also referred to their say in determining the distribution of the surplus. A worker summed it up in these words: 'You get the chance to vote on the distribution of profits—don't you? You also have a right to nominate charities or good causes for the funds.' Several people mentioned their 'right to nominate'. A manager said that work has more meaning to him because it is done in a community and because the Commonwealth gives some of the earnings for charitable purposes.

For a person from the laboratory Scott Bader is 'an organization in which everyone has a say in the day-to-day running of the business. At Scott Bader one is free to say what one likes; and from the work we carry out and the profits we make we benefit those less fortunate than ourselves.'

A final illustration combines the right to dispose of the profits and to give for charitable purposes: 'When you are a member of the Commonwealth you have your own share, money does not just go to dividends. The effort you put into it helps also the local community.

V

Closely related to security and participation is the third major advantage of the Commonwealth, the ownership of ninety per cent. of the shares. The new communal form of ownership was mentioned by about a third of the people of the Commonwealth.[8]

Asked: 'What are the advantages and disadvantages of the Commonwealth?' two people working in the factory referred to ownership: 'You seem to own the firm'; 'after all we are shareholders, while there are shares, we can have a say in them'.

Asked: 'What comes to your mind when you use the word "Scott Bader"?' a person was reminded of his own name because 'I consider it's partly mine. I've got a share in it. Therefore it's up to us to do the best by it.' Another person said 'I feel I own part of the firm.'

In discussing the Commonwealth with a friend, a person with managerial responsibility would speak about 'an experiment to change the ownership of a business, by having a holding company which is owned by the employees of the company —the holding company controlling the trading company. In other words the accent would be on ownership. The transfer from personal to corporate ownership.'

Another manager expressed a similar thought: 'I am back to my practical description. It is, in fact, a trust holding ninety per cent. of the shares of the Scott Bader Company—manufacturing chemists. Certain members of the firm qualify to be-

[8] There were also a number of spontaneous references to the new form of ownership. See p. 327 n.

come members of the body administering this trust. I am not quite accurate there but broadly speaking I would give a purely factual description of the community that might or might not exist.'

Another manager, explaining his feelings of partnership said: 'to work towards the idea of common ownership, democratic integration, has great interest and this is the reason why I stay.'

In the same context, a person from the clerical staff mentioned 'common ownership, giving people a chance to have self-government'. A number of people in the laboratories related common ownership to participation in general. 'The Commonwealth is a scheme for common ownership whereby employees are members of the company and Scott Bader Commonwealth and they have a hand in the government of the company.' 'I should say it's an organization whereby workers and staff alike can participate in the running of the firm, they can all have a say in what's going on, they know about the profits of the company. It's a firm where everyone can take an equal share in responsibility, they can all sit on the committees that run the Commonwealth.' He paused, saying: 'I still haven't told you what it is!' and continued: 'Then I would go on to explain the legal side of it, that it is a charitable organization attached to the company—it holds ninety per cent. of the shares and anyone after two years can become a member holding the shares communally. It's the Commonwealth that decides the distribution of the profits—although it's the Directors that make the recommendations. They have the power to say to the Directors that they don't agree. They have the power to force the full twenty per cent. of the bonus—they never have, of course.' Here is a reference to the right of the members of the Commonwealth to get up to twenty per cent. of the net profits as a bonus.

A worker said: 'I think my first answer would be the material answer—the co-ownership of the shares and the participation—ideally it should be the spirit as well.' Another: 'When you are in the Commonwealth, you're part owner of the firm.'

The new form of ownership was repeatedly referred to in

terms of owning *part* of the firm, rather than in terms of common ownership.[9] These differences in expression may be considered to be merely differences in wording. But this is not the case. As we will see later this idea of part ownership is symptomatic of the difficulties of comprehending the *communal* character of the new form of ownership. This difficulty is a major element in explaining why the new form of ownership has not affected the experience of work of more people and why only about half of those who mentioned the new form of ownership referred to common or co-ownership rather than part ownership.[10]

Another important factor explaining the situation is the need for security and the link between security and property. People mentioned security repeatedly when asked 'What does private property mean to you?'[11] The need for security in an insecure world may be so strong that there is a desire to grasp things if they have a common, indivisible character. The reality of an indivisible communal ownership is then transformed in people's minds into some imaginary part ownership.

VI

Participation in the disposal of profits and the use of a part of the earnings for educational and charitable purposes was closely linked to the rendering of a service to the community.

9 This theme of part-ownership reappears in responses to the question 'Does being a member of Scott Bader make you feel you are a partner in doing an important job?' Three people mentioned common ownership or co-ownership. One person felt 'some of the firms is yours', another, from the factory, also spoke in terms of co-ownership.
Questioned 'If a friend were to ask you "What is the Commonwealth?" what would you reply?' two people spoke about the new form of ownership in terms of common ownership and one person in terms of part ownership. Among the people who mentioned the new form of ownership in connection with their experience of work, co-ownership or common ownership was mentioned about as frequently as part ownership .

10 It is true that there were considerable individual differences in the meaning given to the words used. But these do not explain the systematic tendency towards an experience of part-ownership.

11 Personal interest in what is owned has also been mentioned.

The opportunity for social service was experienced as the fourth main advantage of the Commonwealth. About one fifth of the people spoke about it.

Service may either be rendered through charitable contributions or directly to people since each member of the Commonwealth is expected to give at least eight hours for social service each year.

Some people mentioned both aspects: 'You pack parcels and get satisfaction out of that—you do get satisfaction out of giving the money to charity.' Or they spoke in general terms: 'You have the opportunity of doing social service which you could not do in an ordinary situation.'

Similar was the response of a person with managerial responsibilities to the question about the advantages of the Commonwealth: 'The chance of fulfilling a greater social responsibility than you could do as an individual.'

In the laboratory there were both general and specific references to social service. 'He can have the feeling that he is giving to people less fortunate than himself—giving to people who need help.' Though somewhat indirect and aloof—'he can have the feeling'—there is a clear awareness of helping other people. Another person was more direct: 'As you probably know, we give parcels to old people in the village. I usually take two, spend a quarter to half an hour having a chat—helping chop sticks at Christmas time.'

Social service was mentioned most frequently in the factory, almost always in terms of direct service rendered to the people of the local community. Three workers spoke about 'the satisfaction of being able to assist people when it's most needed'; 'the benefits of visits to old folks'; 'firewood for old folk'. Others said: 'I do help in my own way, with taking parcels to old people and the like.' 'The main function of the Commonwealth is to lend a helping hand to all the needy—especially the old folk of the village of Wollaston.' Or, as another person saw the Commonwealth, 'it's mainly planned to help the poorer folk of Wollaston and the surrounding area to live a happier and better life'. The fact that people 'do not just bring groceries' but visit with the old people has been emphasized.

A number of people combined the rendering of service with other aspects of the Commonwealth: 'The advantages are, of course, this excellent security as far as employment is concerned; plus the fact that you have the opportunity of doing social service which you couldn't do in an ordinary situation.' Or: 'You do pack parcels and get satisfaction out of that—you do get satisfaction out of giving the money to charity.'

With 10,000 parcels and 1,200 bags of firewood distributed in a little over a decade (1951–1963) the experience of social service as something significent is understandable.

VII

To complete our survey of specific advantages of the Commonwealth, we must mention a number of miscellaneous responses and some critical attitudes.

The 'use of the Commonwealth Centre and the annual dinner' and the friendliness of the place were mentioned. 'The great advantage is that we are on Christian name terms with everyone. I'm a great believer in not calling anyone "sir".'

Sceptical were the following comments: 'I don't know any other firm—going back to the book. In the book we have quite a lot to say but in actual fact we haven't.' The book he referred to is the Commonwealth handbook which sets forth the duties and responsibilities of Commonwealth members.[12] Another person felt that he had 'no advantages or privileges' because he was not yet a member of the Commonwealth.

Asked whether there are any disadvantages in Commonwealth membership about one third of the people said no. 'I can't see any. I don't know. If there were any we would try to straighten them out.'

Another third indicated certain shortcomings. They felt that the Commonwealth does not work as it should or that some people do not live up to its demands. Inadequate participation in meetings, lack of trust, greed, unwillingness to con-

[12] See *New Life in Industry*, Handbook and Charter for the Staff of Scott Bader & Co. Ltd. approved by the Staff Conference held at Cambridge on the 28th April 1951. Second Edition, July 1955, particularly pp. 49ff.

tribute and undeveloped communal spirit were among the shortcomings listed.

Less than a third of the people listed disadvantages but they gave to this word a broad meaning. The fact that Commonwealth activities are time-consuming was mentioned several times. A person felt 'certain obligations to staying with the firm' to be a disadvantage. For another person 'it is a disadvantage in case you don't want to do any voluntary work'; or 'responsibilities are piled on you'. 'Cynicism and apathy' have also been mentioned as disadvantages. None of the reasons add up to a disadvantage in the usual sense of the word. Only three points made in regard to money, finances and administration, could be considered real disadvantages.[13]

In summary we may say that the Commonwealth was primarily experienced as giving security in an insecure world and secondarily as opening new opportunities for taking part in various aspects of work and its organization. The new form of ownership and service to the community followed in a considerable distance and were experienced only by a minority of the people.

[13] These points cannot be discussed here without dealing with personal situations. Among the 30 people questioned ten indicated that there were no disadvantages; four said that the Commonwealth does not work properly; six felt that some people did not live up to its values and eight listed various demands made by the Commonwealth and obligations of Commonwealth membership. Two people mentioned other aspects of Scott Bader.

Chapter 10
The emergence of new attitudes

I

While security, the opportunity for participation, the new form of ownership and social service made a clearly traceable and widespread impact, there were new beginnings which were more slowly taking roots among the people.

Asked what comes to his mind when he uses the words 'Scott Bader', a person answered 'a beginning . . . merely a beginning of a growth with an indefinite future—a venture in human fellowship.' This is a modest statement which indicates at the same time the wide new vista opened by the Commonwealth.

How deeply the Commonwealth affected some people's life is indicated in the following response: 'I should say that it's one of my biggest interests, one of my biggest worries and my greatest pleasure . . .' After his wife had remarked 'bread and butter', he continued 'I could quite honestly say it's one of the best things that happened to me . . . I've been brought up in ordinary production factories, ordinary payment by results, squabbles and things, working under artificial light all the time. You go out there and you look out on the lawns, you're more on the level of a country squire. And then I've always been interested in trade union work and social work, and when they decided to form the Commonwealth that gave me an added interest.'

Besides the beautiful surroundings and the contrast to the bad working conditions before coming to Scott Bader he cherished most the opportunity to work for goals unknown in 'ordinary production factories.'

Equally strong was the experience of a person to whom 'Scott Bader . . . does not register like an ordinary firm. It is more than that. On the plane of security and where Christian principles are worked out—tried to be worked out, hoped to be worked out—whichever way you want to put it. Knowing the set-up, you know the foundation is there to build something that revolutionizes industry—if other firms will follow suit. In industry the word Scott Bader means something.' Here is an awareness of the radical transforming power of Christian principles.

One person when asked: 'When you look back to your youth, to things your parents and grandparents told you, do you feel that there has been any change?' 'What were the outstanding events since then?' mentioned the formation of the Commonwealth as 'an outstanding event. I was only about eighteen years then. I didn't really appreciate it, didn't know what it really meant. When I look back on it, what Mr. Bader did, give the factory, give the people their say and their opportunity in the running of the firm, it was a great event.'

II

The religious basis of the Commonwealth was mentioned by a person who saw 'response to the highest, to God' as a general advantage of the Commonwealth. The religious aspect was mentioned repeatedly in answer to the question: 'If a friend were to ask you "What is the Commonwealth" what would you say?' 'It is really a job to define what you would say: just a firm running on principles that they consider better than anything they find in industry. Not just monetary gain, the whole spirit, the right spirit.' Though his experience is somewhat remote—he speaks about 'they' rather than 'i' or 'we'—he too begins to have an awareness of new values.

Another person from the factory started with what he called a 'material' answer—a reference to co-ownership—and ended up with these words: 'I think the spirit is alloyed to anyone with religious-social tendencies. Anyone with these tendencies can't help being a better Commonwealth member.'

A person from the laboratory who was not yet a member of the Commonwealth said: 'From a practical point of view the Commonwealth means not very much. The principles mean quite a lot because they are Christian principles, the right principles.' He welcomed the principles of the Commonwealth but was critical because 'they're not being put into practice'. He felt that some people look at the Commonwealth primarily in terms of what 'they can get out of it' rather than in terms of what they may give to it. 'I think that people should get a living wage—one thing they do. The less fortunate should be helped . . . I have no time for people who sponge—that's where the idea of the Commonwealth breaks down. A lot of people are there for what they can get out of it.'[1]

It is understandable that those people who see the Commonwealth in terms of very high principles have a tendency to be critical about their realization after a relatively short time.

A person from the factory said: 'I've been asked this lots of times, "What is the Commonwealth?" I say it's an ideal, it's a good ideal, not always practicable. I will give you an illustration later on of what I mean. I've already told you I like working there—it's the best firm I ever worked for. But it does annoy me when you ask people why they've joined the Commonwealth, they answer "for the same reason as everyone else", they can't think of a reason for themselves.' After having criticized the attitude of some people towards the Commonwealth, he continued: 'I do help in my own way, with taking parcels to old people and the like. And I do get my own benefits. I tell people what it stands for.' Here again the ideal is upheld in spite of the feeling that only a beginning has been made in its realization.

A number of people refer to specific values, such as responsibility and community: 'The Commonwealth enables its members to exercise their responsibility to the community in the wider sense of the word.' 'Equal opportunities, pacifist tendencies and equality' were also mentioned: 'In the Commonwealth every person is the same regardless of what they do.'

The new sense of values is clearly expressed in the following answer: 'The Commonwealth is a school of life to live out your

[1] In a conversation which took place over a year afterwards he did not remember having used the word 'sponge' but agreed with his wife that he said 'quite a lot join for advantages'.

values—live out your existence in relation to others—to benefit society and those who work with you as well as yourself.'

III

Besides general references to human values and religious principles three ideas recur frequently: sharing, holding something in common and helping.[2]

A person with managerial responsibility saw the Commonwealth as 'an attempt to share one's working wealth in common with others'. This view finds an almost exact echo in a voice from the factory: 'Well, the Commonwealth is . . . the name itself reflects what we're trying to do, that each one who works there should share the wealth of the company, have a share in it.'

People from the laboratory spoke about the 'common' element in work, and about an 'equal share in responsibility'. 'The Commonwealth is an attempt to get the members of the firm together on a common basis for the good of the business and the good of themselves.' The common element was also seen in terms of harmony and community: 'The Commonwealth is an organization designed to bring about a complete unity of workers on a common level to work for one aim: mutual benefit.'

A person from the factory sees the Commonwealth as 'the community organization within the firm where each one is of equal importance and has equal opportunities'. Another said: 'It's a community all right, but what sort of community?' He did not answer this query but continued to speak about community in terms of 'big family life'.

A person on the clerical staff spoke about the Commonwealth as 'a sort of party where everyone helps to help each other'. He added: 'Whether they do it is a different thing—but

[2] In answering the question: 'If a friend were to ask you "What is the Commonwealth" what would you answer?' thirty people gave a total of 49 responses. Of these 19 referred to specific functions of the Commonwealth (ownership 7; participation 6; social service 6); 23 referred to general values or principles (sharing 8; helping 6; new values 9); 3 referred to work and 4 to various other aspects.

they try to help each other. I think a lot of them join because of the extra pay they get when they are ill.' 'Trying to help them along and to install a sense of responsibility into some people' was a response from the laboratory.

People working in the factory referred most frequently to helping. 'I should say the Commonwealth is a charitable organization, governed by a community Council from all classes in the factory. Its main function is to lend a helping hand to all the needy, especially the old folks of the village of Wollaston.' An element of having something in common is seen in 'government from all classes', and help is mainly perceived in relation to the local community. Two other people mentioned help in connection with the services which they render to people in the community.

Queried 'If a friend were to ask you "What is the Commonwealth?" what would you say?' a worker answered: 'Do you know I often thought of that and said I don't know.' With a laugh he added: 'You can read all the highfalutin' language and it all comes down to just helping one another.'

IV

Feelings and thoughts about the Commonwealth become more specific as people speak about the impact of the Commonwealth on work satisfaction. A person with managerial responsibility saw the Commonwealth as 'a body of people endeavouring to make work more satisfying and meaningful for those engaged in it'. Another person working in the laboratory felt that there are 'many different ways of looking at it. To me it has seemed a means of making people feel happy in their job . . . if they want to be happy.'

Some people did not know what to answer when asked 'If a friend asked you "What is the Commonwealth?" what would you say?' 'I don't really know. I don't know what the Commonwealth is' was the response from a person with clerical responsibilities. A person from the laboratory said: 'This will be a stumbling block to me—tongue-tied to give a clear-cut answer . . . the Commonwealth is a set-up which enables all members of the Commonwealth to enjoy the fortunes, good or bad, of the Scott Bader company.'

For one of the workers the Commonwealth is the 'axis of the firm'. Asked what he meant, he said: 'What's an axis? something it rotates on.' In a discussion about how he came to work at Scott Bader a worker said: 'I had been living in the locality. To me, when I came home, it was just a job. Nothing more than that.' But 'due to the birth of the Commonwealth' it means more now. The job provides 'bread and butter' but it also gives 'more satisfaction'.

Another person was more articulate in indicating how the Commonwealth affected his experience of work. His response to the question 'What makes you feel that your job and how you do it is important?' was 'I think everybody's work is important to the establishment and that's the idea of the Commonwealth to show it, that you are not just a cog.' A similar experience was expressed by a worker to whom 'Scott Bader is not a factory'.

The Commonwealth was mentioned repeatedly as a topic of conversation. Asked 'Do you talk with your fellow workers while at work?' a number of people indicated that they speak 'quite a bit' about the Commonweath. 'I get lots of questions from the Commonwealth angle' or 'Commonwealth questions come to me'. Observations showed that the Commonwealth is a frequent topic of conversation.

V

The opportunities to participate in a new venture express themselves in a sense of partnership. We asked two questions about the company: 'Does being a member make you feel that you are a partner in doing an important job?' and 'What about Scott Bader makes you feel that way?'

A good majority of the people had a clear feeling of partnership. About a quarter of these had reservations which in some cases bordered on neutral feelings. Only a few indicated that they did not feel as partners.

A person with clear feelings of partnership said: 'When I

worked in a shoe factory I didn't get there before I had to. Now I'm on the job half an hour before my time—always twenty minutes.' Asked why he gets to work early, he said: 'Before I didn't like the job in the shoe factory and I like the job I'm doing.'

References to the Commonwealth were most frequent among those with strong feelings of partnership.

A manager felt himself a partner because 'as a member of the Scott Bader Commonwealth I am contributing to the development of a democratic . . . organization in a business firm'. Another person said: 'I can be accepted by the people for what I am, not because of the position I hold in the company.' He thus articulates an important aspect of democracy. An active Commonwealth member from the laboratory who had a position of influence in the Commonwealth said: 'Yes, I think it does make me feel I am a partner in doing an important job. You are not just a number or a cog—you can make a contribution towards the well-being of the firm, what you say is considered, not just brushed aside.' Another person from the laboratory felt he was a partner because 'you get a kick out of pulling your weight. You feel you can go to a meeting and hear about the profits. You feel you have made your contribution. I agree with the Old Man that you are a plus to your work and a plus to society.'[3]

People from the factory mentioned the Commonwealth most frequently. 'I feel a partner because I accept the Commonwealth in principle. I mean I was there when the Commonwealth was formed and we had lots of preliminary meetings to draw up the constitution. We felt it was a sincere experiment I could identify with—I have taken it almost literally. If things haven't worked out as I saw things, I've been outspoken—but it doesn't mean that I have lost faith. It's all an attitude of mind if you feel a partner or not.'

Another felt as a partner: 'Of course I do because I'm not only allowed to work freely, I'm allowed to know more about its financial standing, when things are good or bad, than in

[3] Partnership was also related to security. Some people mentioned this connection explicitly.

most firms. You feel more of a partner than you would elsewhere.'

Brief but to the point were: 'You feel as a partner for the simple reason that you are a partner. A sense of belonging. You're helping yourself as well as others by getting along.' 'You are more part of the firm. It gives you a whole sense of responsibility.' And finally: 'Something unique, isn't it?'[4]

VI

Reservations or qualifications about feelings of partnership were more or less articulate.

A person with clerical responsibilities said: 'I think so, yes (I feel as a partner), it's a well-known firm around here. Everyone always thinks it's a fairly good firm to work for—which I think too.' But he added: 'Sometimes I don't.' When questioned he could not give any specific reasons, saying again: 'Everyone seems to think highly of it. You say where you work and they say "Oh yes, I'd like to get a job there".'

A person with managerial responsibilities expressed his doubts in a more articulate way. 'Sometimes I feel as a partner. Sometimes I think the whole business is a stupid sham . . .' Asked when he feels like that, he said: 'When I feel that someone has exercised a brilliant piece of bad management.'

Other people in this group express specific complaints which cannot be meaningfully discussed here. Some quite simply don't feel themselves as partners: 'Well, it's not anyone's fault really. I'm not enough advanced on what's going on there. I don't feel myself a real partner.' One person who feels a 'member' but not a'partner' mentioned the Commonwealth and spoke about the question of participation.

Among those who say that they do not feel as partners, the Commonwealth came up as relatively frequently.

A person with managerial responsibilities said: 'It would be nice to feel that but I don't think so.' Questioned he felt that the company did an important job 'industrially but not socially'. Another person with important managerial responsibilities

[4] Common ownership was mentioned in this connection.

did not have feelings of partnership: 'Sometimes I make important contributions. But this does not mean I am always important. At times I am ordinary.'

A person from the laboratory related his lack of feelings of partnership directly to the Commonwealth: 'It's a formality, going through a formality to become a member of the Commonwealth. Once you have gone through that formality, I don't think it brings about any other feelings about the Commonwealth.' He then spoke about a false sense of security created by the security given by the Commonwealth.[5]

A final response among those who do not feel themselves partners comes from the factory. 'No (I don't feel as a partner), because if I was away from work they'd carry on just the same as if I wasn't there.'

VII

To understand the significance of the Commonwealth in creating new attitudes towards work we must see the feelings and thoughts evoked by the Commonwealth in relation to the feelings and thoughts evoked by other aspects of the work situation. We may classify these aspects broadly in these groups (i) the general atmosphere of work, the location, the physical working conditions and the human contacts, (ii) the goals of the organization and the reflection of the image of Scott Bader in the minds of the people and (iii) other factors not directly related to Scott Bader such as general conditions in the country and the world.

The beautiful place where Scott Bader is located, the friendly and open atmosphere, the relaxed relationships between people and the relatively agreeable working conditions undoubtedly affect people's attitudes. About one fifth to a

[5] He said: 'In fact I think that a false sense of security is created by knowing that you can't be sacked. People go around in a slap-happy way—in a way that people can't do outside.' Though he experienced the Commonwealth as 'a formality' he attributed rather far-reaching consequences to it: it gives people a false sense of security and makes them slap-happy. He sensed certain dangers and made them the focal point of his attitude. See Chapter 7.

third of the people mentioned these aspects in their answers to various questions.[6]

The goals of the organization were mentioned much less frequently. Asked: 'Now we want to discuss what comes to your mind when you use the words "Scott Bader"', about a fifth of the people referred to them but in answering all other questions they were rarely mentioned. There is, furthermore, a strong concentration of responses among management.

A person with managerial responsibility said 'Scott Bader is a potential focal point for wholeness. I see it very often as a series of different letters 'S-C-O-T-T B-A-D-E-R".' He then spoke about the meaning of different types of letters used at different periods and described his feelings: 'sometimes you kind of have an attitude like a farmer has to his land.' Here is an awareness of the integrative functions of the organization combined with a strong sense of belonging and rootedness.

Another person was reminded of 'our tanker going out of the gate' then had a vision of 'the name on our letter-heading', finally of himself coming to work. A third person saw 'his job as a small unit in the whole'. The latter response indicates a feeling of being part of a larger organization, the former had more of an undertone of awareness of personal importance.

Nobody in the clerical group mentioned the organization properly speaking. The ambition of a person from the laboratory was 'to see Scott Bader as a really thriving business concern first of all.' Another saw it as 'a very progressive firm; it always strikes me as being a new firm. In two years I have seen a lot of changes; everything is changing, progressing.' A person from the factory mentioned 'the name of the firm' in a somewhat neutral way.

Asked 'What advantages and privileges do you get because you are a member of Scott Bader?' a person working in the

[6] When asked 'Now we want to discuss what comes to your mind when you use the words 'Scott Bader' 11 out of 30 people and 19 out of 38 responses referred to the general atmosphere, the concrete aspects of work and the human contacts. When asked 'What advantages and privileges do you get because you are a member of Scott Bader?' 6 out of 30 people and 10 out of 41 responses referred to these dimensions.

laboratory referred to the company as 'a small company with a very young Board of Directors.' He liked 'the spirit of the company . . . the willingness to give one's best.'

The goals of the company and the reflection of the public image of Scott Bader were quite incidental in people's comments on their feelings of partnership. 'Scott Bader is reputed to be a high-class chemical producer'. The efficiency of the company was also mentioned. Generally speaking 'the company' and its organization have left little imprint in the minds of the people.

The general conditions in the country and in the world affected the attitude towards work in various ways which we shall explore later. They affected the immediate experience of work in the sense already described: the general insecurity and ever present possibility of unemployment enhanced the good feelings about the Commonwealth, the security it gives and the opportunities for participation which it opened.

VIII

Seen in a broader perspective the Commonwealth appears as the major factor influencing people's experience of work. A brief comparison indicates the crescendo with which it was mentioned in people's replies to different questions:

	Now we want to discuss what comes to your mind when you use the words 'Scott Bader'	Does being a member make you feel you are a partner in doing an important job?	What advantages and privileges do you get because you are a member of Scott Bader?
References to the Commonwealth	7	15*	24*
Number of people	7	15	18

* Favourable references only.

To understand the significance of the Commonwealth we must take into consideration the following factors:

(i) The relative insignificance of the company and its goals in people's experiences of their work is due to the fact that the traditional organization of work considers human values only incidentally. After having listed the advantages derived from the Commonwealth a person was asked whether there are any advantages on the company side. His response was typical: 'Wouldn't have any at all—just like an ordinary firm.' He took it for granted that nobody expects an 'ordinary firm' to give meaning to work. Or, at least, almost nobody.[7]

(ii) The absence of a meaningful contribution of the 'organizational goals of the company' does not mean that these goals do not matter. It means that these goals and the whole structure of value and power which they express are *either* overshadowed by the goals of the Commonwealth *or* they too are simply taken for granted.

The absence of a clear differentiation between what is historically specific and what is universal, removes the basic goals of the organization of work from people's consciousness. Nobody questioned, for example, the historically unique concept of efficiency with its exclusive emphasis on technical-market considerations and its exclusion of man's fundamental need for wholeness and integration. Asked: 'Do you ever sit down and consider how you are doing in your work?' speed and efficiency were the single most frequent criteria used to judge how one does in one's work. Nor are the basic 'forms' and sources of power questioned as long as the power to give orders is implemented in a 'humane' way and leaves enough 'freedom' of action.

(iii) The traditional oppressive aspects of an authoritarian organization of work have been sufficiently modified by the Commonwealth to be neutralized. Without such neutralization the company goals could not have moved as much into the background as they did.

The impact of the Commonwealth must, therefore, be understood as a result of two major attitudes, 'taking the world as

[7] Asked 'What advantages do you get because you are a member of Scott Bader?' only 1 person out of 30 and only 1 response out of 41 referred to the goals of the company.

it is for granted' and 'appreciating whatever changes the Commonwealth has brought about'. There is no evidence that the Commonwealth has given to work much deeper meaning. The reasons for this situation will be explored in Part IV of this book.

However, even after the first decade of its existence the Commonwealth has gone a long way in showing a new way in industry. Those conflicts which make the headlines in our newspapers did not exist any more at Scott Bader. Wages and profits ceased to be in opposition to each other (having again taken their universal meaning and function). Strikes and threats of strikes become meaningless under such conditions. Many of the negative influences upon work were removed and a spirit of sharing and helping has begun to express itself in democratic ways of decision making.

The achievements of the Commonwealth can be best summed up by saying that it has come to a half-way mark in its development. We may measure the half-way mark by three indices. In response to key questions about half of the people mentioned a *specific* aspect of the Commonwealth such as the new form of ownership, participation and social service. The other half mentioned general aspects of the Commonwealth such as sharing, helping and the new values and principles on which the Commonwealth is based. The Commonwealth has also reached a half-way mark inasmuch as about half of the people were aware of the new opportunities for participation. Finally a half-way mark was reached when about half of the people felt ready to have the ten per cent. Founder Shares transferred to the Commonwealth.[8]

With this transfer a new chapter began in the history of the Commonwealth.

[8] See Appendix on Method, p. 375.

Part III

The Constitution of 1963 and its potentialities

Chapter 11

The Commonwealth is coming of age

I

Power was the stumbling block which induced in 1951 the founders of the Commonwealth to retain ten per cent. of the shares with a veto right. Power remained the central problem in 1963 when the time came to make common ownership a full reality.

Did the attitudes of the people change sufficiently during the first decade of the Commonwealth that a full transfer of power could be risked? Was there an awakening of a new conception of power which made this transfer less risky? Or did the experience of the first ten years convince those accustomed to power that their fears were unfounded and that the people could be trusted with the full exercise of power?

As we will see there is some truth in each of these questions.

II

Ernest Bader who started the Commonwealth and who was determined to fulfil his original promise of common ownership was the central figure in the resolution of the problem of power. The basic issues which he had to face was a problem of surrender of power.

Surrender may evoke in us the image of military defeat: unconditional surrender is a word alive in those who lived through the last world war. But surrender also has an entirely different meaning: to give up something important for something more important, something real for something more real, something of value for something of truer value. True surrender ultimately means to give up our little self for our true Self. It is an act of courage and devotion. It is an act through which we take upon ourselves a share of the Cross.

Surrender thus understood is something uniquely personal. At the same time it poses universal human problems. Tillich has indicated clearly the meaning of surrender: 'In order to be able to surrender himself completely, he must possess himself completely. And only he can possess—and therefore surrender—himself completely who is united with the ground of his being and meaning without separation and disruption. In the picture of Jesus as the Christ we have the picture of a man who possesses these qualities.'[1]

In these words Tillich indicates the most fundamental dimensions of surrender. A true surrender presupposes an intimate relatedness to that ultimate reality which to Ernest Bader became alive in Christ. It implies awareness of an other-ness, of a gulf between our attempts to follow Christ and the reality of Jesus as the Christ.

We shall not deal here with the personal meaning of the final act of surrender of his power by Ernest Bader in 1963. We are touching areas of a person's life where the Holy Spirit illumines the most personal experiences. But we must deal with the general meaning of an act of surrender in Western industrial society in the second half of the twentieth century.

Power was surrendered to people who have traditionally been treated as children, that is as 'employees' incapable of responsibly participating in the decisions affecting their working life. In industry people were treated without respect for their essential human dignity as if they were the not too satisfactory products of a mechanical master brain rather than beings created in the image of God.

Abruptly these people were called upon to take a responsible part in the life of a company, to make decisions affecting their own future and the future of all those who are part of the community of work. Suddenly they were addressed as human beings with a dignity of their own.

Equally sudden was the change in the existential situation for the person who addressed them as human beings: Ernest Bader. He, like them, is not only a child of God but also a child

[1] See Paul Tillich, *Systematic Theology*, Vol. 1, p. 143 quoted from A. T. Robinson, *Honest to God*, London 1963, p. 74.

of the industrial culture of the West. He is one of the few people who are still imbued by what Max Weber called the 'Protestant Ethic'. For him work is a calling which gives to success a transcendental meaning.

The people of the Commonwealth are as much imbued by the ethic of success but for many of them it has become secularized; the ethic of a true calling has been largely replaced by the striving for success without an inner meaning. Most of them were furthermore alienated from the spiritual ground on which the Commonwealth grew. This had far-reaching consequences for their encounter: Ernest Bader took it for granted that the Commonwealth was the embodiment of truth while many of the people were struggling to comprehend what it was all about.

Both were caught in the traditional division of people into those who have power, the employers, the bosses or the captains of industry and those who do not have any comparable power—the employees. It is difficult enough for a person to give up power as an act of surrender; but it is as much of a challenge to shed one's second nature as 'the boss' and 'employer' and to become fully democratic in every area of one's dealings. This is particularly difficult as long as the response is that of 'employees' who were not accustomed to freedom at work and who had to discover the potentialities—and responsibilities—which the Commonwealth created for them.

The traditional division between employer and employee is but one aspect of the separation of the spheres of life accompanied by 'the dissociation of the human soul'—to quote again Max Weber.[2] All of us are children of an industrial culture characterized by deep splits. None of us can escape the human situation created by this. To strive towards unity and wholeness in such a culture is a difficult venture which is bound to arouse deep-seated conflicts.

The self-divestment of power on which the Commonwealth is based demanded from Ernest Bader an increasingly full realization of his initial act of surrender; from the people to whom he addressed himself it demanded an increasing ability to re-

[2] See Max Weber, *Gesammelte Aufsätze Zur Wissenschaftslehre*, Tübingen 1922, p. 535.

spond to him as people with dignity and responsibility. In this process a new conception of power came to life. True power was to be rooted in a development of the whole person and was to come from within the person. It was to be rooted in the experience, knowledge and ability of a person. This is the core of the problem of democratic participation. It is also the core of the new conception of power on which the Constitution of 1963 is based.

It is not accidental that the Commonwealth idea has been expressed in terms of democratic integration. Integration means unity, wholeness. True integration implies integrity, commitment and faithfulness to one's true self. To achieve unity and true community in a deeply split human situation and to build this unity on true self-expression of all who are part of the community—this is the deepest problem of democratic integration and participation in industry. To allow men—all men—to move towards this goal is the meaning of the act of surrender which was completed when the power structure of the Commonwealth was reorganized in 1963.

Many people commented how Ernest Bader slowly changed; how he who originally dominated the scene not only by his spiritual power but also by his position as the boss became accustomed to a give and take and to the acceptance of decisions even if he did not like them.

For the people this give and take had to be worked out in relationship to a person who was bound to evoke strong feelings and who provided an ideal screen on which manifold problems could be easily projected. An important aspect of the Commonwealth coming of age was the development of people's ability to meet such a person humanly in freedom.

III

The extent to which traditional conceptions of power still prevailed after the first decade of the Commonwealth is clearly reflected in people's attitude to the transfer of the ten per cent. Founder Shares.

In 1957 Ernest Bader offered for the first time to transfer the

Founder Shares to the Commonwealth. Consequently discussion groups were formed to think through the problems raised by this offer. The groups prepared a report saying, in essence, that they were ready to accept the transfer of the shares provided the regular power of shareholders, particularly the right to appoint the Directors, would be invested in them.[3] Ernest Bader rejected this idea because he felt that a power struggle incompatible with the principles of the Commonwealth might result. He objected in particular to have the directors elected by the Commonwealth.

These events were still in the minds of many people when we asked them in 1959: 'How do you feel about the ten per cent. Founder Shares? Should they go to the Commonwealth?' As already mentioned about half the people felt that the shares should go to the Commonwealth. The vast majority of them were managers and people working in the laboratory. The other half felt that the Founder Shares should not go to the Commonwealth in the foreseeable future or they felt neutral or uncertain. Most of the people working in the factory and those with clerical responsibilities were in this group.[4]

Ernest Bader himself felt that 'it was a good thing to have that ultimate safety control' but he was hoping that the time might come soon when this safety control could be given up. He envisaged a change in the Constitution creating a different type of organization rather than a mere transfer of the power of the Founder Shares to the Commonwealth.

Godric Bader, his son and the Managing Director, mentioned ideas which were soon to be incorporated in the new organization. 'Looking back at it (the retention of the ten per cent. Founder Shares) I'm not quite as dissatisfied or worried about it as I was because it seems to have had a guiding hand in the situation. The time is coming when we have to take some

[3] See Report of Group Meetings to the Community Council, January 20, 1958.

[4] In answer to the question: 'How do you feel about the 10 per cent. Founder Shares?' 15 out of 30 people said that they should go to the Commonwealth (management: 4, laboratory: 7, clerical: 0; factory: 4); 13 people said that they should not go to the Commonwealth (management: 1; laboratory: 0; clerical: 3; factory: 9). 2 people were neutral or did not know (management: 1; factory: 1).

further decision.' He felt that the shares should not merely go to the Commonwealth but that there should be trustees who take an interest in the Commonwealth and create new connections with the outside world.

Other people in management recommended a training period during which people should be given 'the opportunity of exercising the decisions they could make if they actually had the shares'. After having gained the knowledge and experience to become fully responsible they should elect the Directors.

The question of ultimate control and election of directors was central in the minds of many people with managerial responsibility. 'I don't know at what point there has to be someone who says "yes" or "no" in regard to this question of democratic control—can you have a Board of Directors entirely elected by members as a whole? ... We are moving towards that, otherwise the thing is really a farce ... I think this is what the company should aim at ... Some people say that can never be. I think they are quite happy as it is.'

There were also people who felt that the question of ownership was not 'important either way—what is important is maximum efficiency ... It makes no difference whether the ten per cent. Founder Shares go to the Commonwealth or not. The appointment of Directors should not be in the hands of a large body like that. It's a technical matter. I think they would genuinely try to appoint the right directors but they would be misguided.' Others looked at the Founder's Shares 'as a brake, in case of any convulsions within the company ... I like to feel that some person—as an owner in effect—will have an overall interest.'

These responses illustrate the struggle of traditional conceptions of power with a new conception based on Commonwealth principles. Most of the people—except for Ernest and Godric Bader—visualized a transfer of shares including the right to elect the Directors. Within this frame of reference they weighted their doubts and hopes for democracy in industry.

People working in the laboratory were almost unanimously in favour of a transfer of the ten per cent. shares: 'The time should come when the Commonwealth should act as proper shareholders and elect the directors so that the shareholders are having their *normal rights* which they do not have at the moment.'

Doubts, however, remained: 'It's against the Commonwealth principle (not to transfer the ten per cent. Founder Shares) but perhaps it's like the party system. You have the House of Lords as a brake.' The idea of a brake, of a balance, did not prevent this person from advocating eventual transfer of the Founder Shares. 'In the end they will come to the firm—they must if it's going to achieve complete unity but at the moment it may be a good thing; I don't know.'

A gradual approach was widely recommended: 'Like independence, we've got to wait for the right time'; 'we should shoulder our responsibilities, do our best to steer the ship along its path, with the captain playing a smaller and smaller part all the time.' 'There should be some control by the Founder Members because we are still a young organization but the Founder Shares should go to the Commonwealth when they are no longer held by people who had anything to do with the beginning of the firm.' The idea that the ownership of a firm should change after a certain period of time has been systematically developed in George Goyder's book *The Responsible Company*.[5]

In sharp contrast to the views in the laboratory were those of people with clerical responsibilities. Many didn't know much about the situation and wondered whether it would be a good thing to transfer the Founder Shares. Some were afraid that management might manipulate power in their own interest. Others felt 'that the Founder Shares were a good thing. They have built it up. If I were them I shouldn't want to relinquish them . . . I'm rather inclined to believe in something being passed down from father to son.' Or: 'It is all right as it is. It would seem funny if the Commonwealth took over, there wouldn't be a boss. Or would there?' When it was pointed out that the Commonwealth might choose one, he said: 'Then it would be the same as it is now or thereabouts.' The difficulties

[5] See George Goyder, *The Responsible Company*, Oxford 1961.

of going beyond a traditional conception of power are well illustrated by these responses.

Two-thirds of the workers did not feel that the Founder Shares should be transferred to the Commonwealth, only about a third were in favour of the transfer. 'They should definitely go to the Commonwealth'; 'We should try to move away from them in the future but I think the feeling should come from the body of the people. You have to get the real feeling of the majority behind this move, before they do any good'; Or: 'At the moment I feel very much as Mr. Bader. It must be done to make the Commonwealth complete. But he's very cautious—I don't blame him. There's a better team of people here than has been before—we should be able to take it in a few years. Just got to guard against anyone unscrupulous coming along into the firm.' He felt this was particularly important since the transfer of the Founder Shares would mean that 'the directors can be appointed by the people in the firm.'

The majority expressed traditional respect for private ownership, fear that less qualified people may be elected and a general sense of being not ready for complete self-government. 'No, the Founder Shares shouldn't go to the Commonwealth, after all he founded the firm, it was his money in the first place.' 'As a Founder Member of the firm Ernest Bader should be entitled to a bit more.' When it was pointed out to him that Ernest Bader does not get any more money because of the Founder Shares, he said 'Well, I don't think we could have better directors than we have.' Another person said: 'Myself, I don't feel they should go to the Commonwealth; after all, they helped to build the business up.' Asked about the appointment of directors, he commented: 'It comes back to my point. It could get people put in who are in favour of the men but who don't know a thing about the business.' This fear was related to negative feelings about nationalization. The transfer of the shares means 'the same as nationalization—put people in there who don't know a thing about it and the thing is finished.'

Fears were often mingled with doubts about the application of democratic procedures in industry: 'He should hang on to them. I think he knows what's what and should keep control.

What on earth would we do, we don't know who should go on the Board, only the higher-ups know that.' Or: 'The Founder Shares should "definitely not" go to the Commonwealth, not at the present time. I think whatever you have, you must have someone at the top. Otherwise you'll get a clique which is cliqueing together for their own ends.'

The feeling of not being ready for a transfer of the shares was expressed in different ways: 'The Commonwealth is not capable to decide things like who is competent for management jobs. My own opinion is that we would take too much responsibility, we aren't ready for it yet.' This person felt that it will come 'in a long time, not in our generation. We are still influenced by what goes on in the whole of industry. We must regard ourselves as employees, and that's all.' A similar feeling of unreadiness was based on the idea that workers would become executives. 'We aren't ready for them, not until we can train some of our young staff to be executive level, we'd elect a kind of executive, then run the firm as they do now. You see, we still need the firm, the Board. If you had to replace them by voting you'd put them back because they've got the know-how. If you put the roadsweepers there, where would you be?'

Fear that money might be wasted also played a role: 'at the moment there is ten per cent. controlling shares and ninety per cent. worthless shares and the ten per cent. are the bosses which I think they should be.' This worker was very emphatic in stating that the shares should not be transferred now. 'No, I don't, because I think it's easy for one man to spend another's money. I think the directors would exploit others' money.' Not trusting himself, he assumed that whoever has power would misuse it—unless his own money is at stake. Asked whether he thinks the shares should ever go to the Commonwealth, he said 'I think they will go', but there was foreboding in his answer rather than any satisfaction.

Money was mentioned by another person in a very different way. 'I don't particularly want them' he said in speaking about the Founder Shares—'We shall have to buy them out of bonus and when we bought them we still don't have more to say in the running of the company. When we leave, we don't get more.' He felt, furthermore, that 'the firm is opposed to joint consultation. I don't think there will be more joint consultation.'

IV

The main arguments against a transfer of the Founder Shares were: (i) voting is a precarious procedure. It opens the door to manipulations from above and squabbles from below. (ii) It is good to have a system of check and balances, and (iii) the founder is entitled to an ultimate say-so. Workers, long accustomed to be 'employees', intermingled a sense of dependency and acceptance of traditional authority with these arguments.

Those in favour of unqualified common ownership shared many fears with those who were against it. But they felt secure enough to favour the transfer of the Founder Shares. They knew that the main problem was how to foster responsible active participation rather than how to prevent an irresponsible take-over. Some, furthermore, began to have a vision and comprehension of new forms of power.

To understand the deeper feelings shaping these attitudes and arguments we must know something about the image of politics and of people's experience of political democracy. On the whole their image is a negative one as we will see later on. Hence the application of 'political' methods to the election of the Board of Directors was bound to evoke doubts and fears. The attitudes expressed are a stunning comment on the political institutions which, instead of being experienced as models of a living democracy have become examples of a dangerous game of power. One may have to entrust the country's business to this unprincipled game of politics but one must not entrust to it a relatively small business enterprise!

To have found a way out of this impasse, to have moved sufficiently away from the traditional ways to experiment with a new way is a major achievement. It required an act of surrender and a loosening of the old bonds which brought people to a half-way mark where the old came to an end and the new began. It required, furthermore, leadership with a vision and with courage.

Chapter 12
The Constitution of 1963

I

The Constitution of 1963 attempted to resolve the fears and doubts about yielding power to a democratically elected body. The Founders of the Commonwealth gave up the ultimately controlling ten per cent. of the shares and the Commonwealth became the unqualified owner of the business. But the rights inherent in ownership were redefined in a way which can only be understood through knowledge of the whole new organization which was built up.

II

As Diagram 2 shows, The General Meeting, the Board of Directors and the Community Council remained central in the new organization. They continue to perform essentially the same functions as described in Chapter 5.

The General Meeting remained the main legislative body. Every member of the Commonwealth has one vote in approving, modifying or rejecting the conduct of the business and the disposal of the common surplus as recommended by the Board of Directors.[1] The constitutional provisions for the distribution of the surplus remained the same—plough back (sixty per cent. minimum), annual earnings (maximum twenty per cent.) and Commonwealth charitable purposes (maximum twenty per cent.). A new feature is the right of the General Meeting to approve any investment over £10,000 (about $28,000) before the investment is actually made.

The Community Council is chosen in the same way as it was before. Nine of its twelve members are elected by secret ballot. Two are nominated by the Board of Directors and another

[1] The right of the Board to propose the distribution of the annual earnings was qualified later. See below Chapter 16, p. 212 and Chapter 17, p. 219.

one, representing the local community, is chosen by the elected and nominated members and approved by the Board.

There was no change in the relationship of the Community Council to the General Meeting. The Community Council continues to make recommendations for the use of the Commonwealth funds (the 'dividends' of the shares owned by the Commonwealth) and for charitable purposes. It also makes recommendations in regard to membership.

In its basic functions and its composition, the Board of Directors remained essentially the same. It consists of nine directors. The Founder Member rights were abolished but Ernest and Godric Bader became Directors holding office for life until retirement; five additional directors are nominated by the Chairman of the Board—but must be approved by a body of Trustees about whom we have soon to say more; the two Commonwealth directors are as previously elected by secret ballot from a list of a minimum of six people nominated by members of the Commonwealth and approved by the board.

The functional relationship between the Board of Directors and the General Meeting was changed in two significant ways: (i) the right of the General Meeting to approve, modify or reject proposals for large investments before they are undertaken, (ii) the creation of a Panel of Representatives as an organ of the General Meeting.

The Panel of Representatives consists of twelve members who are selected at random. The names of the members of the Commonwealth are put in a bowl and twelve names are taken out. The twelve members thus chosen have to decide whether 'the conditions and atmosphere that exists in the firm justify them in recording a vote of confidence in the Board of Directors'. If the Panel gives a vote of no-confidence, the meeting adjourns for not more than three months, when the Directors shall explain 'what steps they have taken, by reconstitution of the Board or otherwise, to remedy the lack of confidence.' After this explanation, a second panel of representatives is chosen. If this second panel again gives a vote of no-confidence it becomes the duty of the Trustees 'to decide what changes (if any) in the Board of Directors are desirable and to make use of their voting powers if necessary to assist in bringing about such changes.'[2]

This is the second time that the Trustees are mentioned. Who are the Trustees and what is their role in the new organization of work?

The Constitution provides for not less than five nor more than nine Trustees. The first Board of Trustees consists of seven people, two 'Commonwealth Trustees', three 'Nominated Trustees' and Ernest and Godric Bader. The two Commonwealth Trustees are elected by the members of the Commonwealth; they must be members or ex-members of the Community Council—the administrative organ of the Commonwealth. The three Nominated Trustees (also called 'outside trustees' because they are not connected with Scott Bader) are appointed by joint action of the Board of Directors and the Community Council. Ernest and Godric Bader are appointed for life, the Commonwealth Trustees for a period of five years, the Nominated Trustees for ten years.

The functions of the trustees may be divided into legislative and trustee functions. Their role in approving directors and in recommending changes in the Board in case of a no-confidence vote by the Panel of Representatives belongs to their legislative function. When the Trustees act on the basis of a second vote of no-confidence in the Board of Directors, they have a voting power which is equal to that of all the members of the Commonwealth taken together. The same situation prevails in case of any change in the constitution of the Commonwealth; here too, the Trustees have a voting power equal to the membership of the Commonwealth. This means that the Trustees, or rather a majority of the Trustees must agree with the members of the Commonwealth in case of constitutional changes.

In addition to these functions, the Trustees may ask the Board of Directors to take such steps as they 'think fit to restore the profit-making capacity of the company, if at any time the auditors of the company shall certify that the business of

[2] See *Memorandum and Articles of Association Scott Bader Commonwealth* 1963, Article 9, p. 14. This Memorandum will from now on be quoted as *Memorandum Commonwealth 1963*.

the company is run at a loss'.[3] This is a true emergency power in case losses occur which the trustees consider to be due to unsatisfactory conduct of the business.

Before discussing the so-called trustee functions, we must complete the review of the new organization by mentioning the main judicial organ—the Council of Reference.

The Council consists of sixteen members. The members of the departmental committees elect eight of the sixteen members. Four members are elected by the management committee, and four are appointed by the Board of Directors.[4] The Council of Reference is, therefore, based on equality of managerial and non-managerial personnel. While membership in the Commonwealth is a prerequisite for becoming a member of the Council of Reference, the right to vote is independent of Commonwealth membership.

The main functions of the Council of Reference are the same as those previously performed by the General Council. First, the Council is 'to discuss any matter referred to it by any individual member, or by any organ of the company which has not been satisfactorily resolved through the usual channels, and to make recommendations to the Board of Directors'. Second the Council is 'to consider any dispute or matter affecting disciplinary action referred to it by individual members or any organ of the company and to give a final decision on such grievances or appeals provided the ordinary channels have been exhausted'. In all matters affecting disciplinary action including any dismissal, the Council of Reference has the final word, while in all other matters it makes recommendations to the Board of Directors.[5]

[3] *Ibid.*, Article 63, p. 22.

[4] The Management Committee consists of all people with managerial responsibility with the exception of Top Executives and members of the Board of Directors.

[5] *Memorandum and New Articles of Association of Scott Bader & Co. Ltd. 1963*, Article 31, p. 13. This Memorandum will be called from now on *Memorandum Company 1963*.

It is true that the new Council of Reference does not have certain functions which the General Council did have—namely to 'discuss any question affecting the well-being of the company' or 'discuss any matters of expenditure and

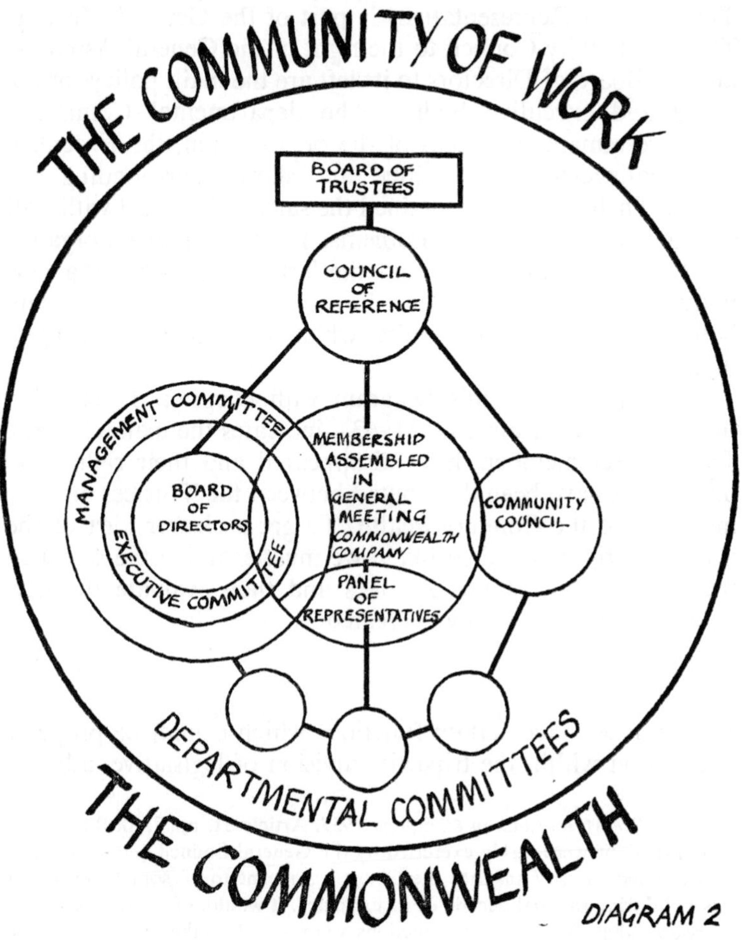
THE COMMONWEALTH SINCE 1963
THE COMMUNITY OF WORK
BOARD OF TRUSTEES
COUNCIL OF REFERENCE
MANAGEMENT COMMITTEE
BOARD OF DIRECTORS
EXECUTIVE COMMITTEE
MEMBERSHIP ASSEMBLED IN GENERAL MEETING
COMMONWEALTH COMPANY
PANEL OF REPRESENTATIVES
COMMUNITY COUNCIL
DEPARTMENTAL COMMITTEES
THE COMMONWEALTH

DIAGRAM 2

Diagram 2 sums up the new organization. It shows the legislative, executive, judicial and trustee organs created by the Constitution of 1963. In the centre we have the legislative body constituted by the membership of the Commonwealth assembled in General Meeting of the 'company' or the 'Commonwealth'. The Panel of Representatives is part of the General Meeting. The Community Council to the right of the General Assembly and the Board of Directors to its left are the main policy-formulating and executive bodies. The departmental Committee structure remains the basis of the organization, the Executive and Management Committee are shown surrounding the Board. Their functions remained the same—they deal with staff and general management problems. The main judicial organ is the Council of Reference and the Trustees appear as a new body in the upper part of the diagram. The largest circle symbolizes the whole community which encompasses all these organs.

A comparison of this Diagram with Diagram 1—showing the organization from 1951–1963—indicates the main changes: The founder members have disappeared and their rights and obligations have been distributed between the Trustees and the members of the Commonwealth. To get a clearer idea of the way these rights are distributed we must examine the so-called trustee functions of the Trustees and then evaluate the new balance of power which was created.

III

The Trustees have certain functions which cannot be properly understood within the tripartite division of legislative, admini-

finance.' (*See Memorandum Company 1951*, Article 31, pp. 7, 8). But in fact these functions were rarely exercised by the General Council and as we have seen this led to criticism that the Council is meant to be something that it was not during the first decade of its existence. It would, of course, be wrong to assume that these broader functions were actually taken away from the members of the Commonwealth. They preserved these rights through their legislative organs. The limitation of the functions of the former General Council in the new Council of Reference constitutes, therefore, primarily a clarification of the functions of the different organs of the Community.

strative and judicial functions. The Constitution of 1963 defines these trustee functions as follows:

(i) To 'have a philosophical oversight of the Community . . . and sponsor the growth of the Commonwealth in accordance with the Memorandum.'

(ii) To veto any measure proposed to be taken by the Directors, the executive members, the Management Committee, the Departmental Committees, as well as of the Council of Reference which, in the opinion of the majority of the Trustees is a 'clear breach of the principles upon which the company is intended to be managed'.

(iii) In addition the Trustees may be consulted by the members of the Board 'in the interest of upholding the principle of solidarity in presenting a united Company policy' or the members of the Board may ask the Chairman or/and Managing Director 'to formally seek their advice or ruling' on problems affecting the well-being of the Company.[6]

The right of the members of the Board to consult the Trustees and the right of the Chairman or Managing Director to seek their advice gives to the Trustees the role of elder statesmen. This opens new channels of participation particularly for the Commonwealth Trustees who are bound to be further from the central decision-making process (or in traditional terms 'below' the Managing Director) than those who ask their advice.

The second function—the right of Trustees to veto any measure which, in the opinion of the majority 'is a clear breach of the principles upon which the company is intended to be managed' is potentially more far-reaching since it opens the purpose of the firm to the scrutiny by the Trustees. The *Memorandum and New Articles of Association of Scott Bader & Co. Ltd.* as revised in March 1963 contains two articles stating the basic purpose of the company and indicating measures to implement these purposes.

The first article states: 'All organs of the organization of the company shall have regard at all times to the fact that the basic

[6] *Memorandum Commonwealth 1963*, Article 63, p. 22; *Memorandum Company 1963*, Article 12, p. 10. and Article 15, p. 11.

purpose of the company is to render the best possible service as a corporate body to our fellow men.'[7] It specifies, furthermore, the basic purpose by reference to the strength of the company, its efficiency, to research, technical education in the plastics and allied industries, etc. These purposes are, on the whole, within the traditional structure of values of a company.

But the next specification of purpose draws a wider circle: 'to provide economic security to its members and to relieve them of their material anxiety or striving for personal advancement at the cost of others.' The Trustees are, therefore, asked to scrutinize business decisions in terms of the security of the members, their 'material anxiety' or the quality of their interpersonal relationships. There are few decisions made in a business which do not affect these aspects of work.

The third purpose mentioned under the general heading 'the best possible service as a corporate body to our fellow men' is 'to produce goods beneficial to its customers and the peaceful purposes of the community at a fair price and of as high a quality as possible.'[8] Most significant in this respect is the emphasis on *peaceful* purposes. This excludes the use of resins for war purposes. Since there are always borderline cases which are difficult to decide and since this principle has not yet been wholeheartedly accepted by the community, trustees may have an important function in this area.[9]

The last specification of purpose, 'to contribute towards the

[7] The veto right applies to measures proposed by the membership of the Commonwealth if assembled as shareholders of the company, because the administrative organs of the company would have to execute these measures. The only measures to which the veto right does not apply are those which the membership takes if assembled as members of the Commonwealth, that is when deciding on the distribution of the surplus for charitable purposes. See also *Memorandum Company 1963*, Article 41, p. 15.

[8] *Ibid.*, Article 41C., p. 15.

[9] The policy of Scott Bader in regard to the sale of its product for war purposes is more important as a sign of protest and admonition rather than as an effective way of preventing its product to be used for war purposes. The company refuses to sell 'any products for the specific purpose of manufacturing weapons of war' (*Memorandum Company*, Article 42, p. 15). But the development of civilian aircraft etc. can not be separated from potential military use.

general welfare of the community, particularly in its neighbourhood' is quite broad but takes a much more concrete significance if read in conjunction with the specific means or measures suggested to realize this purpose. These measures include provision of tuition for students 'from the various sections of industry with which the company comes into contact' and invitations of customers or representatives of research or trade associations to Annual General Meetings.[10]

Even more far-reaching is the demand to 'direct everyday affairs so that the members and employees may fully participate in the firm's activities in relation to their ability, knowledge and experience and co-ordinate all tasks and purposes in terms of service'. This calls for new types of training programmes and group work as well as for new forms of co-ordination of work tasks and of organizing work.[11]

Another principle of the company calls for cultivation of 'understanding and friendship between industrial and agricultural workers' and asks specifically for arranging 'suitable opportunities to the factory employees for assisting the company's farming or market gardening activities or vice versa'. The arrangement of such opportunities may open up new possibilities of organizing work. It may lead to a new conception of the division of labour between industrial and agricultural work and to new types of communities.[12]

In discussing the transformation of wages and profits we mentioned that the firm has been moving towards restituting to 'wages' their universal function: earnings are personal shares in the money earned by a common effort. The Constitution of 1963 recognizes this transformation of wages into shared earnings as a new principle of accounting, and demands the presentation of 'the company's accounts and balance sheet in conformity with the common-ownership principles on which the

[10] *Memorandum Company 1963*, Article 42E, p. 16.

[11] *Ibid.*, Article 42B, p. 15. In 1963/64 Roger Hadley worked at Scott Bader as a personnel and training advisor and initiated various training programmes.

[12] For further discussion of this point see my paper on 'The Humanization of Work—The Judeo-Christian tradition and the future of our Industrial Social Order.'

company is founded'. Specifically it asks for 'the abolition of treating factory wages as "variable costs" and salaries as "overheads", so that the payment of all staff is on a uniform basis of an annual rate.'[13]

Since the nature of costs expresses the nature of the social relationships underlying the organization of work, the abolition of the traditional distinction between variable and overhead costs signifies the abolition in principle of the traditional category of 'employers' and 'employee'—though these terms continue to crop up here and there.[14]

A final principle has far-reaching implications for the whole question of participation, namely 'that members in all meetings should reach decisions without need for a formal vote. To achieve a unanimous decision in this way may not be easy but it is an assurance that it will carry the good-will of all.'[15] The desirability of unanimous decisions poses problems far beyond the technical process of decision making, problems of relationships between people, of respect for different points of view and of the best possible development of people.

The Constitution calls upon the Trustees to watch over the realization and implementation of the various principles just mentioned. This is part of the 'philosophical oversight' which they are asked to exercise.[16]

IV

By redefining the purpose and principles of Scott Bader in the manner just indicated, the new Constitution opens the way to a new value structure. The central value of the organization—a concept of productivity defined in technical-market terms continues to exist but the implementation of the new purposes will at least make a dent in this concept. Yet the most far-reaching change in values consists in the new structure of power which the Constitution put into effect.

'Who really has the power in the new organization?'

[13] *Memorandum Company 1963*, Article 42, C, p. 15.

[14] *Ibid.*, Article 42B, p. 15.

[15] *Ibid.*, Article 42D.

[16] See *Memorandum Commonwealth 1963*, Article 63, p. 22.

To answer this question adequately we must introduce a time dimension. At any one moment of time the power is balanced between the different organs—the legislative, judicial, executive and trustee bodies. The power to legislate is in the hands of the General Assembly provided there is no question of a breach of principles and provided the company does not operate in the red (in which case the Trustees may come into the picture). Executive power and the right and obligation to formulate policy is primarily vested in the Board of Directors and the Committee structure surrounding it, secondarily in the Community Council. Through the Panel of Representatives the membership of the Commonwealth—represented by a group selected by the lot—has considerable control over the Board if the Board does not exercise its functions properly. The Community Council has power because it determines the conditions for membership in the Commonwealth which is a pre-requisite for exercising executive responsibilities. Since nine out of twelve members of the Community Council are elected by the members, they clearly control the Council.

The judicial function is exercised by equal representatives from management and non-management groups.

The Trustees, who have little power in the ordinary course of events, play a major role because they must approve the five directors nominated by the Chairman of the Board. Their second most important function is to approve changes in the Constitution. In exercising these, as well as their important emergency rights in case of financial or other difficulties, the Trustees decide on the basis of a majority vote. This makes the constitution of the board of Trustees of crucial significance.

The principle of balance of power has been applied to the election or appointment of the Board of Trustees. Ernest and Godric Bader have life membership both on the Board of Directors and on the Board of Trustees, special rights recognized for the Founder of the Commonwealth and for his son. But they are clearly in the minority on the Board of Trustees. On the Board of Directors they exercise considerable power, because they take the initiative in recommending the five nominated directors. They also have considerable executive power as

Managing Director and Chairman of the Board. But as trustees they are merely two out of seven people: besides Ernest and Godric Bader there are three Nominated trustees which must be approved by the Community Council and by the Board of Directors. There are also three Commonwealth trustees who must be elected by the members of the Commonwealth. Once appointed or elected, trustees are autonomous for periods of five (Commonwealth trustees) or ten (nominated trustees) years. Within these time limits the ultimate power of the trustees is derived from the members of the Commonwealth and is not imposed upon them.

This does not minimize the significance of the trustees. Trusteeship carries great responsibility and the kind of people selected as trustees is of great importance. Besides Ernest Bader and Godric Bader the first body of trustees consists of the following Commonwealth trustees: Ted Nichols and John Leyland. Ted Nichols, laboratory engineer, has been Secretary of the Community Council since its inception, and before coming to Scott Bader he was very active in the trade union movement. John Leyland is Secretary of the Company. Both are dedicated to the Commonwealth idea. The outside trustees are Mary Danvers Stocks, Robert Edwards M.P. and R. F. Schumacher. Mary Stocks has been active in public life for many years and was Principal of Westfield College, University of London.[17] Robert Edwards has been General Secretary of the Chemical Workers Union since 1947 and a Labour Party M.P. since

[17] *Mary Danvers Stocks*, B.Sc.(Econ.), LL.D., Litt.D.; Member, London Executive Council; Member, Observer and Cassel Trusts; Educated St. Paul's Girls' School; London School of Economics; Assistant Lecturer, London School of Economics, 1916–19; Lecturer on Economics Kings's College for Women, 1918–19; Extension Lecturer and Extra-Mural tutor, Manchester University 1924–37; J.P. Manchester City, 1930–36; General Sec. London Council of Social Service, 1938–39; Principal of Westfield College, University of London, 1939–51. Member of the Unemployment Insurance Statutory Committee and various other Government committees. Publications: The Industrial State, 1921; Fifty Years in Every Street, 1945; Eleanor Rathbone, 1948; History of the Workers' Educational Association, 1953; A Hundred Years of District Nursing, 1960. Plays: Everyman of Every Street; King Herod; Hail Nero!; Dr. Scholefield.

1955.[18] R. F. Schumacher is Economic Adviser to the National Coal Board of Great Britain.[19] He is a noted economist with a deep interest in the human and social situation of our time.

V

The Constitution of 1963 fully implements the principle of common ownership. It constitutes a decisive step forward in overcoming the pyramidal organization of work—though considerable vestiges of the pyramid remained. The new features of the Constitution may be summed up as follows:

(i) The new organization of work establishes a framework of law and order instead of an administrative machinery directed from above and counter-balanced by organized power from below.

(ii) The new framework expresses a broadened conception of democratic government because it encompasses not only a legislative, administrative and judicial function but also a trustee function.

(iii) The Constitution demands the creation of a new value structure by making the development of the principles on which the organization is founded the central criterion in all business decisions.

[18] *Robert Edwards.* M.P. (Lab. and Co-op.) for Bilston since 1955; General Secretary of the Chemical Workers' Union since 1947. Served with Republicans in Spain during Spanish Civil War. Chairman, delegates to Russia, 1926 and 1934. Member, Liverpool City Council, 1929–32; National Chairman, I.L.P., 1943–48; Founder Pres., Socialist Movement for United States of Europe. Vice-President, British Section European League for Economic Co-operation; Vice-President, Economic Research Council; Editor, The Chemical Worker.

[19] *E. F. Schumacher* was born in 1911 at Bonn, Germany, where his father was a professor of Economics. He was educated at Bonn, Berlin, Oxford and New York (Columbia University). He went to New College, Oxford on a Rhodes Scholarship in 1930 to study Philosophy and Economics. In 1937, he emigrated from Germany and took British citizenship in 1946. He served as Economic Adviser with the United Kingdom Control Commission in Germany from 1946 to 1950 and was also associated as Economic Adviser to the Burma Government for some time. He is now Economic Adviser to the National Coal Board of Great Britain.

(iv) The Constitution creates a new power structure with the following characteristics:

(*a*) ultimate power rests with the members of the Commonwealth—because the members have the power to constitute or to sanction the main organs of the Commonwealth and of the company. Members have equal rights which they are encouraged to exercise through participation in accordance with their abilities, their knowledge and their experience. When voting, each human being and not each piece of paper has the same voting rights. When participating in other ways, differences in experience, knowledge and ability are fully taken into consideration.

(*b*) the actual exercise of power at any given time is in the hands of people with widely different responsibilities, different experiences, knowledge and potentialities. They exercise power through organs which assure a variety of checks and balances without in any way interfering with exercise of true authority and true power—that is the authority and power coming from within the person and from within the community.

(*c*) instead of a small group on the top directing 'those below them' there are a number of co-ordinated centres of decision making operating within a delicately balanced distribution of power and responsibilities. Mutuality of relationship is a key to the understanding of the new structure of power and values.

(v) The Constitution implements a new conception of a community of work, of the body politic and of the space-time dimensions of work. It implies a new understanding of the nature of man and of community.

Chapter 13

The body politic and the soul of the Commonwealth

I

When an organization codifies the rights, duties and responsibilities of its members it enters the political sphere.

In true politics men deal with fundamental problems of freedom, power and justice. These are questions of inter-personal relationship as well as relationships to the main organs of a community. The supreme political act is the codification of these relationships in a constitution. Ultimately every constitution expresses a way of life, a basic philosophy of life—or a theology of the social order. It expresses a basic mode of consciousness.

A constitution expresses a basic way of life because it formulates most clearly the quality of the relationship of people to each other and to organized bodies. It indicates their mutual rights and obligations, and defines the conduct of their common affairs.

A constitution expresses a basic philosophy of life because every way of life implies certain ideas, postulates and assumptions about man, nature, history and ultimate reality. Whenever our insights into ultimate reality are made relevant to problems of organized human relationships a theology of the social order arises.

Ways or philosophies of life and theologies of the social order are most concretely expressed in people's awareness of themselves, of others, and of the world in which they live. Only those constitutional provisions which become alive in people's consciousness are experienced in everyday life. Many of the people of Wollaston are followers of Locke and Descartes without ever having heard of these people. But the quality of their actual relationships to each other and to organizations, their whole way of life is imbued by these philosophies. Their ideas on socialism, capitalism, the nature of man, for example, reflect basic philosophical postulates on which our industrial social order is actually built.

In this chapter we shall try to understand some of the philosophical and theological implications of the constitution in so far as they are relevant for the development of a new mode of consciousness. Though a good many of the people of the Commonwealth participated in the shaping of the Constitution and hence in the body politic which it created, few were aware of the far-reaching implications of the organization which they have created and of its innermost meaning—the soul which animates it.

II

At one of the general meetings at which the new constitution was discussed a member of the Commonwealth explained its meaning in terms of a new 'balance of power'. This interpretation is a useful starting point to examine the deeper meaning of the Constitution because the idea of balance is intimately connected with the idea of proportions. To have balance and proportions any-thing or any-body must have form, function, and structure—and must exist in time and space. We can, therefore, best understand the meaning of the new balance of power if we examine the body politic created by the new Constitution in terms of these dimensions.

It is not accidental that the term 'body' has been so intimately related to 'politics'. The human body has a form and structure which expresses the ideal proportions of the 'golden mean' 1:2:3—proportions which underlie important formulations of justice, goodness and beauty.[1] For the Greeks—and

[1] The idea that politics is essentially concerned with power is true only in the sense that freedom is defined by the power of self-realization. If power as such becomes the objective of political action, politics becomes alienated from its true purpose. For Plato politics had essentially to do with ideas and values not with power. The Tyrant, for example, had no true power. (See the *Dialogue of Plato* translated by B. Jowett, M.A., Random House, New York,

which culture has given more divine attributes to the human body?—justice was defined in terms of the right proportions. Such a mode of consciousness is still reflected in our everyday saying 'a square deal'. The square is a rectangle of equal proportions, of the ratio 1:1. This proportion has been considered by Augustine 'the most admirable ratio . . . since here the union or consonance of the two parts is most intimate.'[2]

Not all political philosophers have endowed the human body with a divine soul. Not all have been aware that the ideal proportions of man with outstretched arms are also the ideal proportions of the Cross. But all political philosophers based their theories on their understanding of the nature of man—consciously or through projection.

Hobbes said: 'For by art is created that great Leviathan called a Common-wealth, or State . . . which is but an artificial man.' The reference to Commonwealth is not accidental since Hobbes developed a new theory of the body politic. For him man stands in the same relationship to this political body as a watchmaker stands to the watch he makes. Hobbes saw life as but 'a motion of limbs'. And he compared the life of the body politic to that of 'automata, engines that move themselves by springs and wheels as doth a watch. What is the heart but a spring, and the joints but so many wheels, giving motion to the whole body, such as was intended by the Artificer. Art goes still further, imitating that rational and most excellent work of nature—man.' It is in this context that Hobbes mentioned the Commonwealth as 'an artificial man.' He carried through his analogy of the natural body and the body politic to great detail, and concluded that 'the *Pacts* and *Covenants*, by which the parts of this body politique were at first made, set together, and

[2] See Otto von Simson, *The Gothic Cathedral*, New York 1956, Chapter 2, 'Measure and Light', pp. 21ff. 'Next in rank to the ratio 1:1 are the ratios 1:2, 2:3, and 3:4—the intervals of the perfect consonances, octave, fifth, and fourth.' See *Ibid*., p. 21.

1937, Vol. I, p. 528). Before the fifth century a conception of politics developed which had been opposed to that of Plato and which became predominant in the realm of politics with Machiavelli and Hobbes.

united, resemble that *FIAT*, or the *Let-us-make-man*, pronounced by God in the Creation.'[3]

There are both similarities and differences between such a conception of the body and soul of a Commonwealth and the conception underlying the Scott Bader Commonwealth.

Ernest Bader in an Annual General Meeting spoke about the Commonwealth by suggesting that we must first deal with our 'personal life, our own ego, and self, life or death. Then as a firm, as a corporate body, create a soul and thirdly become part of the larger family of mankind—struggle for life.'[4] When speaking about the creation of a corporate body or soul, he mentioned that people at Scott Bader 'have already one—the Commonwealth, a spiritual entity which one cannot touch but which must be nurtured to make sure that it survives spiritually and materially'.

Here too is a vision of a new body and soul as the essential expression of the Commonwealth. Here too are fundamental analogies between the body politic, its soul on the one hand and man, 'our own ego and self' on the other hand. But there is a world which separates the Common-wealth of Hobbes from the Common-wealth as embodied in the New Constitution.

III

Seen as part of the history of political thought the Commonwealth is an embodiment of the idea that a true democracy and a true aristocracy are identical. A true democracy is a social

[3] See Hobbes *Leviathan*, reprinted from the edition of 1651, Oxford 1952, p. 8.
'*Sovereignty* is an artificial *Soul*, as giving life and motion to the whole body; the *Magistrates* and the officer of judicature and executive, artificial *joints*. *Reward* and *punishment* (by which fastened to the seate of the sovereignty, every joint and member is moved to perform his duty) are the nerves, that do the same in the body natural; the *wealth* and *riches* of the particular members are the *strength; salus populi* (the people's safety) its *business;* Counsellors, by whom all things needful for it to know, are suggested unto it, are the *memory; equity* and *lawes*, an artificial *reason* and *will, concord health; sedition sickness; and civil war* death.'

[4] Annual General Meeting of December 2, 1961.

order which recognizes 'that of God in every man' and gives every person the same opportunity to develop his or her potentialities. A true aristocracy is a social order which reflects in its structure and organization the highest development of each person's abilities and potentialities. True aristocracy and true democracy thus understood are closely related to the Christian conception of man which gave birth to the Commonwealth: 'The Commonwealth was born out of a growing realization of the incompatibility of the existing industrial and social order with a Christian conception and we continue to be moved and inspired by the spiritual force behind such a conception. The Commonwealth is an expression of the age-old ideal taught by all great religions of a brotherhood of all men knowing no restrictions of race, sex or social class and owing allegiance to a living creative spirit. It is seeking through, and beyond, all material ends to foster conditions for the growth of personality truly related to God and man.'[5]

This statement from the foreword to the Constitution expresses the soul of the Commonwealth. It bases the new Constitution on the spiritual force behind the Christian conception of man and the social order. It aims to find new forms of expressing ideals which are age-old because they are rooted in ultimate reality but which must find new forms to be meaningful today. This search denotes a living quality which is in sharp contrast to the outworn formulations of reality underlying our industrial society.

The latter finds its best definition in Hobbes, whose vision of the body politic underlies the present organization of industry. For Hobbes the Sovereign is a 'mortal God' but there are no divine laws to guide the sovereign and hence there is no tension between a divine law and human law. The government of men is based on a contract made acceptable by enlightened self-interest to avoid 'a war of every man against every man'.[6]

Such a conception is the culmination of a trend which is well over a thousand years old but which became victorious only

[5] See *Memorandum Commonwealth 1963*, p. 2.

[6] See George A. Sabine, *A History of Political Theory*, New York 1955, p. 464.

with the rise of capitalism. This trend can be contrasted with the conception of natural law which corresponds to the basic idea underlying the Commonwealth: 'The contrast of nature and convention has begun to develop in two main directions. The one conceived nature as a law of justice and right inherent in human beings and in the world. This view necessarily leans to the assumption that the order in the world is intelligent and beneficent; it could be critical of abuses but it was essentially moralist and in the last resort religious. The other conceived nature non-morally, and as manifested in human beings it was self-assertion or egoism, the desire for pleasure or for power.'[7]

The Commonwealth is clearly in the tradition of natural law. It is rooted in a conception of a 'spiritual force' as the ground of a moral universe, and as the basis of a 'law of justice'. Such a conception is natural in the sense of being the expression of man's true nature or, as is stated in the Constitution 'of personality truly related to God and man'. The Commonwealth is, therefore, in the stream of experience which confronts the existing conditions with a truth rooted in the essential nature of man and his archetypal potentialities. The new Constitution recognizes this explicitly: 'We endeavour to provide opportunity for the full development of us all, both materially and spiritually, unhampered by unjust conditions or crushed by economic pressures, and to take steps towards developing a way of life free from bondage of material things and mere conventions.'[8] Here is an explicit reference to 'mere conventions' which must be overcome if a 'growth of personality truly related to God and man' is to become a reality.

IV

The rejection of existing conventions—in so far as they are not compatible with man's true nature—implies a new conception of power and democratic participation: 'Power should come from within the person and the community, and be made responsible to those it affects. We feel mutual responsibility

[7] *Ibid*. p. 32.
[8] *Memorandum Commonwealth 1963*, p. 3.

must permeate the whole community of work and be upheld by democratic participation and the principle of trusteeship.'[9]

The new concept of power and democratic participation is inseparable from the new concept of balance on which the new organization is built. These concepts express three ideas of democracy: (i) democratic rights based on the conception of the equal worth of all men, (ii) democratic rights based on the idea that everybody should have the same chance to participate, (iii) democratic rights related to the development of people's true abilities and potentialities.

The ultimate power which resides in the members of the Commonwealth when assembled in general meeting or voting in secret ballot is based on an act of faith: namely that all men, no matter how different they may be in emotional, aesthetic, intuitive and intellectual abilities—and the development of these abilities—are ultimately equal in their ability to express the voice of justice. Fears that this faith may be unfounded underlie all attacks on democracy. Bagehot in *The English Constitution* has expressed these apprehensions in the classical statement that *vox populi*, the voice of the people, may under certain circumstances, instead of being the voice of God, become *vox diaboli*, the voice of the Devil.[10]

To base the organization of work on such apprehensions is to deny 'that of God in every man', to cut man off from the spiritual forces contained in ultimate reality. But to completely identify a democratic structure with this ultimate act of faith is to forget about other dimensions of God's creation. Man has the potentiality for goodness and truth, he is made in the image of God, but he may err in the search for his true self and may be alienated from the ground of his being. Hence the Commonwealth Constitution developed an intricate system of checks and balance through which the ultimate power rooted in the equality of all men is exercised at any moment of time.

The second form of democracy—based on the idea that

[9] *Ibid.*

[10] See Walter Bagehot, *The English Constitution And Other Political Essays*, New York 1904, p. 17. Bagehot expressed these fears with reference to the Reform Act of 1867.

everyone should have the same chance to participate—is most clearly expressed in the Panel of Representatives which is elected by lot. The Greeks used this method to choose office holders from a panel formed by election as well as to allocate a nominated panel of jurymen to sit in particular courts or in particular cases. At Scott Bader selection by lot is used to allocate twelve members of the Commonwealth to the Panel of Representatives which combines the functions of a jury and of a judge. Irrespective of its specific purpose the choice by lot is considered 'a distinctively democratic form of rule, since it equalizes everyone's chances to hold office.'[11] Such a conception of democracy is part and parcel of the political philosophy of the Greek city state, particularly of its conception of citizenship.

When we think of citizenship today, we take it often as a 'birthright' or as something 'given to us', as a privilege. 'The Greek, however, thought of his citizenship not as a possession but as something *shared*, much like membership in a family. This fact had a profound influence on Greek political philosophy. It meant that the problem . . . was not to gain a man his rights but to insure him the place to which he was entitled.'[12]

Such a conception underlies the Constitution of the Commonwealth. Participation is understood as sharing of power which allows a person to express his or her true self rather than as a mechanical right to vote. Furthermore, the Commonwealth has been repeatedly compared to a family, a comparison we shall discuss later. Such a philosophy of participation means that forms other than voting are necessary to ensure to each person the place to which he or she is entitled. These other forms demand some criterion for selection.

Selection by lot eliminates the possibility that people are chosen because of qualities not related to the task for which they are chosen (such as influence with other people). But it does presuppose similarities of qualification for the task chosen. If this similarity does not exist, other methods of selection—such as election, nomination or volunteering—have advantages over selection by lot.

[11] George A. Sabine, *op. cit.*, p. 7.

[12] *Ibid.*, pp. 5 and 6. [Italics mine.]

This brings us to the third idea of democracy, namely democratic rights related to the development of people's true abilities and potentialities. People are nominated and elected to perform various functions in the Commonwealth because they have peculiar abilities and potentialities.[13] The use of these powers which come 'from within the person' constitutes the highest form of participation which the Commonwealth attempts to develop. Power coming from within is rooted in knowledge, experience and insight. Ultimately it is—like all true power—the power of the Spirit of Truth and Love. It is not power which is related to a position, it is not status power. It is power which creates its position and which carries its own status rather than being primarily rooted in them.

This third principle of democratic participation implies the synthesis of democracy and aristocracy. It constitutes a radically new conception of power which permeates the whole structure of the Commonwealth. It is expressed in the intricate system of checks and balances. It is also expressed in the ultimate subjection of all functions—including those of the Board of Directors—to the ability to perform them in a way satisfactory to the Community. Finally it is expressed in the whole idea of trusteeship.

V

In the disorder of industry in which we are living today power means the right to make decisions and to tell others what to do. In the industrial order of tomorrow, power means the responsible use and development of man's God-given potentialities. The universal aspects of this new conception of power are expressed in the etymology of the word 'power' as 'potentia', as realization of potentialities.[14] Rooted in a living experience

[13] Volunteering is not a formally prescribed method but it is an informal procedure used in the formation of various Committees.

[14] In the German language, for example, *Macht*, power is not related to *machen*, to make but to *mögen*, being able to do. For this observation I am indebted to Hannah Arendt's *The Human Condition*, University of Chicago Press, 1958.

of the universal ground of all life, this new conception of power differs radically from the tradition conception underlying the present organization of industry.

To understand these differences we must compare the Commonwealth ideal with the ideal traditional conception of power rather than follow the easy path of comparing the Commonwealth ideal with the reality of industry.

We find the highest expression of present industrial practices in the Greek conception of the relationship between the ruler and the ruled. Plato developed this conception in an explicit analogy with his conception of man. The lower nature in man—his passions—constitute what he must master, rule. Reason, man's highest insights into the true nature of things is the governing principle in man. The Greek conception of the true nature of things as the absolute essence in the realm of ideas meant that the governing principle in man is the father principle—the logos principle—symbolically related to heaven. This *inner* governing principle also constitutes the governing principle in the relationships *between* men. To rule symbolizes the highest development of human reason, and reason is the highest of the four faculties in the soul. Faculties in such a conception are not merely categories of classification, 'they are powers in us, and in all other things, by which we do as we do'.[15]

The platonic image of man and of power though it contains elements of universal truth, is in important ways incompatible with the image of man permeating the Commonwealth ideal. To understand the Commonwealth conception of man we must look at recent contributions to dynamic psychology which has given us new insights and new operational dimensions in our understanding of the nature of man. These insights have given new life to the Judeo-Christian image of man.

Bishop Sheen considered the Freudian image of man as ego (man's conscious awareness and will), superego (the rules of behaviour typical of our parental culture) and id., (the instinctual drives in all men) as the modern equivalent of the medieval

[15] See *The Dialogues of Plato* translated by B. Jowett, Random House, New York, 1937, *The Republic*, pp. 741 and 773.

conception of earth, heaven and hell.[16] The value of the Freudian conception is indisputable, but it is inadequate. The function and meaning of ego, superego and id, change as our conception of the nature of man broadens and deepens just as the function and meaning of earth, heaven and hell changed as our conception of the nature of reality broadened and deepened.[17]

To obtain a more adequate understanding of man we must introduce the concept of the Self. The Self may be defined as that dimension in man where the most peculiarly personal merges with the universal. It 'contains' those abilities and potentialities which are truly our own (hence the idea of a true self). The Self has its own centre and symbolizes wholeness or integration around this—our true—centre. Closely related to the Self is our conscience which expresses our personal awareness of universal values and our own true standards of behaviour.[18]

VI

To understand the Commonwealth, we must understand the functions of the organs of the Commonwealth with reference to the conception of man just indicated. But a word of caution is necessary. I am not attempting to outline an image of man and then define the function and structure of the organs of the Commonwealth in terms of such an image. The Commonwealth represents a conception of the body politic which makes the traditional kind of analogy between the body and soul of an organization and the body and soul of man an inadequate analogy. It still retains an important *element* of truth. But it is

[16] See Bishop Fulton I. Sheen, *Peace of Soul*, London, Burns & Oates 1962, p. 8.

[17] See Henry A. Murray 'The Personality and Career of Satan', *Journal of Social Issues*, October 1962, No. 4, pp. 36–54. See also Isidor Chein, 'The Image of Man,' *Journal of Social Issues*, 1962, No. 18, pp. 1–35. See also the answer by Richard E. Carney, 'Man or Men', A Reply to Isidor Chein on Images of Man.

[18] See in this connection the work of Erich Fromm, Abraham Maslow, D. W. Winnicott, C. G. Jung.

false as a model for comparisons because the Commonwealth *recognizes the wholeness and the true centre in each person* and does not identify any particular dimension with a part of the body politic.

The Commonwealth does not say to one group of people 'you are the centre of will power' and to another 'you embody the rules of behaviour' and to a third 'you are the conscience of the Commonwealth'; it says to each person: 'You are a whole person and we want you to enter the Commonwealth in your wholeness, with your will, your conscious awareness, your conscience, your true self. We want you to develop this wholeness and we recognize that you have your own true centre from which you must participate and share the power of the Commonwealth.'

In this sense the Commonwealth principle is a radical departure from the traditional conception that there is a 'head' which has all the knowledge, wisdom and power of the body politic and that the other organs fulfil complementary functions. There is a 'governing principle' in man (in this consists the universal validity of the Platonic conception) but this governing principle is not *abrogated* to a certain group or class of people—who rationalize their usurpation of true power in various ways, for example, with 'managerial prerogatives' (not to speak about the divine rights of the ruler). The recognition of the divine centre in each man implies a recognition of the wholeness of each person within the power structure of the firm and has far-reaching implications for the whole organization of work. It makes all specialized functional assignments *temporary* in nature and makes the people who exercise these specialized functions *responsible to those* in relation to whom specialized power is exercised.

After having stated the new conception of power as coming 'from within the person and the community, and to be made responsible to those it affects'; and after having stated that 'mutual responsibility must permeate the whole community of work and be upheld by democratic participation and the principle of trusteeship', the new Constitution states: 'Common ownership of our means of production, and a voice in the distribution of earned surplus and the allocation of new capital, has helped us in our struggle towards achieving these aims.'[19] The principle of common ownership and the new organization of work evolved from it is therefore the *real* basis of the recognition of the wholeness and true centre in all men as the basic principle of organization. Without such an organizational basis the autonomy of the whole person becomes a mere phrase.

But the need for the delegation of specialized functions remains. A judicial body must exercise the main judicial function for the community. The Board of Directors and the Community Council are necessary centres of direction. In the traditional industrial organization the directors are the ego centre of conscious control and direction. At Scott Bader they function in the same capacity; but they are not the only and certainly not the ultimate centre of will power and direction. The ultimate centre rests in each person acting as a member of the Community. In this lies the fundamental difference. The same is true of all 'organs' which constitute the body of the Commonwealth. They exercise delegated authority limited in time and subject to accountability to the community.

VII

The functions of the trustees must be seen in the light of such a new understanding of the body politic. They are the philosopher-kings of the Commonwealth. For Plato the philosopher-king is the ideal ruler of the state: 'Until philosophers are kings, or the kings and princes of this world have the spirit and power of philosophy, and political greatness and wisdom meet in one, and those commoner natures who pursue either to the exclusion of the other are compelled to stand aside, cities will never have rest from their evils,—no, nor the human race, as I believe—and then only will this our State have a possibility of life and behold the light of day.'[20]

Plato's political philosophy culminates in this conception of

[19] *Memorandum Commonwealth* 1963, p. 3.
[20] See *The Dialogues of Plato, op. cit.*, p. 373.

the philosopher-king. Like all thought of real depth, the Platonic conception has a historically unique and a universally valid dimension. The latter underlies the Commonwealth conception of trusteeship. But the universal core takes on a new meaning because the function of a philosopher-king is given to a body of trustees elected or nominated by the Community for a specific period of time. In their capacity as philosopher-kings the trustees represent the conscience of the Commonwealth because the Community has given them certain rights in case people fail to do what they have agreed to do on the basis of their own free and highest insight. If, for example, the people should try to obtain individual financial benefits by changing the constitutional provisions that receipts from the sale of the company must be used for charitable purposes the trustees have a right to say: No, you yourself have agreed that this is not going to happen. Or, in case measures are proposed which violate the spirit of the Constitution, the trustees act as the conscience of the Community and say: Look again at what you are doing and consider it carefully. Until you have done so, we veto this measure.

Ultimately, the trustees have no power. They are elected or nominated by the community and can be recalled by the community after a certain number of years. But at any given moment of time they have great power. Being human, they could function as a superego following traditional standards of what is right or wrong rather than as a conscience expressing universal truth in a personally and communally meaningful way. Or they could be simply wrong. Hence they are not philosopher-kings by any divine right. They have been given 'the philosophical oversight of the Community' for a certain period of time and been asked to watch that the Community remains faithful to its self-chosen highest values.

Not any one member of the community has abrogated his own conscience; not any one of them has said: 'I am a hand, I am just working here; you, trustees, are my conscience, and you directors are my brain.' Such a conception of man does not express the true meaning of the Commonwealth. The Constitution realizes that the philosopher-kings can only perform their function if each member of the Community assumes his own personal share of responsibility in being a philosopher-king.[21]

VIII

By incorporating the idea of the philosopher-king in their Constitution the members of the Commonwealth have elevated what Simone Weil called 'pre-Christian intuitions'[22] to a central element in the community of work which they want to build. They have developed a new conception of balance and harmony, designed to solve the age-old question confronting any body politic: *qui cavet custodem*? Who watches the Watchman? In the mutuality of relationship the people of the Commonwealth watch and help each other to realize their true potentialities. Instead of projecting their soul into the body politic, they retain their soul, their true wholeness, their ultimate dignity as men created in the image of God.

This is a radical departure from the way in which Platonic ideas of the ruler and the ruled have hitherto been applied to industry—assuming they were applied at their best. The traditional acceptance of the Platonic identification of the governing principle *in* man with the government *of* man implied a projection on the 'head' of a power that essentially belongs to all human beings, not merely to a select few. The demand to take back this projection is implied in the concept of balance and harmony underlying the Constitution of the Commonwealth. This demand opens a new stage in the evolution of human consciousness and the corresponding modes of organizing work.

[21] This is a crucial point because it changes the whole meaning of the philosopher-king idea and makes it part of a democratic understanding of life.
[22] Simone Weil, *Intuitions Pre-Chrétiennes*, Paris, 1951, partic. pp. 129ff.

Chapter 14

The Commonwealth creator of a human space rooted in the universal

I

Every world view has its own conception of balance, proportion, structure and function, as well as of space and time. At a time like ours, when human consciousness and the corresponding forms of the social order are undergoing radical changes, the most fundamental categories expressing the relationship of man to man are changing. As far as the social order is concerned the most fundamental categories are those of time and space.

What are the implications of the new conception of balance, structure and function as regards the life-space of the people of the Commonwealth and the time dimension corresponding to this life-space?

The word life-space may at first seem unusual if not strange. Like the word 'surrender' it is a word which has become best known in the realm of politics: the life-space of a nation.[1] But whenever we speak about a sense of freedom or of being hemmed in, of our ability to move around or to develop our own way—whenever we use such language, we imply a concept of space.

The concept of space is basic in all religious thought because it touches fundamental experiences of man. 'The Kingdom of God', being 'in the world but not of the world', following a certain path or way are spatial concepts in the wider sense of

[1] The German term *Lebensraum* is a concept which has been used in geopolitics. In fact it was often misused in this context as a demand for more life-space, which became a convenient projection for people whose personal life-space had become too narrow and who tried to find an 'outer' solution for an inner problem.

the term. 'I am the Way, the Life and Truth' is central to Christianity; Tao, the central theme of Taoism, means 'the Way'.

We may, therefore, say that life space is a symbolic expression of our fundamental experience of life as a Way, as movement which has direction, or lacks direction. Our experience of the obstacles which we find, our ability to meet and overcome them (or our feeling that our path is blocked) are important aspects defining our life-space.[2]

Each person has his or her own life-space, his own centre and sense of movement and freedom. But people who live in the same culture share basic characteristics of their life-space because each social order divides an 'open space' into definite spheres of life, making one sphere central and grouping other spheres in relation to the central sphere—that is in a definite order or a pattern of values. We will, therefore, begin our exploration of the life-space created by the Commonwealth with a consideration of its central values.

II

The foreword to the new Constitution sums up the central values of the Commonwealth in these words: 'The ultimate criteria in the organization of work should be human dignity and service instead of solely economic performance.'[3] The use of the word 'should' rather than 'is' indicates that we are dealing with a goal and a potential rather than with an established fact. This will become apparent as we examine the meaning of this central value in terms of the life-space it implies.

To define the life-space formed by the organization of work we may ask ourselves what are the characteristic features of work, considered as a sphere of life? How is the sphere of work related to other spheres, such as the family, the realm

[2] We have asked the people of the Commonwealth the following question: 'For some people life moves in a circle, for others it is a process of change and growth, for others it is just an 'up and down', while some feel that life moves like a spiral.' Their answers give a vivid idea of their life-space. However, it would lead us too far from the argument in this chapter to examine their answers to this question.

[3] See *Memorandum Commonwealth 1963*, p. 3.

of politics, etc.? These questions are usually taken for granted, but their significance can be readily seen as we examine the life-space created by the Commonwealth in the light of some historical examples.

The present organization of industry will be one example of a life-space created by the organization of work, the Greek city state another. We shall gain a better understanding of the present by contrasting it with a cultural definition of work quite different from our own. We shall, furthermore, gain a historical perspective because the present has close connections with the Greek world view. Indeed the very word 'economics' is derived from a Greek word meaning 'management of the household'.

The household was the fundamental unit in the organization of work of the Greek city state. In the household slaves performed the work within a clear ruler-ruled or management-slave relationship. Ultimate power resided in the household where the 'father of the family' was the undisputed head. Neither the government nor the state had ultimate power over the organization of work. The sphere of the household was the 'private' sphere, which meant the sphere of privation, where all men, not only the slaves, were deprived of their full humanity. Freedom existed only in the political sphere where those who had the right to enter were equals and in which a fierce competition for deed and fame took place.

The whole evolution of the Western organization of work may be summed up in terms of a dissolution of the household economy and the formation of national economies. Ultimate power now resides in the nation state. Work takes place in a truly political economy, a combination of words which, as Hannah Arendt rightly points out, would have been a contradiction of terms in the Greek city state where 'work' and 'politics' were in clearly separated spheres of life.[4]

Within the national economy the individual company has a degree of autonomy—otherwise no Commonwealth could exist—but it has no ultimate autonomy. The individual company is not within the 'private' sphere of life—as was the basic work unit in the Greek city state. It is not in a public sphere or space

[4] See Hannah Arendt, *The Human Condition*, Chicago 1959.

either since it is based on 'private property'. The modern company is in a 'social sphere' intermediate between individuals and organizations.

In terms of Greek ways of thought the space in which men and women work today may be defined as the playground of the truncated individual—the hand, the brain, the technical expert. Only exceptionally is work a sphere of life which is part of a meaningful experience of life. In the Greek conception of man the truncated individual could best be designated as the technical idiot, where the word idiot is derived from the Greek *idion*, a person who lives in the privacy 'of his own' outside the world of 'the common'.[5] For Aristotle man was a 'political animal' or a 'living being capable of speech'. The idiot was, therefore, the man who was not capable of speech—and the importance of rhetoric in Greek political life is well known.

In the sphere in which work is performed today people are not really capable of speech either—not to speak about their ability to make work part of a meaningful life. Speech is an uneconomical activity in an organization of work whose central value is a purely technically defined concept of productivity or 'economic performance'. To the extent to which speech enters the sphere of work at all it has often lost all human dimensions and has become the speech of well-adjusted, well

[5] The word 'idiot' has been used in the same sense by C. Wright Mills in his book *The Causes of World War III*, London 1959, p. 81. Mills said: 'If we accept the Greek definition of the idiot as an altogether private man, then we must conclude that many American and many Soviet citizens are now idiots. This spiritual condition—and I choose the phrase with care—is the key to many contemporary problems as well as to much political bewilderment.' At first it may seem contradictory that a word which relates to the private sphere is used in relation to the social sphere in which work takes place. This is due to the different meaning of the private and public space for the Greeks and for us rather than to any misuse of the deeper meaning of the term 'idiot'. For us the private sphere is no longer the sphere of privation but the sphere of family life, a sphere in which we can be ourselves and a sphere of intimate relatedness. (Though even today the monotonous repetitiveness of the work to be done in the household is by some people experienced as privation.) But the Greeks did not have a sphere of the family life as we know it because they did not have the Judeo-Christian conception of the nature of man as a person living in community.

behaving automata, acting as 'hands', 'brains' or some other technical function. It has become sales talk. Work under such circumstances ceases to be a truly human activity and becomes a game. The more stereotyped—and hence idiotic—the game is, the more open it is to a universal game theory of behavioral scientists, to the manipulations of the 'glad hand' and to 'the higher immorality of the power élite'.[6]

III

The life-space which the Commonwealth wants to create is the very opposite of the playground of the fragmented individual—the technical idiot. It is a space in which human beings can act meaningfully and be related to a human community. To act means to respond creatively to a human situation. Such a response is the basis for responsible participation. To create a space within which people can participate responsibly is the essence of the new value and power structure which the Commonwealth is endeavouring to create.

The ability to speak is the first condition for such participation. As we have seen, people encountered major difficulties in this respect during the first decade of the Commonwealth. The opportunity for participation, for speech, was there but people had great difficulty to express themselves, 'to speak up'.

The most obvious reason for this situation is lack of adequate training to speak. By speech I do not mean merely the ability to give a talk, but the ability to participate in the solution of a humanly relevant problem which requires experience, knowledge and insight. Two major factors inhibited—and to some extent still inhibit—the development of this ability.

[6] David Riesman speaks about 'the glad hand' in *The Lonely Crowd*, New Haven 1952, pp. 320ff. C. Wright Mills speaks about 'the higher immorality' in his book *The Power Elite*, New York 1957, Chapter 15 pp. 343ff. Mills refers specifically to the absence of any firm moral order' (p. 345) and the institutionalism of the 'higher immorality' (p. 343). He speaks about the inability of our society to 'produce' men with an inner moral sense; 'a society that is merely expedient does not produce men of conscience' (p. 347). The Commonwealth aims to build a moral order, a new structure in which 'men of conscience' can develop.

In industry speech has traditionally been considered a waste of time. Even talking while working was long considered unnecessary if not harmful to work. To encourage humanly relevant talk about work rarely if ever entered the minds of those responsible for the organization of work. Instead of engaging in speech one could produce exchange values. Even at Scott Bader when small groups were first formed, some people frowned on such an activity as a waste of time.

The second factor is the debasement of speech to 'mere talk', 'oratory' or 'theory'. Once speech is thus debased, it is easy to separate it from action. The latter also degenerates once it is separated from speech in the deeper sense of an expression of experience, knowledge and insight. A great deal of what is designated as 'action' in industry today is merely the compulsive behaviour of truncated individuals or technical idiots. Much that is designated as speech is merely 'sales talk'. In line with those spoken words are the written words of that disgraceful journalism of our day which ministers to the needs of the inactive 'citizen' of the nation state. It illumines the extent to which industrial man has lost the ability to speak and act humanly.

An attempt to restore humanly relevant speech in the sphere of industry implies therefore much more than giving people some—badly needed—human relations skill enabling them to participate in meetings etc. It requires the creation of a new space in which human beings can work and act humanly, a space in which reasonable speech and responsible action are interrelated.

The people of the Commonwealth have been deeply moulded by their experience of an industrial life-space which inhibits rather than fosters truly human action. But they are committed to a new beginning and they are trying to restore the ability for humanly relevant speech through a radical change in the value structure of work. To repeat: 'The ultimate criteria in the organization of work' states the foreword to the new Constitution of the Commonwealth 'should be human dignity and service instead of solely economic performance'. As long as a concept of technical productivity devoid of human values is the central value in the organization of work, humanly relevant speech cannot be conducted in the sphere of industry and responsible action is inhibited. True speech and genuine action can only take place when human dignity and service become the ultimate criteria in the organization of work.

IV

When human dignity and service become the ultimate criteria for the organization of work we transcend the Greek conception of man 'as a living being capable of speech' and enter the realm of the Judeo-Christian world view. It is true that there are important similarities between the Greek conception of man and the Christian conception. Otherwise St. Thomas Aquinas could not have accomplished a grand synthesis between Christianity and Greek philosophy—which were considered as irreconcilable in the twelfth century as Marxism and Christianity are considered in the twentieth century. But there remains an important element of truth in St. Paul saying that 'what is truth to a Christian is folly to the Greeks'.[7]

The similarities between the Greek and Christian view of man become apparent as we realize that men's ability to speak is rooted in his ability to grasp the meaning of symbols. This ability distinguishes man from animal and makes society, culture, art and religion peculiarly human realities. The ability to experience symbols is also the basis of the Judeo-Christian conception of man as created 'in the image of God'. His symbolic likeness to God, the fact that man carries the imprints of a divine soul in him, gives to man his true and ultimate dignity.

The experience of this ultimate dignity brings us into a realm which is beyond that of our everyday awareness of life. It is also beyond time as ordinarily experienced because we touch a reality beyond the movement of the clock. But it is not 'beyond' in a spatial sense. It is 'beyond' in relation to our everyday experience. It is 'beyond' in the sense in which our own

[7] The Greek and the Jewish world views were in important aspects opposites. This can be seen in such aspects of consciousness as the 'inner way' of Judaism as contrasted to the fate which the Greeks expressed in their tragedies.

depth is so often 'beyond' us. And yet we know it is there and in moments of true insight we can experience and live this deeper reality. In some form or other most of us had a 'peak' experience—an experience which leads us to the highest because it touches the deepest in us.

To speak about the Commonwealth as 'a family' is an illustration of an experience of the deepest that binds men together. In terms of its ordinary life-space, the Commonwealth is not a family. The Commonwealth is not even within the 'private' sphere of life, and as we will see in the next chapter, it draws clear lines between the working life and the family life. In terms of the body politic the concept of a family implies a head-member or ruler-ruled relationship which is quite incompatible with the fundamental values of the Commonwealth. Nor is the Commonwealth a closely knit community based on intimate relationships. It is meant to be a community of work and not meant to be an intimate familial-communal unit. The Commonwealth aims to be a community of true persons standing in a mutuality of interdependence—corresponding to the actual interdependence created by the division of labour and made visible through common ownership.

To speak about the members of the Commonwealth as a family means, therefore, to walk on a razor's edge between a false sentimental assertion and an affirmation of the deepest truth. We may truly speak of the Commonwealth as a family in the sense in which we speak of the family of man. In times of deep dissension and alienation it is essential to penetrate to this depth of human relatedness to heighten our awareness of our brotherhood. It is also essential because the roots of love and justice lie in an ultimate reality 'beyond' our ordinary awareness.

V

When the deepest aspirations rooted in ultimate reality become alive for a group of people, a movement comes into being, a new vision of a social order expressing new potentialities of human development arises. Though the first decade of the existence of the Commonwealth has left little evidence of such a movement, the conception of a new social order—and hence the necessity for a new social movement—is explicitly stated in the foreword to the new Constitution: 'The Commonwealth has responsibilities to the wider national and international community and is endeavouring to fulfil them by fostering a movement towards a new peaceful industrial and social order.'

The new order is to be peaceful in a more comprehensive sense than absence of war though mankind's survival in the atomic age is the precondition for any new order. The Hebrew word which Jesus used for peace—'shalom'—expresses best the meaning of a peaceful social order. It means to be holy, to be whole, to be completed, to be perfect.[8] As Neumann rightly points out, such an understanding of peace implies the conception of a 'creative balance', of a 'balance of forces' and a 'harmony of proportions'.[9] These ideas convey the deepest meaning of the new 'balance of power' which the Commonwealth attempts to create—within itself and in the social order to come.

The central principle underlying the new creative balance of power is the principle of non-violence. 'To be a genuine alternative to welfare capitalism and state-controlled communism a new peaceful order must be non-violent in the sense of promoting love and justice, for where love stops power begins and intimidation and violence follow'. Love and justice are rightly seen to belong together because all true justice implies love. Indeed love given in the 'right proportions' is justice.[10] Just as peace is not defined exclusively as absence of war, so non-violence is defined as the presence of love and justice, rather than merely as absence of physical violence.

Such a conception of love and justice must be embodied in the new structure of the Commonwealth and the social order of tomorrow if it is to be more than 'mere talk'. The foreword to

[8] See Erich Neumann, *Der Schöpferische Mensch*, Zurich 1959, p. 216.
[9] *Ibid*. p. 208.
[10] This view is in sharp contrast to the understanding of love and justice as opposites by such writers as Reinhold Niebuhr, See *Moral Man and Immoral Society*, A Study in Ethics and Politics, New York 1953. p. 57. p. 73.

the new Constitution follows, therefore, the assertion of love and justice with a reference to the basic principles of organization of work: 'One of the main requirements of a peaceful social order is, we are convinced, an organization of work based on the principles outlined here, a sharing of the fruits of our labours with those less fortunate instead of working for our own private security, and a refusal to support destructive social conflict or to take part in preparations for war.'

The co-ordination of these three requirements is significant. The central requirement is the sharing of the fruits of one's labour instead of working only for one's private security. There is nothing wrong with being concerned with one's own security, but there is something wrong if this concern becomes the centre of one's life. To 'feed the hungry and clothe those in need' must be central. As the centre of a new social order it is complemented by the common ownership principles on which the new organization of work is based on the one hand and the principle of non-involvement in destructive conflict and war on the other hand.

The dynamics of a creative balance implies conflict and tension but it involves creative rather than destructive conflict and tension. Hence destructive conflict is rejected, not conflict as such. There are virtuous circles or rather open spirals in the evolution of human consciousness as well as vicious circles. There are good means—fostering virtuous circles—as well as bad means fostering vicious circles. Good means must be used in a movement towards a new order, virtuous circles must be created and creative tensions are necessary. The new Constitution recognized this fundamental problem of social change: 'We must strive to release the best in man within a free community to live up to the highest that he knows and recognize the interdependence of means and ends as we continue working towards a new and better society.'

The highest is 'the highest that man knows', it is not a utopian ideal of the future. It is a present reality. As the highest—or the deepest—knowledge of man it partakes of the quality of a potential—a realizable potential. By asserting man's true potentialities the new order departs from the present disorder of society. The new order is based on an attempt to move towards the highest we know while the present disorder is based on the lowest common denominator imaginable.

VI

A social order based on this new vision is to be realized in the future. But the new vision has already been realized in the Commonwealth Hall. This is not accidental because in art man becomes most immediately aware of the ultimate dimensions of the human situation. Modern art has, therefore, more to say to us about the present disorder of society and the new order to come than has any other creative expression of man.

Built in 1959 at the initiative of Godric Bader, the Commonwealth Hall belongs to a new mode of consciousness expressing a new conception of time and space. We can best understand this conception by looking at it in a historical perspective.

The space of the Romanesque is the manifestation of the divine in the perfectly human. The Romanesque has the solidity and the rootedness of the earth, opening up to the sky. The walls of a Romanesque cathedral are heavy and firm, the windows are but minor interruptions of the walls. Firmly grounded, the cathedral opens up towards heaven—sometimes with the round of the cupola as the symbol of perfection. In the Romanesque, the eternal breaks into the world of man.

The Gothic, on the other hand, lifts man up to God. Everything in a Gothic cathedral moves towards heaven, the vertical is the predominant line. The solid walls are opened and become mere pillars for the stained-glass windows through which the heavenly light streams in. The Gothic cathedral is a heavenly symphony.

Classicism was man's way back to earth—not to mother earth—but to the Greek ideal of a divine body and soul. The Baroque regained hold of mother earth and manifests an exuberance of nature which contrasts sharply with the clear line of the classic ideal. The Baroque merged its feminine soul with the divine perfection of the round and the human approximation of the ellipse.

The industrial age had no clear style of its own. It built its stock exchanges in the form of Greek temples. But this is a mere façade. Behind it hides an unholiness which manifests itself openly in the ugliness of industry. It is true that the functionalist style expresses a true human potential of modern technology. But the social institutions which have dominated industrialism prevented functionalism from developing its true potentialities: the industrial city is a product of speculative market forces not of a centrally human functional conception of community.

The Commonwealth Hall symbolizes a new order. Neither the Romanesque, nor the Gothic, nor Classicism nor the Baroque could describe the conception of time and space which animates it. Its walls are panels of glass—uniting the inner and the outer, relating the world of man to the world of nature. Its roof is neither low, nor high—it follows the form of a hyperparabola. A hyperparabola is a segment of a circle moving in two lines towards the infinite. It is also a segment of a circle as seen by our human eye which can perceive only a part of the round horizon. A hyperparabola partakes and reaches towards the eternal without claiming the perfection of the divine. The Commonwealth Hall is thus opening man to an eternal reality while leaving him firmly grounded. It expresses a new synthesis of the human form and its divine ground. The 'beyond', formerly experienced as the 'supernatural' opposed to the 'natural' becomes a dimension of depth; it becomes an ultimate reality which permeates all that IS and all that is in the process of BECOMING.

When the Commonwealth Hall was built, a member of the Commonwealth who is also a lay-minister, gave a sermon comparing the process of the building to an act of creation. He pointed out that the hall was built 'from above' so to speak. Instead of the usual way of building from the ground, two pillars were erected and the roof was built resting on these two pillars. The remainder of the Hall was built only after the roof was completed. We may call these two pillars the pillars of love and justice. They ground heaven in earth and give to the earthly its ultimate meaning.

The Commonwealth Hall, symbol of the new age to come, stands in perfect harmony next to the old church of Wollaston which combines the Gothic and Romanesque conception of time and space. One never has the feeling that the Hall does not belong there. As radically different as it is, it reaches into the same ultimate ground of Being and Becoming. The Hall and the Church are, each in its own way, a true manifestation of this ground. The Hall is a beautiful expression of a new form which symbolizes the creation of a human space rooted in the eternal. In this sense it is an embodiment of the soul of the Commonwealth.

Chapter 15
The Commonwealth Ideal of Man

The new structure of the Commonwealth, the functions to be fulfilled by its various organs, the implicit conception of balance, proportion, space and time—all these can become alive only in the extent to which they become embodied in the consciousness of the members of the Commonwealth. Essential is, therefore, a new awareness of the people—of themselves, of others and of the world in which they move and have their being. Such a new awareness is expressed in a new ideal of man.

The 'Schedule of Rules of Conduct' which defines the responsibilities of the members of the Commonwealth contains a fairly comprehensive vision of what kind of a person a member should be. We can pass quickly over such rules as satisfactory attendance at meetings and the obligation to engage in some social service etc.[1] But we must deal carefully with those 'rules of conduct' which express fundamental values.

Mutual help in self-realization is the central characteristic of the new Commonwealth man: 'To be a member of the Commonwealth means . . . to strive constantly to develop one's own capacities and potentialities and to take an active part in helping others to do likewise'.[2] To develop one's own capacities and potentialities means healthy growth, it means to develop one's true self. This is something very different from an ego-centric self-interest, since capacities and potentialities, provided they are truly 'one's own', belong to the true essence of a person and can only be realized by developing what is true for us in relatedness to what is true in others. They call for mutual

[1] See *Commonwealth Memorandum*, 1963, Schedules of Rules of Conduct, point 3, p. 26, and point 4, p. 27.
[2] *Ibid.*, point 5, p. 26.

active involvement. Members are not only asked to develop the potentialities of their own, they are admonished to 'take an active part in helping others to do likewise'.

It is, furthermore, recognized that the development of a person's abilities in the work situation is part and parcel of the development of the whole person. The people of the Commonwealth are not expected to be able to express their wholeness in work—this is only possible in the truly creative work act. But they are expected to make work 'a meaningful and creative *aspect* of their lives rather than a means to an end'. They are given a 'common responsibility to divide work among themselves and to organize it in such a way' that it may be a meaningful and creative part of their lives. The conception of the new man is thus related at a crucial point to a new mode of organizing work.[3]

Work is considered a sphere of life which is related to other spheres: 'The Commonwealth as a community of work does not directly concern itself with the private or family life of its members. However, the Commonwealth stands for a new approach to problems of work and society, and a genuine commitment to the principles of the Commonwealth implies an active concern for the furtherance of these principles in all areas of one's life. Just as a person's working life is inseparable from his whole way of life, so his family life and his participation in communal and political affairs deeply affect his working life and that of others.'[4]

II

The realization of the ideal implicit in these 'Rules' demands persons living in true community. It demands in particular (i) that people meet one another as whole and true people in the immediate contact of work, (ii) that they are able to overcome the false separation of 'the material' and 'the spiritual' and thus be able to experience the unity of life, (iii) that they become actively involved in a transformation of society, experience a

[3] *Ibid.*, point 5, p. 26. *Italics* mine.
[4] *Ibid.*, point 9, p. 27.

tension between mere conventions and man's true self. These demands are interrelated.

In the immediate day-to-day contacts at work members are asked to deal with their problems as participants in a human community rather than as members of an organization: 'If misunderstandings or disagreements of any sort arise it is the obligation of a member of the Commonwealth first to take up the problem directly with the person concerned and give him or her a chance to remedy the situation before the matter is brought to a third person or the Council of Reference.'[5] Members are urged to meet each other as human beings and attempt to work out their problems among themselves. Only if they are unable to do so should a third person or the Council of Reference—the judicial organ—be brought into the picture. The demand for a personal encounter is an important stimulus to grow in mutuality, to help understanding each other, to become responsibly involved—to be able to forgive. It is a stimulus to wholeness and human relatedness.

An aspect of such wholeness is the ability to experience the unity of life by overcoming the traditional separation of 'the material' and 'the spiritual'. The Constitution asks specifically 'to provide opportunity for the full development of us all, both materially and spiritually'. The same idea is expressed in the rules of conduct in regard to the attitude towards money. 'To be a member of the Commonwealth means one deals with money in a spirit of good stewardship. Members share both in the successes and failures of our common enterprise. They should exercise care and economy in spending time and money in the interests of our common purse, on which we all depend for our mutual security and ability to ensure an adequate living standard for all who work with us.' After stressing the communal element in the right attitude towards money, the interrelationship between 'the material' and 'the spiritual' is stated explicitly: 'What we do with our money indicates more than anything else our personal outlook on life and the influence we exert on others.'[6]

[5] *Ibid*., point 7, p. 27.

[6] *Ibid*., point 8, p. 27. It is true that the foreword of the new Constitution

Such an attitude is reminiscent of a principle of the Iona Community: 'The test of our Faith is in our use of time and money and by money we mean all that money represents: all that we call our possessions. There is a sense in which time and money are our only possessions. They are the only things we have to give to other people. We cannot pray for anyone without giving some of our time. We cannot care for someone without giving some of our time and some of our things as well. That is why our constant excuses are "We haven't time" and "We haven't the money". We mean that they are in short supply because they are the only things we have got. Whenever we begin to be serious about our Christian obedience we realize this.'[7]

Once the intimate relationship between the material and the spiritual is recognized, misuse of the material becomes inseparable from misuse of the spiritual. The parable of the seed illuminates this point. 'Some of the seed fell in among thistles, and the thistles grew up with it and choked it'. Jesus explained this passage to his disciples in these words: 'That which fell among thistles represents those who hear, but their further growth is choked by cares and wealth and pleasures of life, and they bring nothing to maturity.' 'Cares' belong as much to the choking thistles as does wealth. Jesus furthermore does not object to the common-wealth but to the misuse of wealth.

To struggle against such misuse is part of the new consciousness of the Commonwealth man: 'Money should not be used to profit from other people's work or to acquire control over other people's lives, such as when seeking additional income from investments and gambling. Such practices are not compatible with membership of the Commonwealth.'[8] This injunction is primarily directed against speculation on the stock

[7] See T. Ralph Morton, *The Iona Community Story*, London 1957, p. 45.
[8] See *Commonwealth Memorandum*, point 8, p. 27.

speaks about 'bondage to material things' as if they were separate from the realm of the spirit. But this would be a misinterpretation of the meaning of this reference. The emphasis is on 'bondage' and not on 'material.' Not the latter but a false attitude towards 'the material' is rejected.

exchange and against investments which give control over other people's lives and/or profits from other people's work. Such activities are considered incompatible with the principle of common ownership. A person cannot be a whole and true person if he shares with one part of his being in common ownership while he profits with another part of his being from the work of others or acquires control over their lives.

Such a demand for consistency amounts to a broadening of the responsibility of the members of the Commonwealth from their own circle of work to society as a whole. 'To be a member of the Commonwealth means working for the realization of the principles of common ownership in all one's religious, trade union and political activities, and Commonwealth members are encouraged to engage in these activities.' This call for active involvement in ongoing affairs becomes even more meaningful through the following amplifications. 'It also means that a personal responsibility and discipline is accepted for each member to become an active participant for the transformation of society in general rather than allow himself to be passively shaped by social forces and pressures from outside.'[9]

Active participation must be understood as the ability to respond to a human situation, to participate responsibly. It is more than merely reacting against forces and pressure around us. As long as we merely react we remain within the frame of reference of the situation we react against. To participate actively means to go beyond the existing situation, to overcome it creatively by developing a new frame of reference. To be able to do this a person must be conscious of the nature of 'social forces and pressures' and of the way in which these forces shape our own life.

Commonwealth members are asked to develop such an awareness which implies a tension between the social forces and pressures which surround us and our true self. The development of a true self expressing our own values is an eminently personal matter. The rules of conduct recognize, therefore, clear limits of general rules, though they equally clearly affirm that growth of a person in community implies

[9] *Ibid.*, point 10, p. 27.

acting from one's own centre and actively shaping the world from this centre. 'To indicate in any specific detail what this means for any particular member of the Commonwealth beyond what has already been said, might violate the freewill of our members. Each member has the responsibility to accept for himself this challenge for growth as a person and as a member of our community. Whatever is done merely "to keep up with the Jones's", to escape the responsibility for one's own convictions, to act with enmity, or in any way do damage to others, is opposed to the spirit in which a person enters the Commonwealth.'[10]

This call to accept the responsibility of one's own convictions and to act in a spirit of love must be seen in the broader context of the development of 'a way of life free from bondage of mere conventions', of a social order which 'must be non-violent in the sense of promoting love and justice' and of a recognition of 'the interdependence of means and ends as we continue working towards a new and better society'.

These statements from the foreword to the Constitution are an integral part of the new ideal of a 'Commonwealth man' and the consciousness which it implies. As is stated explicitly in the rules of conduct: 'To be a member of the Commonwealth means to accept the basic ideas expressed in the Preamble to the Constitution.'[11] These basic ideas contain the germs of a far-reaching and fundamental transformation of human consciousness. They amount to an encouragement to broaden one's awareness by accepting the as yet unrealized potentialities of today as more important than the already realized potentialities of yesterday.

III

The new mode of consciousness which must be realized is in sharp contrast to the mode of consciousness fostered by the traditional organization of work. The latter forms sovereign individuals living in a sovereign nation state. A sovereign individual is a person who considers himself the centre of the world

[10] *Ibid.*

[11] *Ibid.*, point 11, p. 27.

and who is so ego-centred that he is likely to be isolated from his fellow human beings. He is much preoccupied with his little self, seeking status, trying to keep up with the Joneses and fully engaged in the competitive game of an 'affluent' society. In an extreme form he is what Erich Fromm called 'the marketing personality', a person selling himself on the personality market.[12]

In this context the limitation in size of the Commonwealth is significant. Originally the Commonwealth was limited to 250 people. In the Constitution of 1963 the limit was extended to 350 people.[13] These stipulations are an assertion of the mastery of man over the world in which he lives. Size is made a matter of conscious decision instead of being an automatic response to unconscious market forces. It is related to human dimensions of understanding and potentialities of relatedness.

When man's true potentialities of development are made the central focus of the organization of work, forces are activated which foster the development of people's true abilities and purposes. Since all truth has a transpersonal ground and reference, truly centred people are related to their fellow human beings and to the ground of their existence. They develop in a mutual relationship to other people, giving and receiving in terms of their unique abilities, potentialities and needs. Such a development creates communal bonds which relate people to each other and to the web of life.

Communal and community must be understood in this context—in a new—synthetic—way and must not be identified with the group, the organization or a wider entity as such. They mean interrelatedness and interdependency. Community thus understood does not exist apart from or as an opposite to persons but is a complementary aspect of the consciousness of people who are aware of their relationships to others and their interrelatedness with others.

This, in a few strokes, is the picture of the Commonwealth ideal of man: true persons living in a true community; people

[12] Erich Fromm, *Man For Himself*, New York 1947, pp. 67ff.
[13] See *Commonweath Memorandum* Article 5, p. 12.

who are involved in a creative life process and who are able to participate through truly human speech and action in this process; people who are related to the human community and the ground of all Being and Becoming.

Chapter 16
Growing up to responsible participation

I

Responsibility as a person living in community means response to a human situation in terms of one's true self. To be able to exercise such responsibility we must strive to become whole persons and develop the manifold dimensions of our personality. We must develop our emotional, intellectual, aesthetic, intuitive and other potentialities. Such a development expressing a holistic conception of man implies a holistic understanding of participation. In this chapter we will show concretely what participation thus understood means and what forms of participation must be developed if the fundamental conceptions of time, space, balance—and man on which the Commonwealth is based are to be realized.

Participation in the actual decision-making process is an essential aspect of all genuine participation. But it is only one aspect of participation. Potentialities for participation exist wherever there is a potential relationship between ourselves, our fellow human beings and the world in which we are living. Strategic aspects of a holistic participation may be classified as follows:

(i) Relationships to fellow-workers, to tools, machines and the immediate work environment. These constitute our relationships to the concrete aspects of work and include the relationships to the creative work task in the literal sense of a creation of something tangible.

(ii) Relationships to the organization of work, to the purposes in view of which work is organized and to the means used to achieve the goals of the organization. Participation in the decision-making process is an important aspect of these relationships.

(iii) Relationships to the world beyond the 'factory gates'—to the whole social order in its political, economic, psychological and sociological dimensions.

Whenever we establish meaningful relationships with any person or thing or ongoing process in any of these three areas of life, we participate in some way in the human community. Participation in this sense has an inner and an outer expression. We have some inner experience, we are involved in life and we also express our involvement in our behaviour. If we are interested in people, we meet them; if we experience a sense of responsibility for the Commonwealth we vote, talk to people, go to committee meetings etc. If we are concerned about people outside the Commonwealth we take some part in social and political activities.

Holistic participation which is conducive to help the development of our manifold potentialities is not an abstract and unrealistic ideal. There is no expectation that everybody will realize all the possible dimensions of participation. Every person must make his or her own choice about priorities in developing the opportunities which exist. What matters is the existence of various opportunities of which people could avail themselves. Only a community of work which attempts to develop all possible potentialities for participation can offer enough choice to the individual person to allow him or her to grow healthily, develop an inner balance and move towards wholeness centred on the true self. To recognize this necessity and to develop systematically opportunities for meaningful relationships—this is the meaning of holistic participation.

What ways of participation does the Commonwealth open in the three major areas outlined above? What contribution can the various modes of participation make for a balanced, holistic development?

II

People's relationships to each other, to the tools and machines with which they are working, to the product of their work, and to the immediate as well as the natural environment in which work takes place constitute their participation in the concrete-immediate aspects of work.

Within this sphere people meet in flesh and blood, they can see, hear and touch things. As human beings they may meet in their concrete totality, that is, all dimensions of their life are present in a direct encounter with another person. Such a meeting is an essential aspect of a religious encounter. Its importance can therefore not be overemphasized.

Working in groups, having communal tables at meals, discussing problems among themselves before bringing them into the sphere of organization, participation in groups other than work groups—all these will enhance participation in the immediate-concrete aspects of work. Service to the community, visiting old people while distributing parcels and bringing them firewood cut by members of the Commonwealth are other examples.

Also within this sphere is the experience of aesthetic values. These values are an essential aspect of life because they are an outer manifestation of an inner balance and proportions, of the space and time dimensions moulding our life. Aesthetic values enhance the experience of life and participation in these values is of great importance—particularly since they have been so thoroughly disregarded in industry.

The experience of work as a meaningful activity is a final possibility of participation. Participation of this kind takes place whenever we have a positive relationship to the tools, machines, the place of work or to the materials we work with and the product of our work.

Participation in the concrete aspects of work is closely related to the whole value and power system within which work takes place. A person who, for example, is 'high-up' in the traditional type of industrial organization may meet a 'rank and filer' and say to him in a friendly way: 'Good morning, Joe'. We may assume that he expressed a genuine feeling of friendliness rather than merely a conventional duty. Yet in a religious sense this expression lacks an important element because it has been said in a situation in which genuine human equality is absent. The feeling was expressed within power relations which deny the ultimate dignity of men. The friendly 'hello' implied, therefore, an element of condescension, possibly of unconscious pride in having been a good 'person'.[1]

Genuine participation in the immediate-concrete sphere of work presupposes, therefore, a value and power structure which enabled people to participate as whole people in the organizational sphere.

III

To organize means to establish relationships between people and things, between means and ends. Through organization a network of relationships, a structure of values and power arises. People may participate in the satisfactions given by the values and principles which become alive in an organization, such as the common purpose, the reputation of the firm or of the product, the values expressed in the organization of work, etc.

As regards the decision-making process, three types of opportunities for participation exist in the Commonwealth:

(i) opportunities to participate in the day-to-day decision-making process.

(ii) opportunities to participate in policy decisions which are made periodically.

Decisions under (i) and (ii) refer to (*a*) market developments, (prices, purchases, sales;) (*b*) technological developments, (problems of chemical or mechanical engineering); (*c*) developments in any other fields relevant to human development such as knowledge of management, of psychology, sociology or of the theology of work.

(iii) opportunities to participate in the development of the fundamental structure of power and values within which work takes place.

Decisions in the administration of day-to-day business affairs

[1] It is difficult to understand this situation if we take the traditional organization of work for granted. If we were to speak about the friendliness of a man towards a slave, the element of condescension would be obvious. But it exists whenever a new stage of consciousness is being reached which makes the relationships existing under the old (in this case the presently existing) system correspond to a lower level of development.

are made by individuals or by teams chosen on the basis of specific abilities, knowledge and experience and given a clearly defined, delegated authority.

Scott Bader has been attempting to implement Commonwealth ideas by transcending the traditional staff-and-line-relationships which usually imply a rather limited psychological development. The company has been attempting to involve the same person in different teams with different aspects of his or her capacities and with different degrees of authority. A person, for example, may have sole authority in a team to make decisions on service to customers. At the same time he may be a member of a team in which his authority on price decisions is shared with another person who may have the final word in case of a disagreement.

The Board of Directors plays an important role in this decision-making process. The decisions of the Board fall in two broad categories: (i) implementation of basic policy decisions which were previously made and approved by the Community, (ii) formulation of new policies. It is not always possible to separate these two categories clearly. The interpretation of an established policy and the formulation of a new policy are often intermingled. However, in an organization based on a separation of administrative, legislative, judicial and trustee functions, there is a tendency to separate the function of the Board as an administrative organ—namely to carry through and interpret basic policy decisions in the day-to-day decision-making process—from its function as a committee of the legislative organs—in which capacity the Board formulates basic policy decisions which are to be submitted to the legislative for discussion, approval or modification.

The new Constitution attempts to separate these functions as much as possible by limiting the right of the Board to spend money without previous approval by the legislative. As we have seen, all capital expenditure over £10,000 ($28,000) must be submitted to the general meeting and approved by the members of the Commonwealth.

A question of special interest arises in regard to the participation of the Commonwealth Directors—the two elected representatives—in the deliberations and decisions of the Board of Directors.

Beside recommendations on annual distribution of earnings they may participate (i) in the interpretation of basic policy decisions (ii) in the formulation of new policies, (iii) in keeping these functions as clearly separated as possible and (iv) making sure that newly formulated policy is submitted to the appropriate legislative organs.

In each of these areas they may participate (*a*) through contribution of their specific knowledge of technological and market problems, (*b*) through assessment of technological and market problems in wider terms of Commonwealth principles. The first manner of participation has only marginal importance since the Commonwealth representatives as a rule do not have the experience, capacities and knowledge relevant to these decisions. If they had these qualities, they would be in different positions in the firm than they actually are.[2]

But the situation is quite different in regard to the second opportunity based on an understanding of decisions in terms of basic Commonwealth principles.

It is often said that people without knowledge of the market, of engineering and of other sciences are excluded from the most important decisions which are considered 'technical' in nature. This is certainly true if—and only if—business decisions are considered to be limited to the universe of technology and markets—that means if industry is defined as the playground of the technical idiot. It is an utterly false attitude if business decisions are considered to be part of a human universe—that is if man as a whole is taken seriously. There is *no* decision, no matter how 'technical' it appears to be, and no matter how much it is formulated in terms of technology and market problems, which does not have psychological, sociological, philo-

[2] It is conceivable that people are elected to a Board of Directors who do have the necessary technological and market knowledge such as an expert of a union who 'represents' the workers on the Board. But this type of participation which underlies for example the *Mitbestimmungsrecht* of workers in industry in West Germany is based on the existence of two groups each having in *principle* different power. It is, therefore, incompatible with forms of participation based on religious principles.

sophical and theological implications. These implications can be stated in a language understandable to any person no matter what particular 'technical' knowledge a person has in *any one* of those fields.

The notion that people without specific 'technical' knowledge are unable to participate in decisions involving technical dimensions is due to any one or any combination of the following: (i) unconsciousness of the fact that every technical decision constitutes but one aspect of a broader decision involving a total human situation, (ii) inability to see the relationship of 'technical' dimensions to psychological, sociological, economic, philosophical and theological dimensions and to express them in clearly understandable terms, (iii) fear of giving up power or of losing prestige. Such unconsciousness, inability and fear are characteristic of the truncated individual—the man who has developed sheer brain power but is emotionally underdeveloped and without understanding of the human universe.[3]

The Commonwealth Directors can make an important contribution in overcoming the inadequacies of such an unbalanced stage of development. They can insist on an evaluation of policy decisions in holistic human terms. In terms of basic Commonwealth principles this is important in the formulation of policy as well as in the interpretation of basic policy decisions. It is also important in watching that the interpretation of established policies does not involve new policies.

So far we have assumed that the decisions refer to market or technological problems. It is true that all decisions, no matter with which aspect of life they are concerned, have technical dimensions. To organize lectures I must know something about methods of presentation and problems of understanding; to arrange a social event I must know something about cooking, etc.; to give money to charities I must know a good deal about the purposes and resources of various charitable institutions.

[3] The task of sheer brain-power is now being taken over by the computer who can accomplish this particular function much more efficiently than the human species. This, like all technological advance, enhances man's power for good and for evil. To apply this enhanced power for good purposes, a radical change in the power and value structure of industry is essential.

But not every decision centres on market problems and on problems of technology. Only in the world of crippled individuals are most decisions centred on these issues. In a human world central decisions deal with human beings and hence with human values.

There are manifold decisions to be made in the Commonwealth which deal with people and their development. The Community Council and the Council of Reference have a special role to play in this connection. The Community Council deals with problems of membership and thus touches on basic questions of people's attitudes. The Council deals furthermore with the use of the Commonwealth funds. Human values are also basic in the activities of the Council of Reference which is directly concerned with problems of fair play and justice. In addition to these central organs, there is the Social and Educational Committee which has evergrowing tasks if it really is concerned with Commonwealth development.[4]

IV

Basic policy decisions made by the Board of Directors, by the Community Council and by the various organs of the Commonwealth must be submitted to the members of the Commonwealth assembled in general meetings.

As we have seen, participation on this level may go considerably beyond saying 'yes' or 'no' provided people have an opportunity to deal with the issues at stake outside general meetings.

Beyond this there is a need for small groups of up to ten or twelve people if participation in the legislative process is to be responsible participation in the full sense of the word. Some of these groups may be actual work groups; others may consist of people from various sections of a firm. Some groups may be more or less steady groups, others may be formed for specific purposes.

[4] If the Commonwealth is to continue growing towards its ideals its members must develop a deeper understanding of the problems of persons living in community and must be more centrally concerned with the work process itself.

The significance of small groups cannot be overestimated. They are essential because they give a chance to experiment and explore possibilities of participation within a relatively informal situation. Learning 'to speak up' and to gain knowledge is only one of the advantages of small groups. They offer the possibility of a give-and-take, of getting to understand other people, their ideas and their problems. Equally important, they offer an opportunity of getting to understand oneself through the reflection of one's own ideas and attitudes in the mirror of the group. One's own development can thus go hand in hand with development of an understanding of other people. This is an important aspect of community development: dialogue is needed for a true community life.

Small groups must not be considered to be merely a first stage which leads to the 'higher' stage of the legislative assembly. Quite to the contrary: the quality of the proceedings of the legislative assembly is largely determined by the quality of the work done in groups and committees. Without knowledge and insight acquired through groups, the decisions made in the legislative assembly are likely to be based on good intuition, on bad projections, or simply on traditional standards. Decisions thus made are not compatible with the ideal of a true person living in community. Furthermore, if the principle of the company 'that all meetings should reach decisions without need for a formal vote' is taken seriously, small group experiences are essential.

V

Commonwealth development means ultimately a holistic human development. As part of such a development people must learn to speak humanly in a dialogue and to act humanly in terms of a development of their own true self and an awareness of the needs of others. Participation in two dimensions is important to move towards these objectives: (i) participation within a given Constitution, that is within a given structure of values and power. (ii) participation in the continuous development of this structure.

The people at Scott Bader had various opportunities to participate in the formulation of the new constitution adopted in 1963 and they are participating in its continuous development. In 1965, for example, they decided to change the functions of the Board of Directors and of the Community Council in regard to the distribution of the annual earnings (the bonus). Until then the Board recommended the amount of the bonus as well as the way in which the total amount was to be distributed. Since 1965 the Board makes only recommendations about the total amount and the Community Council recommends the way of distribution. Instead of combining the principles of equality of each person and payment in proportion to the salary as was previously the case, the Community Council combined the principle of equality with length of service.[5]

Quite apart from the merits of the principle used, this change amounts to the assumption of a greater responsibility by the elected representatives of the people. It illustrates a movement towards a more democratic structure of values and power and shows that the new Constitution—like any Constitution based on the deepest insights of its time—leaves room for creative tensions between what 'is' in terms of the presently prevailing consciousness and what 'ought to be' in terms of the structure of values and power which the Constitution attempts to realize.

The significance of a growing realization of the basic values embodied in the Constitution is well illustrated by a comment of a member of the Commonwealth: 'If profit is the only motive, it does not matter who runs the firm.' In fact, if profit is the *central* value, responsible participation of persons living in community is not possible. This is why certain forms of participation within the traditional organization of industry amount to 'sharing in the administration of evil' rather than 'participation'. Unless the basic structure of values and power of the organization is 'human', 'democratic', or 'non-violent'—whatever standards we may want to use—participation cannot be 'human', 'democratic' or 'non-violent' either.[6]

[5] See *Fortnightly News*, 7th January 1966.

[6] On the level of the work process itself, there are forms of participation

The ultimate meaning and quality of all participation is thus decisively influenced by the meaning and quality of the structure of power and values within which work takes place. Continuous development of this structure towards its highest potential is, therefore, essential. Participation in this development is a touchstone of truly responsible participation.

VI

Responsible participation as understood here cannot be limited to the gates of a factory, the premises of a laboratory or the walls of an office. In our time there is no other meaningful boundary but the human community, the family of man.

Of strategic importance within this human community is the social order of which the power and value structure of a firm is but a small part. Participation in the development of the social order is, therefore, of vital importance (i) to bring to others the new way of life which is developing within the Commonwealth, (ii) to realize the new structure of values and power embodied in the Constitution of 1963. The realization of the ideals of the Commonwealth is seriously handicapped, if not rendered impossible, unless changes in the social order as a whole take place.

The Commonwealth has recognized its responsibilities to the wider human community. Beyond its charitable and educational functions, it encourages its members to engage in religious, trade union and political activities. Furthermore, at the meeting at which the new Constitution was adopted the members decided that up to 2% of the net surplus may be allocated 'towards the development of Commonwealth firms.'[7]

These are encouraging beginnings. They indicate an awareness of a need for a 'movement towards a new peaceful indus-

[7] The decision of the exact amount is at the discretion of the Directors.

---

developing in industry which are in agreement with the values embodied in persons living in community. The outstanding example is job-enlargement. But most other forms of 'participation' including most profit-sharing plans are incidental to a value system which often denies and destroys human dignity.

rial and social order'. The development of a vital concern for the social order as the strategic focus for involvement in the human community is indeed the second touchstone of truly responsible participation.

VIII

Growing up to responsible participation means to develop the kind of consciousness which allows people to make basic policy decisions in terms of a holistically understood human world. This is not merely a matter of seeing 'the human implications' of technological and market decisions. Basically it is a question of making the holistic development of man—that is the development of persons living in community—central. To accomplish this the structure of values and power must be continuously developed in terms of the highest possible understanding of the true nature of man and of a conception of order, balance, time and space corresponding to such an understanding.

The present cultural situation in Western industrial countries is characterized by fragmentation of man and worship of sheer brain power accompanied by emotional illiteracy and confusion. Under such circumstances responsible participation amounts to a demand to grow up emotionally and intellectually, to grow from a fragmented experience of life which reduces people's vision of the world to a distorted part of reality to an ever widening experience of life. Such a struggle for wholeness is the ultimate meaning of holistic participation.

Chapter 17

Participation in a five-dimensional universe

I

Each person and each culture have to find their own way in the quest for wholeness. But there are certain basic forms of feeling, thought and action which are typical for whole epochs in the evolution of human consciousness and of society. We must, therefore, outline briefly the basic features of the new order which we must build to create a solid foundation for a holistic participation.

A secularized version of hierarchy has been the traditional pattern of industrial organization. The pyramid is the best image of such an organization—a narrow top, a broad base, horizontal lines symbolizing 'staff' and vertical lines symbolizing 'line' relationships. The traditional view of order, of ruler-ruled relationships, of balance of power as well as a three-dimensional space-time universe underlie the pyramidal organizational charts which adorn the walls of many offices.

The appropriate image of an organization based on Commonwealth principles is as different from the pyramid as the conception of balance, order, time and space are different from the traditional conception. The circle or the sphere moving in a five-dimensional universe symbolizes the new structure of power and values.

A circle is a symbol of unity, of wholeness and integration. It is an 'ideal' image of a person because it gives quite literally the picture of a 'well-rounded' person. Circles may be drawn for individuals of for groups of people. The size of the circle expresses the width of the horizon of a person or group, the extent of their knowledge and experience. Since people also have a depth dimension—their knowledge may be shallow or deep—

the proper representation of a person is a sphere, that is, a three-dimensional circle.

Actually, no person is so well-rounded in all directions as to form a perfect circle. We all have our shortcomings and weaknesses. In the actual application of the circular approach to specific problems we might, therefore, inscribe a form into the circle which approximates more closely the development of a person's abilities at any particular moment in time. But this poses problems which we cannot discuss here. We limit ourselves to dealing with the new approach in terms of circles which remain the basic image of the new structure of values and power.[1]

II

We have used circles in Diagrams I and 2 to represent the Commonwealth organization of work. In these diagrams we used circles for groups of people rather than for individual persons. But the principle is the same. A circle represents either a person or a group. The relationships between people or groups of people thus represented by a circle are expressed by the position of a circle in relation to another circle. Unfortunately we are limited here in our ability to reproduce the circles to the two-dimensional space of paper. But the reader may visualize a three-dimensional space relatively easily by thinking of the earth moving through space.

As we visualize different circles—or rather spheres—within such a space we notice immediately that the metaphors of 'level' or 'below' and 'above' are quite inadequate to describe the relationship of the spheres to each other. It is true that there are still levels and there is an above and a below—seen from an arbitrary point of view or stand-point—but these purely spatial descriptions become indequate to describe relationships of spheres within space. Let us visualize, for example, a symmetrical arrangement of various spheres in all eight directions possible in a three-dimensional space. We obtain now the same level on four different planes and what is 'above' is exactly alike

[1] For a detailed discussion see my paper on *Management in a New Era.*

to what is 'below'. Those criteria cease, therefore, to be adequate ways of differentiating between the position of spheres in space and their relationship to each other. They preserve a degree of validity but 'centre' and 'distance from a centre' are becoming the most significant metaphors. It is true that there may be more than one centre in a constellation of spheres. But each centre is clearly related to another centre irrespective of the arbitrariness of our point of view, whether we look at the constellation from any one of the four sides or from 'above' or from 'below'.

Instead of conceiving the organization of work in terms of 'high' and 'low' positions connected by vertical and horizontal lines, the Commonwealth organization of work must be conceived in terms of various centres in the decision-making process. Different people are related to these centres in different ways and they are at different distances from each other. Such a model allows us to overcome the high-low division without in any way denying that different people have different capacities, different functious and participate in different ways in the decision-making process. In Diagram 2, for example, we have circles representing diverse functions and we have different—interrelated—centres of decision-making.

However, each person, no matter how far removed from the central decision-making process he or she might be, has his own circle of activity and decision-making. People are not swallowed up by their functions nor are they considered to be devoid of potentialities of development because they find themselves at greater distances from the central circle.

From his own centre and location in relation to other centres (and circles) each person has a different perception of the firm. We can therefore draw 'a map' or rather a 'relief of spheres' for each person, not only for the organization as seen from an overall point of view. The form of the personal 'maps' differs according to (*a*) the actual position of the person in the firm, (b) the abilities and potentialities of the person and (*c*) the way he or she sees and experiences his or her situation. Everybody has in fact a different perceptual field and a different vision of the organization. The possibility of drawing such personal maps is a great advantage of the circular understanding of the organization of work.

The specific map or pattern of relationship between circles or spheres varies from firm to firm. It depends upon the different functions which have to be fulfilled and the availability of people who are able to fulfil these functions. The general principle of organization may be stated briefly: the size and the position of each circle is determined by the extent to which a person or a group of people have developed their abilities and potentialities. People with the widest horizon and the deepest insights take the most central positions in the decision-making process. There is, however, always more than one centre. We are not dealing with a monolithic constellation around a centre but with a number of planetary systems, each having its own centre and each system being related to the other centres. Within these systems people stand in a relationship of mutuality, of give and take, not of passing orders from 'above' or receiving communications from 'below'.

III

To understand the nature of these relationships we must introduce a fourth dimension: the time dimension. The only way to represent it graphically is to draw two circles or two constellations of circles, each referring to a different period of time. If my horizon today can be symbolized by a circle with a one-inch radius, I would hope that ten years from now my horizon has grown sufficiently so that a circle larger than an inch is necessary to symbolize it. If I am pretty far removed from whatever the nearest centre of decision-making is today, I may also expect to move closer to the centre as my knowledge and experience grow and deepen. The size of the circles and the position of each circle in relation to other circles changes, therefore, constantly. As soon as I am systematically concerned with my growth and development, I will at any moment of time be part of two constellations of circles or spheres—one expressing the potentialities I have already developed, the other the potentialities which I strive to develop in the years to come.

The movement of a person within a pyramidal structure is bound to be limited. Only one person can be on the top—at best a few provided they squeeze sufficiently. In a four-dimensional universe of circles the potentialities for development are much greater. First there is more room within which one can move since the new conception of space is so different from the traditional conception. Second, people stand in a complementary relationship to each other rather than in a primarily competitive one. The growth of one person does not impede the growth of another. The upward movement of a person within a pyramidal structure has a tendency to keep the others more firmly down, whereas the growth of a sphere has a tendency to stimulate the growth of another sphere—may it symbolize a person or a group of people—provided only it is true growth.

Development of a person's inner abilities and potentialities, rather than outer status and prestige are attributes of true growth. To make such growth possible the new structure of power and values must be based on a new conception of power: power rooted in the person or in the community, power coming from within. It also implies a new type of leadership: leadership rooted in inner strength, experience and knowledge rather than in outer position. Such power and leadership create a new field of forces in which the growth of one person stimulates the growth of another person and in which ever new centres of decision-making arise as people grow in knowledge and experience.

We may illustrate these ideas by the change in function of the Board of Directors and of the Community Council in regard to the distribution of annual earnings (the bonus). This transfer of functions has in no way 'diminished' the importance of the Board of Directors while increasing the importance of the Community Council. The change in functions has enhanced the importance of both because it freed energy for the Board of Directors—energy which can be devoted to fulfil its essential function better or to broaden the scope and depth of its activities.

IV

In describing the nature of the new structure of power and values we have made certain assumptions—for example about the nature of true growth—which must now be made explicit by introducing a fifth dimension. This fifth dimension may be called the univeral dimension.

As a symbol of unity, wholeness and integration, the circle itself is a universal symbol. It symbolized these qualities irrespective of the stage of historical development and irrespective of differences in cultures.[2] It is true that as soon as we apply this circle to a specific organization of work at a specific time in the history of man we combine something universal with something historically unique. But the knowledge that there are universal aspects of life and universal laws of development remains basic.

Wholeness, for example, has been a basic need and desire of man throughout the ages though it found the most varied expressions throughout history. The 'organization man' who must belong to an organization in order not to feel lonely and lost is striving for some form of wholeness as much as is the person who joins an intentional community.[3] The wholeness demanded by the Commonwealth also expresses a universal quest in a historically specific form. It can only be fully understood in a specific historical situation—at our time with reference to the truncated individual and to the technical idiot—to people who are isolated and apathetic. It must be understood in relation to the general fragmentation of life.

Though finding historically differing expressions, all truth has a universal core. To speak about a true self, true growth or about true persons and true community implies, therefore, a universal concept of mental health. A minimum of balance is always necessary to prevent us from 'going to pieces'. This is a

[2] See Erich Neumann, *The Origins and History of Consciousness*, Routledge & Kegan Paul, London 1954, pp. 5 ff. See also Gerhard Adler, *The Living Symbol*, Routledge & Kegan Paul, London 1961, p. 343.

[3] The 'organization man' finds wholeness at a relatively low level of consciousness since he is *immersed* in the group, the mass. He is not a person *living* in community.

universal principle to avoid ill-health. A universal and positive conception of health which is in agreement with our most advanced understanding of human potentialities posits additional conditions as essential for true growth. These conditions may be summed up in four propositions: (i) the ability to perceive the world as it actually is, (ii) the existence of a surplus of energy used for growth and development, (iii) the necessity to focus attention on the unique and peculiar abilities and potentialities of a person and (iv) the necessity to develop personal abilities in relation to others.

These four conditions for mental health are interrelated. I must be able to see people and things as they truly are. I must have energy to grow. To grow truly I must develop what truly belongs to me and I must be able to express myself in relationship to other people. I am the healthier the wider and deeper my circle of relatedness. As I strive to realize my true self in relationship to others my circle of relatedness widens and deepens, I become related to a greater, transpersonal Self which is the universal ground of all true relationships, no matter in what terms we may express it. In this sense all true relationships are trinitarian, they are 'I-Thou' relationships.

To be a true person living in true community means this: to penetrate to their common ground, to continuously strive to develop one's own potentialities in a give and take and to become more and more part of the human community. Community thus understood is again a universal quest of man.[4]

The universal dimension is part of all life. It contains the dynamic power of life. To assure continuous growth we must, therefore, constantly attempt to reach beyond the historical form of the universal to the universal ground itself. The first requirement to be able to do this is to differentiate as clearly as possible between the universal and the historically unique dimensions of everything that exists.

By introducing the universal thus understood as a fifth dimension into our time-space continuum we demand a con-

[4] This has been shown clearly in people's answers to the question whether they ever visualized something like an ideal society. The communal element was mentioned repeatedly.

scious differentiation of dimensions of life which were hitherto more or less intermingled. Literally everything—people, things, capital, profits, labour, wages, etc.—must be seen in its universal and historically unique meaning. The universal must be understood consciously in *every* conceivable organization of work and must be expressed in ever new forms.

As we learn to think, feel and act in this way—always diff-ferentiating between the universal and the historically unique, and always seeking the universal ground, we will bring to life a new dynamic of social change; a dynamic of constant change and renewal through relatedness to the universal ground—the living spirit. Hence there cannot be a Commonwealth tradition in the usual sense of the term. To follow Commonwealth principles in building up a new structure of values and power means constant experimentation with new forms. At the same time it means continuity between the old and the new since everything that exists—or ever existed—has both a universal and a historically unique dimension.

In the five dimensional world of which man is becoming conscious co-operation and mutuality will be central. But the universal core of competition, namely self-development—to give only one example—will remain part of the new order. This example shows that the new dynamic of change excludes a simple reaction against what exists. We do not throw the old rascals out to put new rascals in, we do not take power from those 'on top' and give the power to those 'on the bottom'. We must not simply deny the existing values and replace them by their opposites. We must fight *for* what is good in *all* people and in all groups; we must fight *against* what is false in *all* people or groups. We must create a new order which fosters the transformation of all people. Only thus can we transcend the presently existing divisions and oppositions, and move to a new stage in the development of human consciousness.

The transformation of consciousness must go hand in hand with the development of a new organization of work. Without such a transformation the new organization is not viable. Indeed it can scarcely be created without it. On the other hand a new social reality is imperative to enable people to develop new attitudes. The recognition of the interrelatedness of changes in organization and changes in consciousness is therefore essential if we are to build a new order which is truly democratic or non-violent—an order in which persons live in community, an order in which people are integrated around a true centre and truly related to each other.

V

Such a new structure of values and power implies a new understanding of the world in which we live. To show the scope of the transformation—and to give credit where credit is due—we shall indicate now the basic features of this new reality as seen by Tillich.

In his discussion of life processes he states:

> 'The result of these considerations is that the metaphor "level" (and such similar metaphors as "stratum" or "layer") must be excluded from any description of life processes. It is my suggestion that it be replaced by the metaphor "dimension", together with correlative concepts such as "realm" and "grade".'[5]

Tillich points out that 'the replacement of the metaphor "level" by the metaphor "dimension" represents an encounter with reality in which the unity of life is seen above its conflicts. These conflicts are not denied, but they are not derived from the hierarchy of levels . . .'[6] When discussing the concept of realm (which he defines as 'a section of reality in which a special dimension determines the character of every individual belonging to it') Tillich emphasizes that the elimination of a hierarchical order does in no way imply the denial of 'a graduation of value among the different dimensions'. Indeed he formulates a criterion for value judgments based on 'the power of a being to include a maximum number of potentialities in one living actuality'.[7]

The essence of what Tillich is saying may be expressed in these words: the age of hierarchy is gone. We must think in

[5] Paul Tillich, *Systematic Theology*, The University of Chicago Press, Vol. III, p. 15.

[6] *Ibid.*

[7] *Ibid.*, p. 17.

terms of dimensions realizing that there are different dimensions forming a realm and that there are differences of values—that there are different grades—within each realm. These values are directly related to the power to realize one's true potentialities.

The new structure of values and power expressing such a view of life must be understood as a multi-dimensional order with gradations of value based on differences in people's knowledge and experience. There is basic equality in the right and the responsibility to develop one's true potentialities and to contribute to the common good by responsible participation in the development of a new organization of work. By participating in the creation of a new realm—a new space-time reality—people become truly themselves, while becoming truly related to the human community and to God.

True relatedness means the development of a five dimensional awareness of life: within the organization of work such an awareness has three main expressions (i) awareness of the scope and depth of one's abilities and development of one's true knowledge and experience, (*b*) awareness of the time dimensions which are part of all life, and (*c*) a living awareness of and rootedness in a universal. These three expressions are interrelated. To participate responsibly and holistically in the creation of a new order we must penetrate to the universal ground of all life and relate ourselves to people and to the world around us in terms of our rootedness in this ground. Without such relatedness the vision opened by the Constitution of 1963 cannot become a reality.

Part IV

The Commonwealth and the Meaning of Work

Chapter 18
Universal problems of work

I

The vision of the new order implicit in the Commonwealth Constitution of 1963 has brought us far beyond the present reality of the Commonwealth.

To realize this vision far-reaching changes will be necessary. Our next task is to understand the nature of these changes and to assess the problems which arise as we commit ourselves to the development of the new order. By examining the universal dimensions and the basic problems of work we will get the best understanding of the problems of change.

In its broadest, most universal meaning, work is part of an organic life process and may be defined as an expenditure of energy. In this sense both men and animals work. Both participate in an organic life process in which inorganic and organic matter is being transformed into energy, and energy again into matter. Our organs are 'working' and we are working to sustain the never-ending process of transformation from one form of existence into another. We eat, digest, use the energy of digested food to maintain life, return waste material to nature and eventually ourselves 'return to dust', thus participating in a cycle of life which repeats itself year by year, generation by generation, century by century.

But even in this broadest sense of energy expenditure, work means more than a physical process of transformation. Work creates values in so far as it maintains the balance of the forces of nature, sustains and promotes life.[1] However, in the way in which life is sustained and promoted, man and animal differ radically. The work of the animal is an instinctive reaction to

[1] Helmut Thielicke, *Theologische Ethik*, Tübingen 1959, Zweiter Band, Entfaltung, 1. Teil, Mensch und Welt, III. Das Verhältnis Zur Welt in seinen wesentlichen Bezügen, B. Das Wirken des Menschen auf die Welt 2. Die Wirkung auf die Welt in der Form der Arbeit, pp. 395ff.

the environment. At best the animal may change his environment and give it new shape, but it can transform it only through participation in organic and inorganic processes. The animal is, therefore, forever contained in a process in which the promotion of life means also the destruction of life. It helps to maintain a balance which is beyond its awareness and even further beyond its control. The animal cannot create new forms but remains bound to a given 'environment' without being able to create a 'world' of its own.

Man can do all this. He can take the raw materials of nature and make new forms from them, unknown in the organic and inorganic processes of transformation. He can build houses and roads, make tools and fashion a multitude of objects for his daily life, for festive occasions for his own and for communal purposes. In doing so he not only creates objects which have chemical, physical and mechanical qualities. He also creates objects which have a form and are therefore imbued by spirit. This is the most universal aspect of *human* work. Through work man participates in a truly human world.[2]

The creation of form which is the essence of work takes place within five-fold relationships (i) to nature, (ii) to things, (iii) to society, (iv) to people and to oneself and (v) to an ultimate reality.

(i) The relationships of work to nature are manifold. All matter is part of nature; every place where men work is part of nature; all energy resources are part of nature. The organic and inorganic processes mentioned above are part of a natural life cycle.

Arendt uses this criterion to distinguish between work and labour. Referring to Locke's distinction between 'The labour of our body and the work of our hands' [3] she says: 'unlike *working*, whose end has come when the object is finished, ready to

[2] It should be noted that I said 'man creates objects which have a form' and not 'man creates form'. Strictly speaking man does not 'create' form. He only creates objects to which he gives a certain form. All form is divine. It can be 'discovered' but not 'invented'. Seen on a human plane it is archetypal. It manifests itself in the work process and expresses itself in the whole 'style' of an age.

[3] Hannah Arendt, *The Human Condition*, Chicago 1949, p. 79.

be added to the common world of things, *labouring* always moves in the same circle, which is prescribed by the biological process of the living organism and the end of its "toil and trouble" comes only with the death of this organism.'[4]

Labour thus understood is that element of the world of work through which man partakes of the natural life cycle defined as 'a process that everywhere uses up durability, wears it down, makes it disappear, until eventually dead matter, the result of small, single, cyclical, life processes, returns into the overall gigantic circle of nature herself, where no beginning and no end exist and where all natural things swing in changeless, deathless repetition.'[5]

The satisfaction of our daily needs—food being a prime example—requires labour. The labour of the housewife illustrates well the endless repetition of the daily tasks of maintaining and developing life. But in the world of man labour is always subordinated to work, to the creation of form. The form may be 'invisible' as in the case of the housewife who creates a style of living, a pattern of relationships, a way of life. Nevertheless it is the result of work and not of labour.

(ii) When man through his work creates visible form with the help of nature 'things' arise. All work is performed with the help of things, with tools, implements, machines. Things always partake of different realms: matter and spirit; nature and society, the inanimate and the animate. As form they are both matter and spirit and hence belong to nature as well as to the web of social relationships which man has created. A thing is inanimate, but men alone 'animate' it, transform it from a dead artefact into some-thing by entering into a relationship with it.

(iii) The relationship to society is most clearly expressed in the inclusion of things into the means-end relationships which are part of the organization of work. As things, the products of man's work constitute use-values. They have certain physical, chemical, biological, aesthetic and other qualities which makes them useful. They have a concrete form and an inherent purpose. For this reason the purpose and meaning of work is much affected by the use of the product of work.

[4] *Ibid.*, p. 98 italics in original.

[5] *Ibid.*, p. 96.

When these use-values enter the wider organization of work, for example, the market, they become transformed into exchange values. They take a new form and become part of the whole organizational structure of values and power. Exchange value is an abstraction from the concrete qualities of a product. It is expressed in a price tag which brings a thing into the realm of money. In terms of exchange value people can acquire power over things and thus indirectly—over people.

Compared with exchange values, use-value has a quality of both concreteness and totality, it expresses something essential about 'the thing itself'. This essential quality is the universal aspect of the product because it refers to the use and quality of the product irrespective of the historically specific circumstances under which it has been produced. The chemicals which Scott Bader produces—or licences—are the same whether produced in Wollaston, in Czechoslovakia, in South Africa, in the United States or in Russia, though the systems of organizing work and market exchange differ greatly in these countries.[6]

(iv) From its earliest beginning work was performed in relationship to other people. Whenever a person does not produce everything needed to sustain his or her life, work creates interpersonal relationships. Through work we meet not only people of blood and flesh. Through work we enter the world of human values which are inseparable from the universal problems of work. These universal problems are problems of human relationships, of the criteria and values used in the decision-making process. They are problems of power used to implement the values chosen. Justice and freedom are some of the basic issues arising in this connection.

Through relationship to people (and things) we also establish relationship to ourselves because we relate to people (and things) with certain aspects of our own being. My relationship to work may be superficial or deep, work may evoke in me a desire for status and prestige or for true-fulfilment and creative

[6] Exchange-value on a formal level is also universal, because it is pure form without content. But as a social reality it is always time-bound.

expression. The world of work may be meaningful to me or I may be alienated from it.

(v) Wherever man and human values enter, there is an ultimate dimension. Justice, freedom, alienation—they all have an ultimate meaning. True being is rooted in the universal ground of all life.

The relationships which work establishes to these five realms are interrelated. The interrelated web of these relationships constitutes the mode of participation in work or the meaning of work.

III

The experience of work as a calling—which had a major influence on the development of modern industry—may serve as an illustration of these interrelationships.

The experience of a calling is contingent upon a certain development of human consciousness. It requires an experience of oneself as someone distinct from the group, from the collective. Hence the idea of a calling was most clearly formulated when the medieval world came to an end and the Reformation took place. But the experience of work as a calling has a more universal basis. To speak of work as a calling is an acknowledgement that the meaning of work is decisive for the meaning of life because work is an essential aspect of man's destiny.

Freedom to choose one's true destiny (thus accepting the higher necessity of work) depends upon a degree of freedom from participation through labouring in the natural life cycle. If we all had to grow our own food and basic necessities of life we would be quite literally 'tied to the soil'. We would be extremely limited in creating things and relationships expressing the form true to our being. To do the latter means to follow an inner voice, the vocation given to man by God.

Today in Western industrial countries man has a large degree of freedom from active participation in the natural life cycle and hence potential freedom to participate in a meaningful work process. But instead of making this potentiality a reality man has subordinated meaning and spirit to a mechanical life cycle where 'no beginning and no end' exists: the assembly line, the continuous work process of the factory. This process of labouring has until now defined the problem of freedom and necessity of many people in industry. They live in a realm of necessity which is as harsh as the necessity of participation in the natural life cycle but lacks the experience of the eternity of all that IS.

When Arendt speaks about a 'changeless, deathless repetition' she refers to a borderline experience where the endless cycle of time merges with the timeless circle of nature. Those who labour on the land partake of the endless cycle of time and timeless circle of life. To understand this we must look at such paintings as *The Sower* by Millet or by Van Gogh. Eternity is alive in these paintings.

For the assembly-line and for the shift workers the 'changeless, deathless repetition' is transformed into a 'changeless, lifeless repetition' of certain movements. They participate in an endless cycle of time but they have lost immediate contact with the timeless circle of life. For them the problem of necessity and freedom poses itself with an overwhelming power. The question which their life situation poses is an equally crushing one: Have they lost the freedom to choose their true destiny?

Cybernation opens new potentialities. It frees man not only from participation in the endless cycle of nature. It also frees him from participation in the mechanical life cycle. But these potentialities do not solve any more the basic problem of freedom than did the liberation from the natural cycle of life. The organization of work, the human relationships within which work takes place are decisive for the meaning which work takes. Without the possibility of creative participation no technological development will bring freedom for true self-realization—for the development of true persons living in community.

IV

In posing these questions about freedom and necessity in work, we have asked questions touching man's ultimate destiny, questions affecting the totality of a life situation. We have asked religious questions. We must now formulate these questions with reference to certain strategic dimensions of work which we will examine in the following chapters: (i) people's relationships to nature, to things and to each other, (ii) their relationship to the values and power structure created by the organization of work, (iii) their relationship to society, and (iv) to ultimate reality.

For each of these realms we will ask certain questions which define people's mode of participation in work.

(i) Is there participation in the concrete aspects of work, in things which can be seen, touched, heard, smelled?

(ii) As regards the structure of values and power we are already familiar with the impact of the Commonwealth. Now we must dig deeper into the meaning of this dimension of work by asking questions such as: are the means-end relationships through which things enter the organization of work and become part of the structure of values and power in harmony with man's true way of life? Are the goals of the organization in agreement with man's true purpose? To be true, they have to express that inner voice, that vocation or that way and purpose which is both peculiarly our own and which has, at the same time, its root in a universal and hence eternal realm of experience.

(iii) Do people participate in society in a way which strengthens or weakens true self-realization? Are the means-end relationships typical of society as a whole conducive to such a development or do they hamper it?

(iv) These questions establish a direct link between work and ultimate reality. Means and ends—as categories of understanding work—'correspond' to the Way and the Purpose—as categories used to understand our relationship to an ultimate reality. Since means and ends are nerve centres in the organization of work we have a direct way of testing the ultimate meaning of work by asking the question: Are the means and ends used in the organized work process in harmony with the true Way and the Purpose of our life? Are they in harmony with the one who said 'I am the Way the Life and the Truth?'

It is important to understand the meaning of the word 'in

harmony' in this context. We are not sugar-coating industry with a sweet and pious so-called 'religious' crust. Nor do we confuse the realm of work with ultimate reality. We simply assert the fundamental unity of all life. We recognize that life manifests itself in spheres which have a measure of independence, a degree of lawfulness of their own. But we assert that these spheres must be in harmony with each other and with the central and fundamental values giving form to life. To say that the means and ends in the organized work process must be in harmony with an ultimate, true Way and Purpose is an assertion of the unity and interrelatedness of all life.

Specifically we relate the problems of means and ends to the problem of values and power as well as to that of freedom and necessity. These constitute the three-fold expression of the problem of meaning and participation in work as defined from a religious vantage point.

V

To build an organization of work fostering the true potentialities of a five dimensional universe, interrelated changes must occur in our relationship to the strategic dimensions of work just mentioned.

Work must become part of a meaningful life and must make some contribution to the meaning of life other than being a mere means to make money. Society must be experienced as a web of meaningful relationships with a wider world; we must have a sense of participation in the events shaping this world. An ultimate reality which transcends the historical and cultural uniqueness of all socieites must somehow be part of our consciousness of life. We must be rooted in a ground of universal humanity and Truth.

To examine how such a consciousness may be created would go beyond the theme of this book. But we must examine here the deeper meaning of work for the people of the Commonwealth. We will only touch upon the meaning of society and of ultimate reality as far as they are essential for an understanding of the meaning of work.

By exploring the actual meaning of work in the light of the basic questions raised above we shall lay the foundation for an understanding of the changes which are necessary if the potentialities of the Commonwelath are to become the realities of industry.

Chapter 19
The basic experience of work

I

The essential quality which work gives to the life of the people constitutes their basic experience of work—their experience of work as a whole. Strictly speaking, the whole can only be grasped intuitively. We can only approximate such an understanding by an attempt to comprehend all known aspects of reality and reach the depth of human experience.

We have asked the people of the Commonwealth certain questions specifically designed to touch their deeper experience of work. It is true that in their answers to these questions the wholeness of their experience has been broken up like the prism breaks light into its constituent colour-parts. But the feeling tone of the response, if not the image conveyed by the response itself, helps us to understand their basic experience of work. In addition, we have touched a wide spectrum of reality by asking over 300 questions pertaining to the world of work.[1]

In this chapter we will draw on many questions relevant to our exploration but we will organize the presentation of the material around people's answers to two questions:

'When you think about your place of work, what comes to your mind?' and 'What do you first think of when you think of work?' These questions open a vast perspective while providing a fairly concrete focus on work. They touch something basic in people's experience of work.

The objective possibilities of choice opened by these questions cover a wide range and refer to many dimensions of work.[2]

[1] See Appendix on method.

[2] The concept of objective possibilities of choice is an important one. The obvious objection to this concept is that people do in fact have no choice unless they know (and maybe experienced) an aspect of reality. This is true. But I have chosen the concept 'objective possibilities of choice' intentionally to emphasize the need for a widening of our consciousness—and our choices.

People's responses give, first of all, an indication of the feeling-tone which work has. They introduce us into the atmosphere created by the daily work just as by entering a house, we get a feeling of the atmosphere which permeates the house. Good, bad, indifferent; positive, neutral, negative; leaving us cold or creating a sense of warmth; friendly or unfriendly—these are some of the possible attributes describing the atmosphere of work.

These feelings indicate the life space within which work takes place. The manifold dimension of awareness within such a space may be explored and classified in different ways—each classification expressing a certain point of view and ultimately a world view. We shall explore the strategic dimensions elaborated in our discussion of the meaning of work and follow the classification elaborated there: (i) people's relationships to nature, to things and to each other, (ii) their relationship to the value and power structure created by the organization of work (iii) their relationship to society and (iv) to ultimate reality.

(i) People's relationships to nature, to things and to each other have a unique quality because these are aspects of life which have a concrete dimension. We can see certain aspects of them, maybe hear, touch and smell them. The natural surroundings, the buildings where work takes place, the machines and tools, the product, the people who stand, move or walk around—have this immediate—concrete quality.

(ii) Not as clearly visible to the eye is the organization of work conceived as a structure of means and ends, a structure of power and values. The name of the firm, what the firm stands for in the eyes of the public or in one's own inner awareness may express this structure of values and power. People may feel positively or negatively about the goals of the organization, its practices, its way of getting things done and the people in the centre of decision making. People may feel as significant members of the organization or they may feel like cogs in a wheel.

(iii) Means and ends, values and power are not only aspects of the experience and perception of the organized work process. Each firm is embedded in a wider network of relationships which form more inclusive structures of power and value.

Markets relate different firms to each other and bring the product to people—in the case of Scott-Bader—all over the world. A vast web of organized relationships arises which includes the economic and political aspects of society. Work may be seen as a nerve centre in the network of market and economic relationships, as an essential aspect of the social order.

(iv) Finally work has an ultimate dimension of meaning or lack of meaning. Work may be experienced as a means to an end or as an end in itself. A person may work to 'make a living' or to express an inner meaning. Work may also be experienced as a necessity or as a creative expression which gives a sense of freedom. It may provide an outlet for a person's abilities and potentialities.

Related to the experience of work as freedom or necessity is the experience of work as a labouring activity or as an activity which gives form to things. The element of 'labouring' may manifest itself as strong physical exertion, mental effort or as participation in the 'endless lifeless' process of mechanical production. These are significant aspects of the deeper meaning of work. Another aspect is the time dimension which manifests itself as time passing slow or fast and more fundamentally as time being full (because it has a creative content) or to be filled (because it confronts one as potential emptiness). Since all creativity is rooted in the universal eternal ground of life, the experience of time as full is closely connected with an experience of the universal aspects of life. When time becomes a purely historical phenomenon—measured by the endless movement of the hands of a watch in equal increments—the activity going on in time tends to be experienced as superficial, monotonous, and empty.[3]

All these dimensions listed under (i) to (iv) indicate the objective possibilities of choice open to the people of the Commonwealth. Which of these possibilities have they chosen?

[3] On this point see also my book *Towards a Democratic Work Process*, the Hormel—U.P.W.A. Experience, Harper & Brothers, New York, 1953, pp. 192–195.

II

In answering the questions 'When you think about your place of work, what comes to your mind?' and 'What do you first think of when you think of work?' the overwhelming majority of the people expressed positive or neutral-positive feelings. Only a few were indifferent or ambivalent. There were no outright negative responses and even critical comments were exceptional.[4]

The all-pervading trend was the experience of a 'happy atmosphere'. A clearly positive expression of such an experience was : 'I find pleasure at work. I never feel like not coming. I am happy at work. In other words I don't come here and say "I wish it was five o'clock" when I get here.' A neutral-positive response also coming from the factory was as follows: 'What do I first think of? The particular plant I work in—the reactors—what should be going on in them.'

Significant are the many comments indicating that work is not experienced as something negative. 'I don't dread Monday morning' is a theme which appears in different variations. A young man from the laboratory said : 'I don't dread going in on a Monday morning. It gives me the feeling there are people far less fortunate than myself who perhaps have to get up on Monday morning and stoke a boiler.' 'On Sunday nights I don't have the dread of thinking "Oh Monday morning". I would rather come to work than stay at home. It is nice to have just that bit of responsibility and better than just stopping at home doing the dishes.' For this person—a clerk who does a fairly repetitive job—a sense of responsibility and the avoidance of the routines of the house make work satisfying. Along similar

[4] When asked 'When you think about your place of work, what comes to your mind?' 11 out of 30 people had a positive response (office 3; laboratory 5; factory & maintenance 3) 16 a neutral-positive (office 3; laboratory 3; factory & maintenance 10) and 3 were ambivalent-negative (office 1, factory & maintenance 2). In answer to the question 'What do you first think of when you think of work?' 6 out of 30 had a positive response (office 2; laboratory 2; factory & maintenance 2), 21 had a neutral-positive response (office 4; laboratory 6, factory & maintenance 11), 3 were indifferent-ambivalent (office 1; factory & maintenance 2).

lines is the experience of a manager: 'I don't get a feeling of "Oh dear". The thought doesn't depress me.'

A number of people from the factory were equally clear in saying that work is not disagreeable. A shift worker: 'I can tell you this: since I worked at Scott Bader I have never felt I didn't want to go to work.' A day worker felt similarly: 'Doesn't disturb me at all. When you work in a factory you don't like Mondays, but being at Scott Bader is not a factory to me. Monday is like Friday.' He does not experience Scott Bader as a factory because a factory means something destructive.[5] The replacement of something bad by something good is clearly expressed in the words 'When I have been in other places I never had any interest in work, I got up in the morning and said, "Oh, bloody work". Here it is different; work is a pleasure.'

A number of people working in the factory expressed this feeling of pleasure directly: 'Well, I find it interesting. I'm perfectly happy in the work I do. If I wasn't I would go somewhere else. The people I work with are a good crowd. In my department they are a good team'; or, 'I always had a happy feeling about things at work—it was never tedious.' One person even spoke about his place of work as 'home from home'.

'I think that all the attributes of the place are conducive to work. If someone won't work here, they are blackguards, I think.' Another person also from the laboratory was reminded of 'the spaciousness, the sense of freedom, the general happiness of the place . . . I think this is the most important thing, the happiness of the place.' Here is a good illustration of the interrelationship between the experience of the physical place and the psychological space: the sense of freedom and happiness unites them.

Not all of the people of the Commonwealth could share this experience. Indifferent or ambivalent responses were, 'If some-

[5] All except two of those who started their answer by saying that they did not dislike work were classified as neutral-positive. One was in the positive group and one was in the neutral-positive group in his response to one question and in the indifferent group in his response to another. Most of the following responses were in the forthright positive group as regards one of the two questions asked and in the neutral-positive one as regards to the other question.

body says what do you think of Scott Bader's as a place of work I say, "Well, it's not too bad at all".' Or, 'I don't think about it until I get there.' A third person asked 'The actual work?' and then said: 'I don't think about it, I just do it. When I leave here I completely cut myself off from it. Of course I realize there is a certain amount of risk involved with chemicals—better not thought of.'

The above conversations all took place with factory workers. In the office and the laboratory qualifications were less frequent. A person from the laboratory was 'most of the time . . . quite happy to work hard but there were times when I was a bit lazy and thought "Oh blow it. I shan't bother."'

There were a few who felt it difficult, at first, to answer the question. 'Lost for words', 'can't make it out'; 'stumped for an answer' are illustrative of such feelings.[6]

We may sum up the general atmosphere by saying that, on the whole, work evoked a positive-neutral image and created a happy feeling. The paucity of negative feelings is remarkable and one gets the impression that there is a positive influence at work which enables people to give some meaning to work. This influence affects different people in different ways and to a different extent. People who use mechanical tools and implements are somewhat less strongly affected. On the other hand they are often more explicit in acknowledging the difference between working at Scott Bader and other places they know.

These findings are supported by the large number of people who say that they are often thinking about their place of work.[7] Work does not evoke any resistance in them, their mind is open to it. A person who indicated that he does not often think about his place of work said: 'Because we are so spoilt about it. I don't realize how pleasant it is.' Another person who thinks 'quite often' about the place said: 'Some of my friends working in local factories often say that they heard about that cranky place of Scott Bader.' He laughed after he had said this and con-

[6] One of these worked in the laboratory, two in the factory.

[7] What really matters in this context is not how often they actually think about their place of work but that thinking about their place of work does not evoke any resistance in them, that their minds are open to it.

tinued: 'I tell them about it. They get the general opinion that it is a free sort of place.' In a world which has difficulties in preserving a sense of sanity Scott Bader is indeed a 'cranky place'. It is a deviation from what is considered the norm.

What is the meaning of the positive-neutral basic image evoked by work? How are these feelings reflected in the strategic dimensions of work?

III

The work environment and the setting of the buildings in which people work were mentioned repeatedly: 'I have a mental picture of a garden factory of which I am very proud . . . I don't think about my office or any particular place.' Similar was the response of a person who thinks of 'the whole factory' and who felt that it is 'rather a nicely set out place, an orderly place.' A person in the office spoke about the 'pleasant grounds. I like the old building. I like the setting.' Some people in the laboratory were equally aware of the beauty of the surroundings: 'A very pleasant setting of a situation, a wonderful pleasant spot to work. I always tie it up with the places I saw in Birmingham. Here you couldn't have a better environment. Most people in most laboratories look out into lovely scenery—which must help them with their work, I'm sure, rather than looking out onto slums.'

The place and implements of work also influence the basic experience of work. Three people mentioned their office, one indicating that the space is inadequate and that the office is, therefore, 'cramped, untidy, and dirty'. The instruments, tools and machines with which people work mere mentioned more frequently: 'I naturally think of the resin plant, the reactors, what process is going on in the plant.' Another worker simply mentioned 'reactors and chemicals'. A clerk said: 'the first thing that comes to my mind is a desk and a chair.' Typewriters were also mentioned. A person who said 'I think of paper' has mainly managerial responsibilities.

But on the whole the working place, the machines and tools which people use were not a vital part of the basic experience of work.[8] 'My office'; 'a desk and chair'; 'a reactor'—are rather colourless expressions, indicating a fairly neutral aspect of work. This conclusion is borne out by the answers to the question: 'What stands out about working conditions?' Positive feelings are clearly much stronger than negative feelings but first responses are finely balanced between positive, neutral and negative.[9]

The actual work process was mentioned even less frequently than the implements of work. 'The process going on in the plant'; 'everything is all right—going through'; and 'getting the materials through' are typical responses from the factory. They convey a sense of a flow and reflect the nature of the work process which requires more manipulation and control than contact with materials, handling of machines or labouring activity. Only one person mentioned his hands.

Other concrete aspects of work do not form a more vivid part of the basic experience of work. The product was mentioned only exceptionally and incidentally. Only one person from the factory spoke about 'past batches' and 'wondered whether they reached the approval of the labs'. Nobody else mentioned the product as such. This may be explained by the fact that the end-product is almost literally a formless chemical. But as we will see other factors are decisive.[10]

People too were mentioned rarely though somewhat more frequently than the product. A worker felt that the people he is working with are a 'good crowd' and make a 'good team'. A few others mentioned people more or less directly. When thinking about his place a factory worker asks himself 'mostly "what's going on there? How are the chaps getting on?" At

[8] This conclusion must be somewhat qualified if we take into consideration the observations made by Roger Hadley. These observations suggest that certain machines have considerable significance. See p. 260 n.

[9] First responses on work place and equipment: positive 4; neutral 3; negative 4. Total responses: 11, 4, 6 resp.

[10] See 00 below p. 00. One of the more important factors is the relative lack of knowledge of what the liquid resin is being used for. The lack of real knowledge of chemical processes which may have affected the relatively infrequent references to the work process should also be mentioned in this context. These are aspects of work which have been made part of a systematic training programme initiated by Roger Hadley.

present two of the shifts are short-handed, how do they manage?' A manager was reminded of 'people coming into the office all the time' and a person from the laboratory was concerned with those people who 'don't have a sense of urgency' and do not work well 'without supervision'.

People seem to take it for granted that they work with other people. It is true that there is relatively litte team work establishing direct mutual relationships. But people see and meet each other every day. They sit together at tea break and few are isolated in their work. The relative absence of people in the basic experience of work is, therefore, due to other factors.

An analysis of the questions 'Who do you work with?' and 'Do you consider any of these people your friends? In what sense?' shows that there are clear feelings among the people irrespective of their place in the organization. We find relatively few traces of authority in the sense of power attached to a specific position and exercised over other people. An important explanation of the paucity of the human element in the basic experience of work lies, therefore, in the absence of conflicts typical of a more traditional structure of power. Another factor is the relatively superficial quality of friendship. The overwhelming majority considered the people they work with as friends, but their conception of friendship is more of friendliness than of any depth of feelings.[11]

To conclude: the basic experience of work is affected by the natural environment, the instruments and machines, the production process, people, the actual place of work and the product. The people of the Commonwealth mentioned these aspects in the order listed here: the natural environment was mentioned most often, the product least frequently. There are significant differences according to the place and kind of work. People working in the factory mentioned the natural environment only exceptionally, the production process most frequently. References to instruments and machines were more typical for the office than they were for the factory. Altogether

[11] A person who expressed 'hope' that the people he works with are his friends was asked what he means by friendship. He said: 'Not intimate but they are all right'—See pp. 280, 281.

the concrete aspects of work were mentioned by about two thirds of the people of the Commonwealth.[12]

IV

There are few traces of the impact of organizational goals. A few people mentioned their concern with the consumer. One worried 'about different customers, whether we are getting more orders from them'. Another wants 'the product to be first class'. When he thinks about his work he first wants to see 'that all the products are turned out first class, so we got no bad orders, so the customers are okay.' For these people—both of them shift workers in the factory—work has some meaning because it is related to the goals of the organization. They referred to the relationship of the goals of the company to the market for goods; but nobody mentioned either markets as such or the whole network of organization which relates the work done at Scott Badar with the economic organization of the country and the world. The Commonwealth was not mentioned either.

About a sixth of the people saw work as a means of earning money and are, in this sense, related to the monetary-market mechanism. 'Well, the first thing is earning a living. In other words: money.' Another person when questioned 'What do you first think of when you think of work?' asked: 'You are not supposed to put down your pay-packet?' To the comment 'Whatever you think of' he responded 'I have been out of work. I know what it is like.' Money is uppermost in his mind because of his experience of unemployment. For others work is 'a means to live by, something that must be done to live' or 'a means of livelihood . . . also of interest . . . most of the time'.

Most of the people who mentioned work as a means of

[12] Asked 'When you think about your place of work, what comes to your mind?' 14 out of 30 people mentioned the concrete aspects of work (work environment: 5; work process: 3; place of work: 2; instruments, tools and machines: 2; product: 1; people: 1;). Asked 'What do you first think of when you think of work?' 10 people mentioned the concrete aspects of work (instruments, tools and machines: 4; people: 3; work process: 2; place of work: 1).

making a living were in the factory though none of them was a shift worker. A person from the laboratory was reminded 'of enjoyment. I like what I do. I do it with a purpose which is earning my wage.' This is a borderline response since the idea of *earning* a wage has a different quality from sheer making of money. As we will see later the concentration of the experience of work as making a living among people working in the factory indicates that there are certain satisfactions missing in the factory which pople in the laboratory and in the office either have or do not expect.[13]

Even if we include the responses about money—which are at the borderline of people's experience of society and ultimate reality, the organizational aspects of work were mentioned about a third less frequently than were the concrete aspects of work. This may be partially explained by the greater ease with which something concrete lends itself to the formation of an image. But there are other, very different, reasons for this situation.[14]

V

Two of the people who just spoke to us did not speak about making a living as such but spoke about 'a means to live by, something that must be done to live'. This expresses an experience of an elemental and a universal aspect of work: work as a necessity of life. The way in which this aspect of work enters people's experience is most revealing.

'What do you first think of when you think of work?' 'That's a good one. A sense of livelihood, life and death. There is no other means of living—not for the likes of us.' This person related the most elemental experience, the experience of life and death, to work as a means of living. Yet the universal element of this experience is weakened by the division of people into

[13] The alternative explanation would be that workers are more interested in money than other people.

[14] The fact that money has been mentioned relatively infrequently may indicate that other satisfactions have come to the foreground for the people of the Commonwealth. It may also denote a lack of significance which the goals of the organization have for the people of the Commonwealth.

those who have to work and those who do not have to work. 'The likes of us' are those for whom 'there is no other means of living'. The others are those who instead of working for money let their money 'work' for them.

This is a factor of great importance in understanding the basic experience of work. The people of the Commonwealth like all people in Western industrialized countries live in a society where a living does not necessarily have to be made by work. On the whole people do not experience this situation as objectionable, as indicated by their answers to the questions: 'You either work to make money or you let your money work for you. Could you comment on this?'[15] Their responses show that—for reasons to be clarified later—their ethical view of the world is stunted. Yet the need to give an ethical meaning to work is strong.

A person experienced work 'As a means of providing my family with the necessities of life and something to keep my hands and mind gainfully employed during the hours of daylight. To be gainfully employed means to do something that I am interested in. When I say gainfully employed I think of this as opposed to bookmaker's clerk at a racecourse—seems a waste to me.' He transcends the sheer necessity of working by seeing in work something interesting, productive and ethically positive.

The need for ethically meaningful or creative work is a relatively exceptional attribute of the basic experience of work. This does not mean that it is not a deeply felt need. It means that this need has been so inadequately satisfied that it no longer enters into people's expectations.[16]

Only one person answered the question: 'What do you first think of when you think of work?' by an explicit reference to

[15] Only one person spoke about 'sponging on other people', two spoke about 'the idle rich'; one objected to money acquired 'dishonestly'.

[16] In a world in which 'capital' enters human consciousness as a 'creative' agent on the same or on a higher plane than man, the experience of true creativity must be numbed or relegated to a sphere of life which is separated from the world of work. This is an important factor which must be seen in connection with the whole conception of society which decisively influences the experience of work.

work as a creative act: 'You are here to express life, to create, you help keeping things in order.' Here is an elemental experience of work as creative formation of the human and social order and as creative participation in life. This person also expressed a concern for deeper values than present-day 'materialism' and a desire to create opportunities for 'a better life', to 'start something different and to see it grow.' Work thus experienced becomes a participation in the creative process through which man—made in the image of his Creator—realizes himself.[17]

While this response is important because of its uniqueness, it expresses a potential experience which manifests itself in some form whenever it has a chance. At Scott Bader this is particularly pronounced in the laboratory where we find the clearest traces of an awareness of work as something productive and potentially creative. A person who mentioned first 'analysis of competitor's products, chemical analysis' spoke about 'finding out, discovering. Knowing that nothing is going to be the same because you don't know where you are ending up when you start.' The nature of the work done by this person is unlikely to lead to any great discovery but he experiences participation in a process of discovery and development.

A similar feeling is expressed by another person working in the laboratory. He answered the question: 'What do you first think of when you think of work?' in these words: 'Certainly something that is very pleasing and good to do. Something that there is an incentive to work at. It's not dirty work. You are building things up all the time. Something where the future is unknown is more interesting than something that's routine.' This response which contains various aspects of work experience emphasizes the creative element of developing a potentiality which may bring fruits in the future.

[17] This view of work finds its clearest expression in the original Hebrew view of work according to which work meant participating in the creation of a world which was not yet fully created and hence needed the collaboration of man and God. See Adriano Tilgher, *Work through the Ages*. New York 1930. See M. Sibley and others, *Personality, Work and Community*, Chicago 1953, Part II, p. 94.

When the nature of the work is such that an experience of a creative contribution is more difficult to have—as it is in the factory—the need for productive participation expresses itself often in pride of doing a job well and in a sense of responsibility for the work.

A person who had a deeply rooted commitment to the Commonwealth said: 'Well, going there is not just a matter of going to work. It's more of a pleasure.' To the comment of his wife, that it is bread and butter, he responded 'It's more than a job, I take pride in it.' The rejection of the idea that working at Scott Bader is just having a job is significant.

A sense of responsibility was shown by a person who thought first of the reactors and wondered 'what should be going on in them'. Another expressed his interest in speaking about 'the production angle, getting the materials through, getting them made, out to the customer'. He specifically mentioned his concern for 'getting more orders' from the customers. Other people wondered about the quality of their work and asked whether 'the previous work is satisfactory'. Such expressions as 'I think mostly "What is going on there"' or thoughts about 'the difficulties we might meet up with' show at least an incipient sense of responsibility.

About half of the people in the laboratory mentioned a creative aspect of work and between one third and one half of those working in the factory mentioned some responsible involvement with the work process. One person who has a very simple work task even keeps a little note book. 'Well I often make a list out what I am doing next day; I think it is better to do this at home than in the hectic factory. In business generally people rely too much on memory—they could jot it down in a little note-book.'

Management, taking its responsibility for granted, is more impressed by the magnitude of the work to be done. 'I can't say I leave the office and forget; the problems come back.' Or: 'I think first of all of piles of paper—the thought of getting through masses of documents, letters, making decisions.' 'I think of a big mass of something that has to be moved.'

In these responses the 'labouring' aspect of work emerges as a mental 'labouring' activity. In the laboratory and in the factory the 'labouring' aspect appears more in connection with the experience of work as a necessity than in connection with the responsibilities or the painful aspects of work. This is confirmed by the answers to the questions about fatigue. Though people are tired after work, they are not exhausted and after some relaxation they are able to do other things.[18]

The absence of pain is not equally balanced by a presence of joy in spite of many positive aspects of work. It is remarkable that work is relatively rarely reduced to a job. Only three people spoke about a job when asked 'What do you first think of when you think of work?' A person working in the laboratory said 'I think of my job, the two go together.' A factory worker: 'It is a case of going there to do a common job'. Another: 'I just more or less wonder what job I will be having the next day. Or about the job I'm already on. If the previous work is satisfactory—if it's holding good.' These people use 'job' more in a colloquial sense than as an indication of a meaningless task to be performed.

However, evaluating all responses, we must conclude that the link to an ultimate reality is tenuous.

VI

Work and the place of work evoke manifold and divergent ideas in the minds of the people. But we can discern clear trends marking the basic experience of work.

The outstanding feature is the neutrality of people's basic experience of work. Neutrality does not merely mean that the image of work is rather colourless. It is true that no vivid images are evoked by the first thoughts about work. It is also true that the working life is experienced as a fairly uneventful life, as shown in the answer to the question: 'What event in your working life has given you the greatest satisfaction?'[19] But

[18] Asked 'Does your job make you physically tired?' over one third answered with a straightforward 'no', about one third with a 'yes', others mentioned mental fatigue.

[19] Awareness of one's own power, promotion and approval were mentioned most frequently.

neutrality means more. It denotes the following pattern of awareness.

(i) The outright negative aspects of work have been largely eliminated. Work is neither a harsh labouring activity nor is it performed in a bad environment and under the lash of a stern foreman or supervisor. Typically work is not merely a means to make money.

(ii) There are beautiful natural surroundings and a happy atmosphere. There is a developing sense of responsibility.

(iii) And yet, the basic experience of work is marked more by absences than by presences. Elemental qualities come to the foreground here and there but a deeper sense of purpose and meaning is little developed. Only some people experience work as a creative activity. There seems to be little awareness of an ethical or religious universe.

There are systematic differences between office, laboratory and factory. The creative element is more strongly expressed in the laboratory. In the factory work is more often experienced as a concrete process and as a means to earn a living. The lack of creative expression is compensated by the search for a responsible participation. However there are common elements which are well summed up in the following response: 'The first thing I think of when I think of work is that work is a necessity for life. If it can be done in a happy atmosphere that we got at Wollaston—it's very much better than if it is overcrowded by insecurity and unhappiness.' The necessity is made acceptable because a 'happy atmosphere' has replaced 'insecurity and unhappiness'. But the necessity is not transcended in a meaningful activity.

Undoubtedly the Commonwealth has been the decisive factor in creating a happy atmosphere at Scott Bader. But nobody mentioned the Commonwealth when talking about the first impressions of work.

This could be explained by the tendency to turn towards the actual work process rather than towards the new structure of power and value within which work takes place. This explanation has validity which is substantiated by the fact that the Commonwealth was mentioned repeatedly in answering other questions pertaining to the experience of work.[20] However, it does not adequately explain the failure to mention the Commonwealth in connection with the basic experience of work.[21]

We can understand this situation if we ask ourselves what the fundamental meaning of the Commonwealth in the sphere of work would be. It would mean an experience of work as a meaningful personal-communal activity with a human purpose. This is exactly the kind of experience which is largely absent. The Commonwealth has affected the basic experience of work by creating a new atmosphere but it has not yet penetrated to its inner core, its ultimate meaning.

As we further examine strategic dimensions of work we will better understand this conclusion.

[20] The Commonwealth was mentioned by a sixth of the people when asked 'Now we want to discuss what comes to your mind when you use the words "Scott Bader" '.

[21] People, for example, mentioned the product, the work process, the work place and physical environment when questioned about Scott Bader—but they did not mention the Commonwealth when questioned about their work and their place of work.

Chapter 20
Things, means and ends

I

The meaning of work is decisively influenced by the role which things play in the world of work. People work with instruments, tools and machines. They produce a product. All these are things which have a concrete aspect; they are the 'stuff' with which work is directly concerned, the 'material' to be formed.

In this chapter we are primarily concerned with the things with which people work and only incidentally with the product. When we look at these things as concrete objects we find certain mechanical, chemical, physical, aesthetic or spiritual qualities. These qualities give a specific form and purpose to the object. A sewing machine, for example, has the qualities which make it suitable for sewing. A weaving loom has quite a different end: it is meant to produce cloth. Since the purpose of a thing which is defined by its mechanical, chemical, physical, aesthetic or spiritual qualities is independent from the particular social system within which the thing is used, we call it a universal purpose. A universal purpose is a human purpose, not a purpose peculiar to a capitalist, a communist, a socialist, or a mixed economy. In the language of economics, thinking in terms of universals means thinking in 'real terms' as distinguished from 'monetary terms'. To think in real terms means to abstract from all social relationships (symbolized by money) as well as from the institutional framework within which work takes place. 'Real terms' deal with the *thing as such.*'

The universal purpose of things must be understood in relation to the people who use the things in the work process as well as in relation to those who use the product resulting from this process. Seen in relation to the worker, the universal meaning of the things used as instruments, tools and machines is to facilitate the work process, to make it less fatiguing and to reduce the time necessary for work.

When things enter the organization of work, they enter into mean-ends relationships different from the universal purpose which they fulfil as concrete means of production. Within the organization of work things serve the purpose of the organization. The organizational purpose differs for different social systems. In a capitalist society, for example, the organizational purpose of production is to sell at a profit. 'Things' become capital and are subject to the vicissitutes of markets. In such a context a machine may destroy the meaning of work since its use is not primarily related to human values. It may make work repetitious and monotonous or may even displace workers. These are not universal qualities of the machine but are results of the specific *way* in which a historically unique social system uses the things necessary for work. For example, a machine may enhance the meaning of work when used by a worker for one hour and the identical machine may destroy the meaning when used for eight hours a day. The specific meaning of the machine depends upon the social organization within which the machine is used, not merely upon its universal purpose, *the thing as such*.

The meaning which things have in the world of work is, therefore, determined by (i) their universal purpose (ii) by the specific purpose which they fulfil in a given system and (iii) by the interaction of these two aspects. The universal is always present and interacts in some way with the historically specific. Even if the organizational purpose is to sell something on the market, the thing in question must satisfy a human 'need'. And even if a specific social system uses machines in such a way that they destroy the meaning of work, they still may reduce effort and fatigue.

II

To get an understanding of people's experience of the things with which they work we asked them: 'Do the things you work with mean anything to you?' The objective possibilities of choice opened by this question are delineated by the universal aspects of instruments, tools and machines and by the specific roles which they play in different social systems.

As universal agents, machines and tools may evoke interest in the processes which they perform, the functions which they fulfil and the tasks which they accomplish. They may be experienced as co-operating with men, as means of facilitating work. There may be a sensory relationship, an aesthetic experience or an awareness of things as part of the whole life process.

As agents of a historically unique system, instruments, tools and machines may be experienced as means to realize the goals of the organization or one's own goals. The goals of capitalism, socialism—or of the Commonwealth—may affect people's experience. If capitalism is decisive machines may be experienced as competing for job opportunities, or even as the 'cause' of unemployment.

To distinguish as clearly as possible between various factors influencing the meaning which things have in the world of work, we divided the people into four groups according to their primary instruments of work (i) those with managerial responsibilities whose primary instruments of work are their brains and imagination, (ii) those with clerical responsibilities who use typewriters, calculating machines etc. (iii) those whose primary instruments of work are test tubes and related apparatus and (iv) those who use highly mechanized semi-automatic chemical reactors, machines or mechanical implements.[1]

A person in the first group almost defines his existential condition in his answer to the question: 'What do the things you work with mean to you?' 'to dictate letters, use the phone at the right moment, getting wheels to go in the right direction for the benefit of the company.' These activities objectify them-

[1] Asked 'Do the things you work with mean anything to you?' 13 out of 30 people mentioned universal aspects (management: 4; laboratory: 3; factory & maintenance: 6) 13 people mentioned the things they work with as means to an end (management: 5; laboratory: 4; factory & maintenance: 4) 2 people from the factory mentioned common ownership and 7 people mentioned other aspects of the things they work with.

selves in 'the balance sheet, figures, letters, presentations of reports of the company'.

Another person said: 'Most of my work is done with my head or with a telephone . . . I find this a very difficult question. The things I work with are mainly an extension of my personality . . . only their use means something . . . accomplishing certain ends—making a sale or satisfying the customer.' Probed whether he thinks of himself as an end, he commented: 'I was thinking about that angle. To a very large extent I am using my own personality and my own ideas. This is important because you represent Scott Bader as much as yourself. To a very large extent the people with whom you are dealing form their opinion of Scott Bader as an industrial undertaking and of the Commonwealth on the basis of what they see or find in you . . . It is very difficult to see where you are going personally in your work. You do not have the same criteria as an artist and a craftsman. An artist can see himself in his completed work.'

This person has a clear awareness of the things he works with as means to an end and as an extension of his personality. But the meaning of the things he works with is ambiguous since he is not sure about the meaning of his own work. This illustrates the relationship between the inner meaning of work and the meaning of the things with which people work.

For most of the people in this group the work process has an inner meaning and some experience it as part of a life process: 'I get a sense of thrill from making decisions.' Or: 'There is nothing I do that has no meaning to me; every action I do has a meaning. If I am asked to produce a set of figures for a certain purpose I do understand the purpose; in fact I might even have originated the purpose.' Another person considered his work 'a crusade' from which he cannot separate himself and which manifests itself eventually in 'sales figures'.

The physical instruments of production have almost disappeared from the awareness of most managers. They reappear again among those who have the highest integrating function in management. The whole firm entered into their perception of the instruments of work and they were aware that 'some of our reactors are exceptionally well fitted for our purpose, both in size and in their way of working.' This person felt 'very proud to have this equipment as a means for us to work . . . it works out our salvation in a way, because it gives us the income we need.'

He perceived the universal aspects of the tools and machines and their use as means to provide the income needed to live and to build up the Commonwealth. The market situation entered into his vision of means and ends but it is a broad vision. This is indicated in the word "salvation" and expressed more directly in the perception of production as 'co-operation with machinery in a creative manner.' Machines are thus seen as co-operative agents in a creative endeavour. 'I am anxious to see that new plant should be the best and most suitable to us, glad that the equipment is taken care of, is being appreciated for its importance, treated correctly, with proper engineering practice.'

This was said by 'a commercial man' not by an engineer. He is a commercial man with a heart and wide vision, manifesting itself in a perception of the 'things' he works with as encompassing the tools and machines of the whole firm.

A person much closer to engineering brings into the open more problematical aspects of work. He is concerned with managerial and scientific problems and their practical application. Asked what the things he works with mean to him, he first indicated that he is 'satisfied working at a chemical plant' and then spoke of 'a tool which is creating something. The actual physical creation is satisfying, but there is a type of frustration which one gets as a research worker who produces an idea which has no physical reality. It is the abstraction of it which is frustrating.' He contrasted the abstract idea with the actual physical production and the fact that 'from increasing efficiency you see an actual return in money for it, it can be directly interpreted in money values. This is very difficult to do with research ideas.' Asked whether the actual physical process of production and money are on the same or on different levels, he said: 'They are similar, a certain amount of chemicals means a certain amount of money.'

This conversation raises some basic problems pertaining to

the 'thing' character of work particularly the problem of alienation from the concrete aspects of work—and life. The person who spoke to us experienced this problem as abstraction from physical reality. There are good reasons why he is particularly sensitive to this problem.[2] Many people attempt to compensate for this abstraction by concretizing the most abstract of all conceivable things: money. Money after all is either an insignificant little coin or a piece of paper; or a mere figure on a sheet of paper.

To understand this problem of abstraction and concretization we must realize that the 'thing' character of work, the concrete relatedness of people to the physical reality and to the instruments of their work is an aspect of man's relatedness to matter. And matter is symbolic of the maternal, of the feminine.[3] The separation of man from the concrete reality means, therefore, on a deeper level, separation from the earth quality of life. What does man thus separated from his own creative femininity do? One way is to identify with efficiency and money. The inadequate experience of physical reality is compensated by relating things to the presently dominant conception of technical productivity which is devoid of human values. 'Chemicals . . . mean . . . money . . . ' exchange value—not use-value—a thing to be used.

III

The second group—those whose instruments of work are typewriters, calculating machines etc.,—did not have clear feelings about the things they work with. They 'do not really' mean much. 'That's an odd one. I think we will pass that over' indicates ambivalent feelings rather than the neutrality of a blank mind. Noteworthy among this group is only the absence of a negative experience of the instruments of work.

The third group, comprising laboratory technicians of various skills experienced physical instruments on the whole in

2 These are related to his personality and cannot be discussed here.

3 Etymologically 'matter' and 'mater' have the same roots. 'Mater' is the Latin word for 'mother'. The whole 'earth' symbolism of the Chinese relates to the feminine principle of Life.

a positive way but they do not play a significant role. 'The things I work with mean only something as a means to an end. I had to work with electronic equipment in the Forces. A piece of equipment is a piece of equipment. If it does the job, it is good enough. I wouldn't have a piece of equipment that doesn't work in the place.' This is a matter-of-fact attitude which looks at the equipment purely in terms of its functional possibilities, its ability 'to do the job'. Another person spoke about 'precision-instruments' into which a lot of thought has gone and which he sees as wonderful achievements in engineering.

Similar ideas were expressed in the following responses: 'Well, I look upon them as an aid to doing the job I am given to do better and quicker.' Or: 'It does give me a great sense of satisfaction when you achieve something that's workable. You do experiment after experiment without achieving anything. You tend to get a bit frustrated . . . in a way, (the equipment) means something, but it's difficult to explain. The equipment we use is necessary for the job . . .'

Some people's thought turned towards the chemical process of transformation when asked whether the things they work with mean something to them. 'Yes, I think so, I understand or try to find out the chemistry of things'.

'I regard them as the tools of my trade,' expresses a personal feeling which gives to the tools a symbolic and not merely an instrumental character. They become symbols of participation in a corporate body. This person also indicated that he 'can't stand dirty equipment. Can't work with anything that looks inferior or obviously has got a defect.' Here a different aspect of the symbolic character of the equipment comes to light; values which are emotionally charged are attached to it.

Another person spoke about 'a certain nostalgic feeling as you go into the lab. and are surrounded by resin and so on,' adding as an afterthought, 'in a way you are working with pretty dead material.' But his mind came back to the original expression of a nostalgic feeling connected 'with the whole environment, the smell of the place, you get an attachment to it. You feel it is part of your life. If you are ill three or four days and you go back, it feels sort of good to be back—you know.'

The physical atmosphere becomes here a symbol of the psychological atmosphere experienced at work.

IV

The fourth group of people consists of those who do factory or maintenance work. By some of them the instruments and machines are primarily seen as means to an end: 'They have no sentimental value. They are just my assistants', 'They mean a great lot; for the simple reason if you've got a good piece of machinery you know you can get a job done. . . . I want to have as much care taken of them as possible.' Or: 'What do you mean the things, the tools, that's everything except the human—they are just there to do the job, that's all. In my job there's not many things.' Actually there are quite a few things with which this person works but he does not experience them strongly, except in so far as they make the actual work less burdensome: 'they prevent you from going home more tired than you do—as a means to an end'. He perceives a universal function of machines which was mentioned in various ways by other people. 'You can turn out products much better and easier.' Only one person mentioned a negative aspect of chemicals. 'It means dermatitis.' He laughed after having said this—though dermatitis is a skin disease which affects some people as a result of handling certain chemicals. 'Other things mean nasty smells.' Specifically asked about the reactors, he said; 'They need lots of patience.'

There are clear differences in the strength of people's experience of the things they work with. They may mean 'a great lot' or they are 'just there to do the job; that's all.' To judge from people's responses as well as from observation the general feeling among the people is in between these extremes.[4]

'You don't mean the Commonwealth you mean business' was the way a person began to speak about the things he works

[4] Observations made by Roger Hadley have shown that typewriters, for example, are of considerable importance to the people using them. They talk about the different machines and will invite each other to their offices to see a new model.

with 'it must mean something. It means repetition . . . Sometimes it means, not new discoveries, but new methods, new processes.' This person has a strong desire to give a meaning to the endless process of batches going through the reactors. He can see an element of variety, of new processes and methods being introduced. And somehow the Commonwealth lurks in the background. Another person stressed the variety. 'Reactors and that, you mean? Yes they do (mean something) there is quite a variation in their performance, variation in their temperature and something different going on with them all the time.'

A person who is more concerned with maintenance than with process work relates his tools and the materials he works with to learning about his job. 'They help you learn more. . . . You learn different things about different metals, hardness and softness and things like that.'

An even wider meaning is given to the machines and tools by a person who said: 'I suppose they mean my life to me . . . the whole concept of work, where I am and how we are working is life to me. It is my life, working.'

A number of people derived meaning from the common ownership of the things they worked with. 'I feel we own them.' 'They are a means of earning a living, of producing something that will be of use to somebody else, and, in our particular case, they're part of something we ourselves own.' Note the progression in this response: first he thought of machines as a means to earn a living, understandably so since he had experienced unemployment. Then he expressed a sense of productiveness: 'producing something that will be of use to somebody else'—a rather exceptional reference to use-value. He experienced machines as meaningful because they produce something that satisfies human needs. His awareness was in terms of human values rather than in terms of a price-tag, the marketability of the product. Finally he spoke of the common-ownership as the culmination of the meaning which the things he works with have for him. He thus expressed the highest awareness of the machines and tools which we find in the factory.[5]

[5] There are a number of people for whom the machines and tools mean various things without having a very clear meaning. A shift worker answered

V

The general picture of people's experience of the things they work with has a few clear marks of orientation but, on the whole, its lines are not too sharply drawn and its colours not too pronounced. A neutral tone predominates and the 'things' have more often an instrumental character rather than a symbolic quality.

Historically unique aspects were mentioned only exceptionally. There are several reasons for this. They are more likely to be negative since they manifest themselves in competition between men and machines, in unemployment—or in repetitiveness. The absence of a negative awareness may therefore be considered a result of the impact of the Commonwealth. But it is also due to a tendency to close one's eyes to those aspects of the social order which conflict with the prevailing perception of society.

References to the universal aspects of the instruments and machines were more frequent—they were scattered all over the picture. They appeared as awareness of technical processes, of the time and effort saving aspects and of the creative possibilities of the things with which people work. There was also a sense of participation in the life process and occasionally an awareness of things as instruments for the creation of use-values. But only exceptionally were these universal aspects part of an articulate experience of work as humanly meaningful. Hence the dominant experience was of things as means to an end, as instruments within an organization which is taken for granted because it is removed from the focus of attention.

The experience of the things with which people work varied greatly for different occupational groups. Thrill and involvement in work can be found among managers but they give little evidence of a relationship to the concrete world of work.

---

the question about the meaning of the things he works with by asking: 'What do you mean? I got no tool except a shovel'. Asked about the reactors, he said: 'I like to see them all clean, looking all right.' Another person also answered with a question: 'The reactors or the chemicals?'. To the comment 'both' he responded: 'Yes, certain chemicals mean certain things.'

Among the clerks in the office we can discern neither enthusiasm nor relatedness to concrete objects. People in the laboratories experience the things they work with mainly as means to an end. In the factory we find the most varied experiences: on the one hand no meaning to speak of, on the other hand, the meaning of creative participation and common ownership.

This polarity is typical for the factory. People working in the factory are most affected by those forces inherent in the present organization of work which do violence to human development and destroy human values. At the same time they have the deepest need for a more human organization of work. Being strongly under the influence of destructive forces, they have a good deal of apathy but once this apathy is overcome, they are more open to a new world.

They also show their sensitivity to the forces shaping the world of work by the ornamentations which they give to their place of work. They create their own aesthetic in a world which has traditionally lacked any aesthetic quality. These ornamentations—pictures of 'pin-up girls'—are not visible to the casual visitor but they are easily accessible to those who work there.

Such pictures are typical for our factories and offices. At least partially, they result from a deep need to compensate for inadequate contact with the concrete and feminine aspects of life. The present organization of work has a tendency to cut people off from these aspects and to inhibit the expression of true feelings, of immediately experienced human values and of 'reason'.[6] As a result the undifferentiated-feminine, the commercialized collective sexuality of the not too discriminating woman is likely to assert itself. It asserts itself to maintain some semblance of sanity in a world which has lost a true sense of what is sane and what is not sane.

Though it is difficult to make comparisons, the image of collective sexuality may play a smaller role at Scott Bader than it does at other places. If true, we can discern here the influence

[6] Reason as used here must be distinguished from rationality. Reason combines thought and feeling. Reason as such is not feminine in quality but contains a feminine element absent in rationality which is pure logic.

of the Commonwealth. But the commercialization of sex remains symptomatic for a fundamental aspect of people's relatedness to the things they work with—the concrete aspects of their work. It expresses most clearly the impact of a historically unique organization of work which uses technology without adequate regard for human values.

Chapter 21
The product, use and exchange values

I

The product is the end-result of the work process. It links the firm with a market economy. It is also a link between the world of concrete realities and the world of organization. Being at the cross-roads of these worlds the product is particularly suited to evoke a fundamental orientation towards work. It demands a choice of direction from us. It calls upon us to give it some meaning.

The final product which the people at Scott Bader produce is quite formless. As a liquid it is among the least differentiated 'things' we could imagine. What we can 'see' in the product depends therefore not so much upon our eyes but upon our minds. It depends more upon the whole range of feelings and thoughts which are connected with the product, its creation and its use rather than upon the concrete vision of the finished products in which the formless liquid is eventually to find form.

As we listen to what the people of the Commonwealth have to say in answering the question: 'Does the product mean anything to you?' we shall get an understanding of what they can see with their senses as well as with their inner eyes of experience.

The objective possibilities of choice are primarily defined by the two basic properties of any product: (i) its concrete mechanical, chemical, physical, aesthetic and spiritual attributes, which allow the product to satisfy a human need and constitute use-value, (ii) the possibility to express the value of a product in monetary terms. The product has not only concrete qualities but also an abstract form. It has not only use but also exchange value for which we account in terms of costs and which finds expression in a price.

People may be aware of the product as a use-value or as an exchange value. The latter opens the world of markets and organizations to the possible vision of the product. Awareness of the concrete reality of use-value means awareness of the universal aspects of the product. Awareness of the world of exchange value, means awareness of specific historical dimensions.

Since the historically unique dimensions are expressed in different organizations of work, different structures of power and value, the meaning of the product differs as the goals of these organizations and the nature of these structures differ. The range of possible choice may be defined in terms of the values of the existing capitalist market economy on the one hand and a social order as visualized by the Commonwealth on the other hand.

A developed awareness of the product in terms of Commonwealth principles would manifest itself in an awareness of tension between the existing market economy and a social order as envisaged by the Commonwealth. This is particularly true since the Commonwealth introduces a limiting principle into the world of exchange values: its product may not be sold for purposes of war or preparation for war.

Besides belonging to the world of use—and exchange value, the product belongs to the person or group who has created it. In so far as people are related to the product, they bestow on it certain qualities of their own: good workmanship, a sense of achievement, success, etc. In so far as people are alienated from the product it may lose all meaning. The range between a positive experience of meaning bestowed on the product and meaninglessness denotes an important possibility of choice.

II

The experience of the meaning of the product is related to the specific 'product' of one's work and does not depend exclusively upon the finished product. Those who work in the factory are closest to the finished product, even if they do not see much of it before it gets filled into drums. For the people working in the laboratory the finished product may be a reaction in a test tube. The product of the office staff is either an idea which sets into motion some productive process; or it is a piece of paper containing words, sentences, figures, graphs and once in a while even a picture.

The following conversation introduces us to the vision of people whose main product consists in ideas and the activation of ideas.

RH: Does the product mean anything to you?

He: What, the balance sheet? That's the product that one's aiming for. Certainly the product is that we've done things through the Commonwealth. There's a very definite satisfaction in that.

RH: What about the physical product?

He: Yes, if one has been away for some time one has a sort of homely feeling almost, in regard to the factory smells, like a baker would feel after he'd baked a batch of successful loaves—the smell means money. For me, the smell of resin is exciting, like a farmer smells manure. The worse the smell the better the farmer!

The balance sheet—pure exchange value—springs immediately to his mind whereas the exciting smell comes to consciousness when he has been away from the place for some time. The smell is inhaled as a chemical substance but becomes quickly transformed into a vision of money and security. The more fundamental satisfaction, however, is attached to the Commonwealth. The product is experienced as a symbol of a useful human service rendered through the Commonwealth and made possible by the success of the business. It is not seen in terms of substantive qualities of use-value. The managerial task gave rise to a vision of 'successful loaves'. There are good, warm and fresh loaves of bread, and there are old and stale loaves. A loaf of bread is a symbol of earth, of growth, of the bread of life. Like the farmer's smell of manure 'a successful loaf' conjures up images consisting of a mixture of these elements.

While for this person the values of the Commonwealth were an essential aspect of success, for others success alone has become the meaning of the product: 'I have tended to identify my success with it' Or: 'I want to be successful, I want 'X' (name of the product) to be successful'. This person felt very much emotionally 'entangled' with the success of the product and looks each month 'with great excitement upon the sales figures wanting to know how well we are doing, whether we are better than we were last month'.

The excitement and the emotional entanglement are concentrated on the movement of the sales figures—on pure exchange value. The product appears not only as a symbol of success but the striving for success seems to have swallowed up the product. Such a preoccupation with success is very widespread in industry particularly when the managerial task is reduced to a game devoid of the concrete reality of things and the ethical reality of human beings. At Scott Bader there is a tendency to see the managerial task in connection with the human community. Whenever this happens the product is seen not merely as success in a game but as success in a humanly relevant task which is contingent upon the success of the business. Though concern for the latter is very strong, we find at the very centre of managerial responsibility an awareness of the product as use-value as distinguished from the exchange-value of obsessional success and the game of power.

'Yes, the product such as synthetic resin which contains a lot of brain power in its nature is certainly a remarkable achievement.' This person saw the product as the result of man's power to partake of creation. He mentioned a new product, spoke about its uses and the improvements it makes possible. He considered it 'a source of satisfaction to know that the product is a service that we can render' and he mentioned 'the ordinary pride of the manufacturer who is able to produce something worthwhile in the context of friendly competition'. Here is a clear awareness of use-values and the rendering of a service.

For a person who combines managerial responsibility with technical work the 'quality' of the product 'and its quantity is a measure of the efficiency of the plant process. You must have one to measure the efficiency of the other.' The quality—and the quantity of the product constitute the concrete reality of the product. For this person this reality is swallowed up by the idea of efficiency—a successful loaf is an efficient loaf.

On the whole people with managerial responsibilities were as much aware of the product as use-value as they were of exchange value. Success is primary, efficiency secondary.

III

For the people whose instruments of work are typewriters, calculating machines, etc., the product meant very little 'No, not really, I type about it but I don't see it afterwards. We had a tour round the factory but they used such technical terms. I know what things they make but not what materials they use.' Or: 'It does not mean very much . . . we are not told very much about it. You are given an open day once every ten years.'[1] A desire to know more about the product and to see it more often was strong among this group. But a vision of the use of the product was exceptional: 'I think it is interesting in as far as the things it ends up in, car bodies and radomes.'

For the people who work in the laboratory the product often meant a sense of achievement: Use-value was a subsidiary experience, awareness of exchange value is absent: 'The work we are doing is analytical. The product of our analysis gives me a sense of achievement.' Or: 'There again, the sense of achievement, the fact that you produced something from something else. In a way it's like looking on Johnny as a product of Ruth and I, we are proud of him as I am proud of the things that leave us.' Here the product is perceived as the child of one's work, as creative achievement; it is like little Johnny, his son.

'We try to achieve the best. I can hardly say perfection. All that we do is concentrated in getting people to use the material to its best advantage.' This person perceived the product in

[1] On open days all departments and sections of the firm are open to anybody. There have been only two open days before 1963 when induction courses for all employees started. These courses include talks on the organization of work and tours of the laboratories and factories. There were also talks and discussions on the structure of the Commonwealth and the opportunities for participation.

terms of achievement and in terms of use-value. The latter forms the main theme in the following response: 'We put a lot of effort into giving people a good product.'

'I don't touch the finished product but I'm interested in any change in raw materials that have gone through my hands.' Here participation in the technical process of transformation is primary; the product itself seems remote. 'We don't see the finished articles. In actual fact we are working with creative material but we don't use them creatively. You can make something hideous out of it or something beautiful . . . you feel you have pretty complete control of the product, you get what you want from it. In a sense you are boss of the resin you are using. You can cure it quickly and slowly, you have control of it.' Creativity, the possibility of a beautiful or ugly end product, control over work, rather than being controlled by it are elements of this, very sensitive, experience of the product.

IV

The people who work in the factory and on maintenance had a strong desire 'to see' the product. They had some sense of achievement and satisfaction, an awareness of the use-value of the product and of the potentialities of human relatedness. They also kept an eye on the market situation, on exchange values.

'Well, I'd like to see what it's turned into . . . We know what it's used in.' The desire to see in spite of the fact that he knows the use of the product indicates the need for more than a visual image. It shows that a meaningful experience is lacking.[2] 'No I don't suppose the product means anything, except it's a product. You don't see the end product. It is nice to think of it as an end product.' Actually he thinks of 'aircraft, car bodies, children's toys and new corrugated lights'. But in spite of these visual images he misses something of importance, because he does not experience any meaning in the product.

Others, though they also missed something, found some

[2] There is a person who gains satisfaction 'when I know what it is.' But for others knowledge without seeing something more in the product is not enough.

meaning in producing the product: 'I don't make a finished product that you can see in the shop. But to turn out a good product means satisfaction whether you see it in a shop or not.' Or: 'It means problems and a challenge. You're always meeting a challenge to do something about these things.'

For some people, the sense of satisfaction is connected with knowledge about the product. 'The product means something when I know what it is'. 'I know a bit, which makes it more interesting.'

A large number of people derive satisfaction from the quality of the product or its use. 'Yes, it means a lot. They all have different uses and we have quite a range of products. Everything means something different as regards the various products.' 'I feel proud of it because it's new, with a future.' Or: 'It means a lot to produce something that's good. If we produce something useful to the community, I am proud of it. It is nice to know your products are improving things for people. Plastics in the home is marvellous. There is not enough of it.'[3]

A number of people mentioned the quality of the product in connection with exchange rather than use-values: 'Yes, it wants to be the highest quality we can turn out at a price to suit our customers and get a fair profit.' 'Yes the product means something as long as they can sell it. It is a waste of time to make anything that does not work out right.'[4] 'It means something in a good many ways. If it goes out first class we're almost sure to go on getting the orders for it. Then the firm will go on all right. Apart from this it's our living too, isn't it?'

Here the product is seen as part of an organization of work which makes unemployment possible. The fear of unemployment—in spite of the security given by the Commonwealth, comes out most clearly in the following response: 'The product means that it keeps me in work'.

[3] A similar response was: 'I believe we're making something that eventually goes into products that are a great deal of use to people—it goes into so many products that eventually practically every member of the public can get benefit from it.'

[4] This person also indicated that he gets a sense of achievement if the product comes out right.

Exceptional is the awareness of the deeper ethical or religious meaning of use-value. 'Whatever I do, whether it is working or leisure, I want to make it part of my life. I don't want just to work eight hours a day and then be finished; make it part of your life. I find satisfaction in it. Our product is used for something that will bring enjoyment. A product that is contrary to my principles and beliefs—I wouldn't handle it. That's a good question. You put something in my mind.'

V

Different existential conditions of work give rise to different experiences of the product.

People with managerial responsibilities identify the product with success. They are about equally aware of exchange and use value. The experience of people with office responsibilities is rather colourless. Use-value emerges incidentally but the outstanding feature is yearning for a meaningful vision. People connected with the laboratory have a predominant sense of achievement. They are aware of use-value but not of exchange value. The experience of people working in the factory and on maintenance is the most varied one. The extremes range from relatively little meaning to awareness of a service rendered to people and strong relatedness to a human community. For some the experience of use-value is connected with a sense of good workmanship; awareness of exchange value is often due to fears about one's work opportunity. A deep quest for meaning is also apparent in this group.[5]

The differences and similarities between these four groups are significant. The predominant theme in the first group is success, in the second a certain haziness, in the third achieve-

[5] Asked 'Does the product mean anything to you?' 30 people gave 37 responses. Of these 11 referred to the quality bestowed on the product (management: success: 3, other: 1; laboratory: sense of achievement: 5; factory: good workmanship: 2); 11 referred to use value (management: 3; clerks: 1; laboratory: 3; factory: 4) 3 referred to exchange value (management): and 4 to both use and exchange value (factory); in addition there were 8 'other responses'. Of these 4 indicated that the product had not much meaning, 4 referred to other aspects of the product.

ment and in the fourth a good deal of emphasis on use and exchange values combined with a certain difficulty in giving meaning to the product.

Success is an ambivalent goal since it can be relatively easily divorced from the concrete reality of things and the essential qualities of a person. It may be measured by a curve on an office wall, going up (and down) from month to month and year to year. This possible split is an occupational risk connected with managerial activities. The Commonwealth and the implicit awareness of use-value has a tendency to counteract this risk.

The prevalence of 'achievement' in the laboratory indicates that participation in the technical process bestows meaning on the product. The absence of the perception of the product in terms of exchange value has various reasons: (i) The work in the laboratory is not directly connected with exchange value as is the work of management; (ii) people derive enough satisfaction from their work to make escape into abstract substitute satisfactions unnecessary. Finally, (iii) they did not experience unemployment in a way which makes them anxious about their work opportunities as did many workers.

The fear that the product may not find a market and that there may not be any jobs available comes to the surface in the factory. It is expressed in a concern with exchange value. Workers have as much of a desire and need to bestow meaning on the product as people in the other groups. But it is more difficult to do so in the factory. Hence 'good workmanship'—which is the factory equivalent to success and achievement—cannot assert itself as a strong trend, and use-value though strongly experienced by some is not a prevalent theme.

The common element in all four groups is the desire to 'see' meaning in the product, not just to see a product. Indeed, the latter is much more than a physical reality—it is a symbol of visible purpose combining the need for a relationship to the concrete reality of things with the need for a purposeful meaningful activity.

The difficulties encountered in giving meaning to the product are primarily due to the difficulties of seeing something with one's inner eyes rather than to the difficulties of forming a visual image. Not distance from a finished product but distance from a meaningful purpose is decisive in evoking complaints that the product can not be seen. Whenever there is some meaning connected with the product distance from the finished product is not decisive and does not prevent a visual image arising.

On the whole people are neither alienated from the product nor do they have a strong meaning attached to it. The link between the product and the overall organization of work is rarely seen. There is no awareness of a tension between Commonwealth ideals and the actual market economy. This indicates certain limitations of awareness. The reasons for this situation will become apparent soon.

Chapter 22

People and service to the community

I

Our relationships to things and to the product of our work cannot be separated from our relationships to people. Purpose and meaning are attributes of man and of the human community. They are inseparable from our experience of ourselves, our fellow human beings, and our involvement in the human community. They express themselves in our sense of service to the community.

The quality of people's relationships to each other is determined by (i) the development of human potentialities (expressing itself in a certain 'structure of being'), (ii) the development of social organization (expressing itself in a certain 'structure of work')[1] and (iii) their interrelationships.

(i) Among the manifold aspects of the development of human potentialities two points affecting our awareness of each other must be mentioned here. First the significance of an awareness (or lack of awareness) of human potentialities which are common to all men and not rooted in a specific culture or social order. Second the significance of an understanding of 'projections' in people's relationships.

Unless there is something universally human, people could not meet as human beings at all. A universal human quality enables people to meet spontaneously, to express feelings and thoughts quite independent from the particular organization of work within which they meet. But whenever people meet, two factors enter into their awareness of each other: (*a*) the extent

[1] The concept 'structure' is usually not used with reference to work. It denotes organization and technology. In the actual experience of work these two dimensions are intermingled. It is, however, of great importance to distinguish clearly between them.

to which they are able to see the qualities which other people actually have and (*b*) the extent to which they see certain qualities in other people which these people in fact do not have at all or have to a much smaller—or greater—extent. This latter process is called 'projecting'.

A person may be seen as kind, harsh, considerate or aloof; as lazy, hardworking, as a good or as a bad member of the Commonwealth. A particular person may in fact have these qualities. But it may also be that the person activates something in me which makes me attribute these qualities to him or her though he or she does not have them. I may also underestimate or exaggerate certain qualities which a person actually has to some extent. Whenever this happens we deal with projections rather than awareness of an objectively true quality or situation.

Projections are particularly easy to evoke when people meet who are at different 'levels' in the organization of work—to use a traditional metaphor. People who have power over us or people over whom we have power are often seen as quite different from what they actually are. This is all the more true when the power is resented or if there is a need to rationalize power exercised over other people. The presence or absence of projections is therefore a good indication of the tensions created by the organization of work—as well as of the general state of development of man's potentialities.

(ii) The organization of work affects the quality of people's relationships since it attributes roles to people and makes them perform certain functions. Organization gives rights, privileges, obligations and responsibilities. These are bound to effect the quality of relationships between people. We often meet another person as a 'functionary' rather than as a human being. We play roles rather than being ourselves. We carry respectable masks instead of expressing true feelings. Roles and functions may become all embracing and penetrate our whole being. We may lose sight of our own values and our true individuality and become the role which we are expected to play.

The division of work among the people is an important element determining roles and functions, obligations and responsibilities. We must see this division in a wider historical perspective. In the early stages of social development the division of tasks and responsibilities was rudimentary. A family produced most of what it consumed. Gradually this integral work task was divided among more and more people. Today we literally depend for our livelihood upon thousands if not millions of other people. We are part of an organized network of relationships which influences the quality of all relationships to people —outside as well as inside a firm. It determines *who meets whom* in a particular firm as well as *the way* in which people meet.

(iii) The interrelationship between the development of human potentialities and the roles and functions which people have is so intimate that the distinction between these two elements needs more illustration than their interdependency. To be able to differentiate between these we must be aware of the universal dimension of life. The universal quality of human relatedness allows people (i) to meet as human beings at any particular time or stage of development and (ii) to grow and move from one stage of development to the next.

Without this universal quality people could only meet in a worker-chargehand, a manager-managed, a chairman of committee-committee member, etc., relationship. These relationships would be completely mechanical and stereotyped. They would be without meaning and purpose because meaning and purpose have their roots in the soil of human universals. Without this universal quality people would furthermore be forever contained within a given historical organization. They could neither develop an existing nor build a new organization of work.

The purposes and goals of any particular organization are historically specific expressions of human potentialities corresponding to a given stage in the development of human consciousness. Roles and functions change, therefore, as new potentialities come to the surface and demand expression. But the central reference point of these developments remains the human universals, those needs and aspirations which all men share. To be truly related to other people we must be aware of this universal quality whether people meet within a firm or in a wider community.

Since people and things are intimately interrelated in the work process, we can express the necessity of an awareness of human universals as a necessity of awareness of use-value. To establish a link between work and a wider human community people must be aware of use-value because the latter expresses the universal attributes of a product. Without a consciousness of the product as use-value we are not able to experience work as a service to man.

II

We get our first understanding of the quality of people's relationships as we analyse their answers to the question: 'Who do you work with?' Do people consider (i) other individuals, (ii) the immediate work group or (iii) everybody in the department as co-workers?[2]

The clearest pattern emerges for the shift-workers in the factory. They all indicated that they work with their fellow shift workers. Only one of them included the plant manager. None of the shift workers mentioned a day worker though the shifts rotate in such a way that they meet each other during two out of three weeks. Equally a day worker, although he comes into contact with shift workers, mentioned only the other day workers. A maintenance worker spoke only about his own workmate. On the whole people considered those as co-workers with whom they have direct and frequent interactions and/or people to whom they have an immediate relationship of responsibility.

Among those who mentioned everyone in the department there are two rather distinct sub-groups (*a*) those who work together in a room although they may not be part of a work group encompassing the whole room and (*b*) those who are in charge of a work group. The latter have more group-feelings than feelings of authority. One person for example talked about 'a group of people in the plant', another said: 'there are fifteen of

[2] The following analysis was made by Roger Hadley.

us' and a third, although referring to his supervisory position when saying 'I've had quite a number of them there' continued to speak in terms of 'we' and 'us': 'We work in conjunction with others as well. We've had them in with us when we've been pressed.'

A comparative analysis of the answers of those who mentioned everyone in their department and of those who mentioned only individual people shows that these differences are often the result of individual differences, peculiarities of experience, and personal difficulties of establishing relationships. Most people who consider only specific individuals as their co-workers worked closely with other people, but somehow felt cut off from them.[3]

Up to a certain point the group of those who were considered co-workers had a tendency to increase with increased responsibility. The plant managers experienced all the people in their plants as co-workers. But in general managerial circles people limited their references to the group of people they work with directly. They did, as a rule, not refer to people more than one step removed from them. This pattern is due to a variety of factors. Most of the plant managers are more part of the work team than being merely supervisors. They may give a hand with work when needed. In appearance, most of them are indistinguishable from the workers. They usually wear the same kind of work clothes—green overalls—as the day and shift workers. They have their tea with the workers in the canteen. Outside work, plant managers and day or shift workers also have a good deal in common.[4] Many have a similar background and live in the same kind of housing. Most of them mix quite readily outside work. None of these factors apply to the general managers. The more pronounced difference in work tasks between general managers and workers as compared with plant managers and workers plays also a role.

[3] In some cases their work was not directly related to the work of other people. But this was not true in all cases.

[4] In assessing these attitudes the local situation should be taken into consideration. The bosses in the local boot and shoe industry are said to be or familiar terms with their workers.

While this situation makes it easier for plant managers to include the workers into their experience of co-workers, the workers do not always reciprocate the plant managers' experience. This indicates a loosening of the traditional hierarchical structure without new clearly communal forms and corresponding feelings having emerged yet.

III

To get an understanding of the communal bonds between people is an extremely difficult task. People may be rather matter-of-fact and even cool yet when a real problem arises, they may show qualities of a deeper commitment.

The overwhelming majority of the people of the Commonwealth consider the people they work with as their friends:[5] 'I consider all of them to be my friends' . . . 'Normal sort of friendly relationships I expect to exist among workers.' Or: 'As far as I am concerned, I'm just one of the company—everybody is my fellow-worker.' The word 'company' preserves here some of its original meaning of 'compagnons' who join their fortunes in work.[6]

For most people friendship means a friendly attitude, not something 'intimate'. Often it includes giving a helping hand: 'you have grown to get on with each other well and help each other when you get behind.'

People in the factory expressed most frequently a willingness to help each other: 'How would you term "friends"? I would term "mates" rather than "friends". A friend is someone you would confide your trouble in. I don't think you could confide your troubles in your workmates.' Or 'Well, what should I say, workmates? . . . A friend is one you meet outside work'. Another person referred to his co-worker as a friend 'when in a

[5] For a good majority the people whom they consider their co-workers coincide with the people whom they consider their friends. For about a fifth the group of friends is smaller and for about the same number the group of friends is larger than those they work with. These differences are largely explained by individual circumstances which do not concern us here.

[6] Originally the word 'company' was related to the word '*compagnons*', that is fellows who eat one bread.' See Hannah Arendt, *The Human Condition*, Chicago 1959, p. 25.

good mood' because they are 'the only two who dare argue . . . we are not "going-out" friends, he is a mate at work. I never meet him out of work. I hardly meet any of them.'

These responses express quite clearly the meaning of a workmate as a person with whom one shares a circumscribed, though important aspect of life. The expression 'mate' has the quality of *copain* and combines a genuinely human feeling with the sharing of an existential situation.

A person, who had been ill, said: 'I like all of them. They'd do anything for me. They lend me books to read now that I'm here. Jack has been round several times.' Another took it as a sign of friendship that his fellow-worker 'supplies me with my Sunday dinners' when they are both working on weekends. Others draw the circle of help wider. 'When I say a friend it's a person who is always willing to help me out. I'm thinking of buying a van and he's willing to come with me in it till I'm ready to pass the test. He has advised me on buying a van, etc.,' Another considers a friend 'someone I would go to in time of trouble and expect some help—not just financially.'

Ideas on friendship different from the main stream of experience were expressed by people from all groups. For a person from the factory a friend is 'a person who has the same ideas as you, who is ready to support you as you are ready to support him, who is always sincere, open.' The references to sharing of ideas and a common purpose were exceptional: 'Well, we work together towards a common objective in a good friendly spirit.' The Commonwealth was mentioned only once as a factor entering into feelings of friendship.

A few mentioned reliance and confidence as attributes of the friendship which they experience at work: 'they're the sort of people you can rely on and do things for.' Or: 'someone you could rely on. Someone you could place a confidence in.' He added: 'It is difficult to think of a director as a friend.' This comment was made in a particular personal situation and yet it expresses something typical, namely a certain compartmentalization of the feelings of friendship and difficulties in developing communal feelings in the firm as a whole.[7]

[7] There are also lines separating friendship at work from friendship outside

The people in the office, the laboratory and the factory have relatively little contact with the people from sections other than those in which they work. A minority is brought through their work into contact with people from other sections—primarily people from the office and the laboratory rather than from the factory.

To understand these feelings we must relate them to the organization of work:

(i) The Commonwealth has modified the impact of the hierarchical structure. It has taken the sting out of it and created a friendly atmosphere.

Asked: 'Who do you think are the high-ups?' and 'How do you feel about them?' Many people spoke about 'high-ups' with whom they do not have daily contacts. They expressed, on the whole, feelings of approval without showing any deeper attachment. There was a certain element of remoteness and communal feelings were not apparent. But—and this is an important point—there is no indication of negative feelings.

We indicated that projections are easily evoked by tensions arising between workers, chargehands, foremen, plant managers; between laboratory technicians and supervisors; or between clerks and managers. As a rule, these relationships do not evoke negative projections.

(ii) However the people of the Commonwealth have preserved a fairly traditional conception of authority. Asked 'When we say a man has authority what does that mean to you?' the majority saw authority in terms of 'giving orders'; 'the power to tell you what to do'; 'the power to command'; 'the right to make decisions'. Only exceptionally was authority linked to 'responsibility' or 'maturity of character'.

The answers to the question 'What do you think are the most important qualities that a foreman or supervisor should have?'

---

the place of work. A person said: 'Yes, I like to think that they all are friends —not because I'm a snob but because the majority of my friends I've known for some time and I think it's good to have friends other than those you work with.' Two people from the factory indicated specifically that friendship at work and friendship away from work went together. One of them said: 'I certainly do consider them my friends. Socially as well as at work.'

showed similar attitudes. People did not speak about a responsibility of the person in authority to the group. Nor did they express a desire that the basic authority should originate in the group. They did not have an awareness of a community of maturely interdependent people who meet each other in a mutually meaningful relatedness. Nor were they aware of the ethical implications of the division of labour and differentiation of work.[8]

(iii) These limitations of a communal relatedness and the paucity of a sense of common purpose led to tensions between the felt potentialities and the actual realities of the situation. As a result projections arose and were concentrated on one person: Ernest Bader, the man who represents the Commonwealth more than anybody. He has been the magnet who attracts all the glory, hopes and unresolved problems of a community of work which has resolved to make service to man a basic objective.

IV

The industrial system in which the people of the Commonwealth live is not organized on the basis of service. It is oriented towards profit and market chances, and service is—as far as the market economy as a whole is concerned—quite incidental. In contrast to this situation, the Commonwealth attempts to develop a service orientation to a wider community as well as within the work community itself. In this endeavour it is at one with all genuine socialist as well as religiously inspired thought.

Service may be rendered (i) through the product, that is through use-value satisfying a human need, (ii) through immediate contact with people at work, (iii) by giving money to worthy causes, that is through exchange value obtained through work and (iv) through a combination of (ii) and (iii), such as bringing somebody a parcel of food or firewood bought with the receipt for the product of one's work.

The Commonwealth aims to foster all four forms of service.

[8] This was shown clearly in answering the question 'There are certain disagreeable jobs which have to be done in every society. Who should do them?'

Here we are most interested in the extent to which awareness of service leads to an awareness of people and human values. The awareness of use-value is of particular significance in this respect because of the intimate relationship between use-value, the universal properties of the product and people's awareness of human values and a human community.

Their answers to the question: 'Do you see anything in the work you are doing now that would help people?', followed by the question: 'Is there anything else you do that makes you feel you help people in any way?' gives us an understanding of their experience of service rendered to people.

Over eighty per cent. of the people felt that they do something that helps people. Money given to worthy causes, parcels and firewood given to old people were mentioned most frequently. The product and services rendered in direct contact with people at work less frequently.[9]

People with managerial responsibilities had a tendency to emphasize the immediate service to people, 'direct contacts at work in seeking mutual development'. Or: 'I have a desire to talk to people whenever there is an opportunity, encourage, to be of help in giving advice, whenever this is asked. . . . I cannot claim any systematic service or effort except through the Commonwealth. I take that for my work, my duty, I take it for granted. The care and thinking about the well-being of our group is my constant concern'. Another person said 'I am trying to do what I can as far as the Commonwealth is concerned. I think I have developed a reasonable sense of social service.'

In other responses human needs and use-values were central: 'I make a contribution to a joint effort—the firm producing things that somebody needs.' But many people had difficulties

[9] Asked 'Do you see anything in the work which you are doing now that helps people?' and 'Is there anything else you do that makes you feel that you help people in any way? only 5 people did not mention something that may help other people.

Service through the Commonwealth was mentioned 16 times (management: 2; clerks: 2; laboratory: 3; factory: 9); direct contact with people was mentioned 10 times (management: 4; laboratory: 2; factory: 4); service through the product was mentioned 9 times (management: 2; laboratory: 1; factory: 6); other aspects were mentioned 16 times.

in seeing the product as a vehicle for service: 'it's not the main purpose of the work—if we weren't making resins others would make them.' This is a realistic evaluation of the market situation and hence helping people was experienced in connection with 'the way we do the work' or in 'providing a service to the customer'.

People using typewriters, calculating machines, paper and pencil were not very clear about the help they gave to people through their work. None of them mentioned personal contact with people or the use of the product. Only the Commonwealth was experienced as an instrument of service, particularly the help given to people by distributing parcels. 'I should think that this Commonwealth idea is not a bad idea, giving everyone a hand and that. If he's trying to spread that idea I would say it was helpful.' Though the spreading is left to other people, the value of the idea was recognized.

People working in the laboratory mentioned all aspects of service often showing a technical orientation which deprived use-value of its truly human meaning. My work gives 'support to those without technical knowledge in the plant. They feel they have something to learn.'

Awareness of a useful product was rare: 'The plastics industry is just in its youth, it is growing up, developments that will be forthcoming will help people very much. Just take our kitchen, the top of the work bench, that is all plastic although not the particular one we are concerned with. It cuts out the drudgery of the kitchen, makes the place more pleasant to live in.' His wife who was present added, 'more things are wrapped in plastic, you even get potatoes in plastic bags now, vegetables looking fresh.' Another person said: 'Any advance helps people—even if you do only a small fraction of that.'

More technically orientated are the following responses: 'We are only helpful in as much as we are giving other industries what they want.' Or: 'I look at the product more in a scientific light, what can be made from it. I don't look at the end product. I never seem to relate this thing to people.'

A person of great sensitivity who tends to bring in the open problems inherent in a situation responded in a questioning mood: 'Help the general public? No, you help only specific people. It is not like some jobs you could mention. Nursing or even market gardening where you are growing something for people—the better you grow it, the more you enjoy it. Something like we are engaged on, to 99·9 per cent. of the public it means nothing. The number of domestic uses you can put our resins to are small.'

Other people mentioned the Commonwealth 'I feel distributing these parcels to the old people is a great help. It must be pretty rotten for these people to live by themselves. The parcels which we give them come out of the company's profits, we don't miss that money but to these people it is a great help. Also profits are distributed in other ways to less fortunate people. We are contributing in general to a better standard of living. We have just given some money to spastic children. This does not hurt us at all. To them it is a great help.' Or: 'Of course, our Commonwealth. I think that's the way we help people. Making individuals feel they count. I'm thinking of the gifts we give to dependent relatives. The little things that don't matter so much in terms of value but mean so much in thought and deed.'

People working in the factory were more aware of helping people by the service rendered through the product and through the Commonwealth than were the other groups. They take a certain solidarity for granted.

'Yes, according to what we're told they're using our stuff for lifeboats and things like that. Surely that's a great help'. 'As regards what I make, yes I feel I am helping people. Without chemical processing the world would be in a very poor state now, everything you touch has got something to do with synthetic resins, etc.,' Or: 'Well, I can't see any help in what we are doing but the stuff we make helps them, it makes life easy for people. You can even get plastic shoes now.'

Exchange value and service to people at work are major elements in the following response: 'That's a bit of a funny one. That wants putting in a different way. The finished article only helps those who buy it. In your work you more or less only help your work or your mate if you're helping him. That question is more suited to a hospital nurse or a doctor. Of course you do help other people by doing your work *right* and not wrong whatever job you do.'

This person combines a strong awareness of the universal aspects of life and of the deeper meaning of service with a keen perception of the peculiar nature of the industrial world of exchange values in which we live. Though his work tasks are simple his whole mode of consciousness is remarkably akin to that of Benjamin Franklin. His sense of what is 'right' is an admixture of a natural sense of right and a Puritan sense of rightful duty easily accompanied by guilt feelings. Work is a help to other people: 'Doing your work right whatever job you do' and 'help your mate'.

An awareness of exchange values more typical of the twentieth century was expressed in these words: 'It makes work in other trades, we don't make any finished articles, do we?'

A number of people experienced difficulties: 'I don't see how we can help people except that it is a raw material.' 'We are not helping people personally because the product we produce is for industrial use. There's no personal gain attached to it at all.' As already noted the fact that the product is a raw material does not adequately explain the difficulties in seeing a use-value. 'I could see a way of my friend using it in his job' illustrates an awareness of use-values. Other factors account for these difficulties which are enhanced for those who maintain the plant. They felt that they 'make nothing' in spite of the fact that the 'product' of their work is tangible and of immediate use to other people: 'We help by keeping machinery going, we don't make nothing.' Or: 'It's difficult because we are not producing anything.'

A willingness to help was expressed frequently: 'I am always willing to help anyone that is in trouble if I can.' Or: 'I help anyone. I help the lady down the road. When she said "How much?" I said: "Can't charge. That's the Commonwealth." '

Many people in the factory mentioned the Commonwealth. They spoke about the distribution of parcels, visits to old people, distribution of money for charitable organizations, eight hours of voluntary work as well as the Commonwealth in general. 'We work and make a profit for the company and a percentage of that profit goes into charity.' Awareness of a service rendered through the Commonwealth was often separated from work itself. 'I help not in the ordinary work—in the Commonwealth yes.'

The broadest view of helping people was expressed as follows: 'Other people have something to learn from us. Apart from practising Christian charity, being neighbourly.' Or: 'I do think that what we're doing and the Commonwealth attitude is good for people outside. I think it does help. The whole attitude, the Christian approach to industry is worth being associated with.'

V

The questions about helping people aroused a good deal of puzzlement.[10] 'A social worker', 'nursing or even a market-gardener', 'a hospital nurse or a doctor' may be expected to render service to people. But industry is not expected to do so. It is seen to be more concerned with markets than with men. Awareness of use-value does not come 'naturally' in such a world which moulds human nature in the image of exchange value.

The Commonwealth has only begun to penetrate this experience of the world of work and is often seen as an adjunct of the presently prevailing pattern, as something complementary rather than the centre of a new world. This is a major reason why people are not aware of a basic conflict between the service orientation which the Commonwealth wants to develop and the existing organization of industry. This lack of awareness is intimately related to people's experience of society, particularly their difficulties in perceiving its universal dimensions. The service orientation—which is a universal aspect of work—is therefore only dimly seen. People, furthermore, do not see that only a social order organized in view of the satisfaction of

[10] More than half of the people asked for clarification of the questions, irrespective of the kind of work they were doing or their position in the firm—although there was no ambiguity in the wording of the questions themselves. The idea of helping people was unexpected and people felt the question odd.

human needs could possibly allow a genuine development of service. As a result relatedness to people is weakened. Inner tensions making for apathy and lack of human involvement arise and inhibit the development of creative tensions between the desires to render service and the difficulties of doing so in the presently existing market economy.

We must, therefore, not be astonished to find that many people of the Commonwealth do not see in the product which they produce a carrier of human service. The objection that this is so because they do not produce a finished product is only partially valid. More important than the physical distance is the psychological distance which the lack of the experience of work as a creative form-giving act and the lack of a service orientation in the overall organization of work imposes on the people's inner vision of use-value.

But even over a hundred years of experience of a society reluctant to consider human values in the organization of work could not eradicate the desire of people to be humanly related to their fellow human beings. This desire shows itself as an underlying feeling and comes only exceptionally to the surface. In response to the question whether he does anything that helps people a worker said: 'No, I don't do anything like that', adding 'I wish I could'. For most people such a wish is not any more part of their conscious expectations.

The experience of community must remain a limited one as long as this desire and need can not be adequately satisfied. We have seen that communal feeling was more or less limited to the actual community of work and the local community. But even there we have noted major limitations in the experience of communal bonds. This shows the difficulty of feeling deeply about one's neighbour and fellow workers without having a real feeling about mankind.

Chapter 23
Work and society

I

The relationships of people within a firm are part of a larger web of human relationships. An office, a factory and a laboratory are microcosms reflecting the macrocosm of society and culture. The relationships within a firm are, therefore, decisively influenced by the whole fabric of society, its economic and political structure and the ethical climate which permeates them.

To grasp the deeper meaning of work an understanding of the basic interrelationships between work and society is essential. In this chapter we sum up the result of investigations which will be published in a separate volume and illustrate them with an example. Three questions are relevant in this connection: (i) How do people experience the society in which they live? (ii) To what extent and in which way are they involved in their society? (iii) How does their experience of and involvement in society affect the meaning of work?

II

The key to understanding these questions lies in the distinction between historically specific and universal dimensions of society. We have referred repeatedly to this distinction and will now illustrate it with reference to labour and capital.

Labour and capital are fundamental in any industrial society. They are realities of everyday experience, they refer to power-groups and they are fundamental categories of social organization. An understanding of people's perception of capital and labour is, therefore, of crucial importance for an understanding of the impact of society on the world of work. It serves as a good illustration of work and society.

We asked the people of the Commonwealth: 'Does labour

create capital or does capital create labour?' The significance of this question becomes apparent as we become acquainted with the objective possibilities of choice in regard to 'labour', 'capital' and 'creation'.

(i) Labour may be understood as wage-labour, as a commodity on a labour market. This is the actual role of labour in a capitalist society. There is a supply of the services of labour and there is a demand for them. There are employees and employers. These categories belong to the same type of organization of work, to the same 'ethical' universe.

(ii) Labour may be seen as the true creator of wealth. Such an experience implies either a deep humanistic ethos or the living awareness of God as Creator who enables man to partake in the creative process.

The first mode of awareness is historically specific since a labour market is a historically unique institution. The second refers to a universal dimension since labour is the only true creator of wealth irrespective of the specific form of social organization.[1]

It may be objected that machines too create value. Is it not unrealistic to omit machines in talking about the creation of wealth, particularly in an age of automation? This is certainly true but not the issue at stake. Machines are essential in the work process but only human beings can suffer or enjoy work —and get a share in the product. It is a serious comment on our time that it is necessary to make this fundamental point clear: that man and man only can 'create' wealth in a human ethical universe and that in this sense labour is the universal creative force. To put machines on the same plane as people amounts to 'animism' because it 'animates' a dead artefact and makes it a living agent or the source of values.[2]

[1] Labour may also be understood as a labouring activity—as an exertion of effort, an expenditure of energy—or as a working activity which finds expression in craftsmanship.

[2] It is true that machines are adequate substitutes for mechanical brain-power and for sheer horse-power. On both counts they are much superior to men. But machines are and remain dead artefacts, they have no blood in them, they have neither heart nor spirituality, and thus lack the essence of

The twofold conception of labour has its counterpart in a two-fold conception of capital.

(i) Capital may be seen as investment of money to create a demand for labour. This is an historically unique perception because it implies the existence of a market for labour and—for capital. It presupposes a 'capitalistic' organization of work in which some people do and others do not have power to organize work and to make decisions.

(ii) Capital may be seen as a means to enhance the power and ability of man to create things or to render services. This is a universal dimension of capital. Whether we deal with the primitive economy of Robinson Crusoe, with the British and American economies of mid-twentieth century, or with Soviet Russia, capital is a means to facilitate production. It is a means to render man's creative efforts more effective.[3]

Creation too may be seen in two ways (i) as a genuinely creative act of 'creating' new form or (ii) as a mere act of re-producing given forms.

III

We shall explore the following types of awareness of historically unique and universal dimensions of capital and labour:

[3] Capital seen as a means of exchange also has a universal quality. Capital thus understood becomes synonymous with money and implies the existence of a money—as distinguished from a barter economy. A money economy is a stage in the development of human consciousness, which has become more or less universal in the West since the end of the medieval world. We do not barter one good for another but we enter into all kinds of exchange relationships. Hence money is used as a means to facilitate exchange. This again is true for the economy of Great Britain and the United States as well as Soviet Russia. Because it is related to a whole system of exchange, the perception of capital as money is a very complex perception.

---

what makes man human. They can neither create nor discover form; they can only reproduce forms developed by man.

The habit of many economists to speak about machines in the same way as about men is an expression of false consciousness. It implies the principle of 'misplaced concreteness' (to use a philosophical term) or animism (to use anthropological language) because it considers machines as if they were living agents.

(i) Exclusive awareness of historically unique dimensions. This group compromised almost one third of the people of the Commonwealth.

(ii) (*a*) Exclusive awareness of universal dimensions or (*b*) awareness of universal and historically specific aspects of capital and labour which do not form a clear and coherent picture. This group consisted of somewhat less than a third of the people.

(iii) Awareness of both universal and historically unique dimensions ordered in a clear picture of reality. Only a few of the people had such an awareness.

(iv) People who did not really know accounted for the balance of the people.

(i) People in the first group can only see historically unique aspects: labour is identical with wage labour and capital with investments. Typical responses to the question: 'Does labour create capital or does capital create labour?' were: 'I think it's very much a two-way thing. If one invests in a company and builds up a company, one creates labour for people to work in the company. On the other hand, if one has people working for you it does create more capital.' 'What comes first, the chicken or the egg? I should say capital started labour. Without capital you can't start labour. You can have the labour without money and it's no good at all.' Or 'capital creates labour because it takes capital to create the plant, the factories and they come before the labour. If a man has a job he is working for a capitalist, therefore the money he earns on a Friday—he must see that he has something in him from Sunday to Saturday—you can't work on air can you?'

This is, in simple terms, a clear statement of the 'advance-fund' theory of capital which in the past has often been used as an argument to keep wages low. To such a position Henry George would have answered: 'To say that a man must have his breakfast before going to work is not to say that he cannot go to work unless a capitalist furnishes him with breakfast'.[4] The need for breakfast is a universal phenomenon. It is rooted

[4] See Henry George, *Progress and Poverty*, Everyman's Library, London 1930, p. 54.

in man's biological nature. But the 'advance of money' by a man called a capitalist is not a universal phenomenon. Yet thought-forms can be so completely dominated by what is historically unique that the aberrations of a system become the norms of perception. If labour would not create capital 'the boss would not employ you'.

(ii) People who were only aware of universal aspects said: 'I undoubtedly think that labour creates capital. I think it creates wealth and this is a way of defining capital. That wealth can be used to increase the productivity of labour in order to create even more wealth I should say. It originates in labour and not in capital.' Labour is here conceived as 'living' creative power. Or, as another person put it: 'Labour creates capital because originally someone must have built up the capital.' Here the universal dimension is put back in history, it is not really alive in the present.

The same is true for those who can see universal aspects in conjunction with historically unique ones but only in a muddled way: 'I think that labour creates capital because it actually creates something, produces something. Nevertheless the capital enables it to do so. It has a catalytic effect, it enables, it relates the creative force of labour, it directs it.' He animated capital and gave it a creative power. He, like others, did not draw clear lines: 'Labour creates capital. I suppose you could even say that labour is capital . . . somebody needs capital to start an industry, but once it grows it needs labour. It depends to a large extent on labour. Capital by itself is useless.' Or: 'That's rather a deep question. As things are in present society, the things go together. It's impossible to express labour in terms of money merely and, therefore, to put the problem this way is hardly right.'

The common element of people in this second group is lack of movement: they simply accept what is. They do not experience creative tensions.

(iii) The world looks quite different to those who see universal and historically unique elements in a clearly ordered way:

RH: Does labour create capital or does capital create labour?

He; Is it an either-or question?

RH: Do you think it is an either-or question?

He: I should have thought labour created capital.

RH: Why?

He: Well, if you get work and the right sort of work and people pulling together, it creates capital.

RH: Is there such a thing as capital creating labour?

He: Someone floats shares and give work out. It works both ways.

RH: Is it possible to create capital without labour?

He: Most certainly it is, through speculative buying, tea shares. They slumped one half. Then overnight the Chinese cease fire. They leaped right up. If anybody bought these shares when they were low, he could have made tremendous capital gains without effort. There is also buying and selling of property. You reap dividends when development takes place.

FB: Is it possible to create labour without capital?

He: Yes I would think in a set-up like the Bruderhof community. Have you heard of this? They do this without . . . only a minimum of capital is required. They work from nothing to produce profits to live; they exist from the fruits of each other.

In this conversation labour seen as a co-operative effort of human beings creates capital. There is also awareness of an organization of industry in which labour is dependent upon those who 'give(s) work out'. In such an organization capital 'creates labour' or at least opportunities for people to work. The universal meanings of labour and capital are seen and it is recognized that they are distorted because we live in a world in which you can create capital 'without labour'. On the Stock Exchange you can 'cash in' on a war or on a communal effort. The opposite of such a situation is the Bruderhof community where labour can be creative 'without capital'—or rather almost without capital, because people work without dependence upon a labour market and capitalistic investment; people live 'from the fruits of each other' and the universal creative power of labour becomes effective.

When universal and historically unique dimensions are seen in a clear perspective, the present economic system is often regarded with scepticism: 'Labour creates capital because something like 90 per cent. of this country's wealth is in the hands of ten per cent.' This person has an awareness of inequality in power, of concentration of capital, and of labour as the creator of all things—and hence also of the capital owned by ten per cent. of the people.

Also critical is the following response: 'I think labour creates capital. I never felt that one man earning money alone could earn a million—except on the Stock Exchange'. There 'a man alone' can make a million but in industry only the universal creative power of labour can create value.

Tensions arise in all groups and are sometimes referred to explicitly.[5] But they become the more pronounced, the more articulate the awareness of a universal dimension which is violated by the specific historical organization of work. A person who said that 'labour makes life out of something that is inanimate' but who also recognized 'that capital brings life to labour as the economic system is organized' expressed a strong discomfort: 'I don't like to think in terms of capital and labour. I don't want to. I want to think in terms of life generally.'

The following conversation illustrates how conflicts arise with awareness of a universal dimension:

FB: Does labour create capital or does capital create labour?

He: I should say capital creates labour, because you got to have the capital to start with. If you have capital you can get credit. You need that. It's no good to have labour if you have no capital to start the things with.

FB: And where does the capital come from?

He: I don't know, I haven't got much, I like to have more. That's an awkward question, why do you ask me that?

FB Where does it start?

He: Maybe in the brain of a person, he starts, works hard, gets

[5] After having spoken about capital and labour in the present system, a person spoke explicitly about the situation being 'the cause of much tension' and then referred to the Commonwealth as an attempt to resolve the problems which arise.

> a little capital, wants more labour. The more labour they get, the more capital they make like the ICI (Imperial Chemical Industries). It has been done in this village. A person knowing something started a boot and shoe factory in an old shed. Somebody gave him a hand. It expanded. Did you see the factories which are here now. Capital made this one man, he started in a small way. Mr. Bader started in a small way, he had to work hard.

This conversation started with an emphatic statement that capital creates labour—quite in harmony with system-determined thinking. When challenged where the capital came from he became uncertain and annoyed—'an awkward question, why do you ask me that?' He looked for a way out of this tension by referring to the man who started from scratch and worked himself up—a universal phenomenon of labour creating capital. But instead of leading him to a new outlook on life and bringing about a creative tension, the recognition of labour as a universal creative agent was almost literally—in the same sentence—swallowed up by the transformation of the little man into the giant Imperial Chemical Industries. As soon as this happened, his thought went back to other little men—in the boot and shoe industry (a much less dangerous thought) and it ended with the comforting statement that Ernest Bader too started in a small way and had to work hard.

Ernest Bader's solution was the Commonwealth. The person we had this conversation with is deeply involved in the Commonwealth. It has personal meaning for him and expresses truly human values. Yet it has not sufficiently penetrated his experience of work and society to open the way to a new experience of work and life. Somehow he remained caught in a world in which capital 'creates' labour.

In such a world conflicts arise because man's creative power is not adequately recognized. An attempt is made to minimize these conflicts by the image of the 'little man going to the top'. This is an unreal image because not all little men can go to the top. But it has real value as long as man's true creative powers cannot find a meaningful expression.

IV

The awareness of labour as a universal creative agent is quite widespread among the people of the Commonwealth but its meaning is blurred and hence work is not experienced as a creative activity. 'To create', 'to make' and 'to cause' are used almost interchangeably with reference to making things—and money. For most people the awareness of creativity is stunted because their basic experience is moulded by a system in which breakfast depends upon a capitalist advancing wages to pay for the breakfast. In such a world the miraculous power of money to beget money—particularly on the Stock Exchange rather than the creative power of man dominates experience and awareness.

How strange such a world would have been for a person living in pre-capitalist America is indicated in the words of Abraham Lincoln: 'Labor is prior to, and independent of, capital. Capital is only the fruit of labour and could never have existed if labor had not first existed. Labor is superior to capital..'[6]

The Commonwealth ideal is in full harmony with such a view. But people's awareness of capital and labour does not yet adequately reflect this conception. Their awareness may be summed up as follows:

(i) Those who are only aware of historically unique dimensions suffer from a complete black-out of those aspects of capital and labour which are universal. These are the people who are ordinarily considered 'perfectly normal' but who are unable to see half of objective reality. They relegate the universal aspects of the world of work to a dark corner of their unconscious.

We may expect that the people in key positions of decision making are most strongly moulded by the existing organization of work and see the world animated by the life-blood of capital. But this is not so. The incidence of 'capital creates labour' responses is overwhelming—in the factory.[7] There we

[6] Quoted in *The Catholic Worker*, Vol. XXX, No. 9, April 1964, p. 2.

[7] Out of 8 first responses, 6 came from the factory, 2 from the laboratory and none from the office—neither from clerks nor managers.

find the people who have borne the brunt of capitalism, who have carried its greatest burden and who bear witness to its power.

(ii) Those who were only aware of a universal dimension or who were aware of universal and historically specific aspects without having them ordered in a coherent perception either do not see half of reality or, more typically they are confused because they intermingle two aspects of reality. We may call them the hopefully confused people because they do not suffer from a black-out of half of the world in which they live. They are considerably healthier than the 'normal' people who seem so well adjusted to the world in which they work.

(iii) People who have an articulate awareness of both universal and historically unique dimensions experience a tension which may or may not become creative depending upon the combination of these dimensions.

(*a*) If the historical uniqueness of the world of work as organized at present is clearly seen and if the universal aspects are identified with the vision of a classless society then we have a marxist view. There are no such marxists among the people of the Commonwealth.

(b) If the historical uniqueness of the world of work is clearly recognized and if the universal dimension is expressed in a vision of a new order or alternative new orders—without any of these new orders being *identified* with the universal, then a genuine religious awareness arises. Such an awareness is not absent but is quite exceptional among the people of the Commonwealth.

Few people have developed their awareness of the universal dimensions of capital and labour to the point of relating it to the social order as a whole. Hence the formation of a dynamic picture of the social order and a sense of active involvement in creative change are thwarted.

V

Whenever an aspect of reality is denied its rightful entrance into awareness, it has a way of coming in through a back door. This is what has happened to many if not most of the people of the Commonwealth. Being unable to distinguish clearly between what is universal and what is historically unique they often give universal meaning and hence absolute sanction to what is merely a passing historical phenomenon.

This accounts for the perception of capitalism as something unavoidable because it is rooted in a universal human desire for money. This is why most of the people indiscriminately accept competition as a good thing. They elevate it to a universal principle of justice, order and harmony. Without competition men are perceived as animals rather than as human beings who desire to grow and strive to do their best. The tendency to give universal meaning to historically unique phenomenon is also a factor in explaining why few people know how to overcome the supremacy of markets over men. Supply and demand are seen as universal and unalterable forces beyond the control of man.

The tendency to universalize is a central feature in a pattern of awareness which has the following features:

(i) A tendency to leave out of one's awareness whatever does not fit into an idealized image of society. The dark sides of the social order are not seen. This selective process manifests itself, for example, in the widespread lack of perception of the labour-market as an aspect of capitalism. The result is a shrinkage of consciousness: essential aspects of reality remain in the dark.

(ii) The impact of this type of selective process is enhanced by the tendency to dissolve social systems into individual attitudes. Capitalism is often seen as equal to the sum of individual capitalists. A corollary is the view that only individual striving or forces are important. There is no clear awareness of social, collective forces.

Since people give universal meaning to individual attitudes which are historically unique the dissolution of the 'system' into a sum of 'individual' attitudes reinforces the process of universalizing a historically given situation.

(iii) This process is further strengthened by a separation of the spheres of life which makes it possible to transfer an aspect of reality which cannot be completely denied from one segment of the social order to another segment. An example is the relegation of potentialities of development to the realm of 'mere' ideas or abstract noble sentiments. The separation of the spheres of life amounts to a fragmentation of life and implies a reduction of reality to 'observable facts'. Life is not seen as a dynamic reality with potentialities which are real though they are not yet realized. As a result universal forces are without influence even in so far as people are aware of them.

The large majority of the people of the Commonwealth *do* have an awareness of universal dimensions of life and a genuine ethical impulse connected with it. They show this for example in their stress on the communal element in their vision of a good society and particularly in their attitude towards the destruction of foodstuffs in the thirties which they wholeheartedly condemn as wrong. But their awareness and their ethical impulse cannot become operative because they are not part of a clear vision of society as a whole. Few people for example, experience a creative tension between what is and what ought to be because such a tension presupposes a differentiated awareness of the universal and the historically unique dimensions of life. Most people see Western-industrial man formed by over a hundred years of capitalism as the prototype of the human species—that is, as universal man. This is a powerful factor in stunting people's ethical impulse. What, after all, can man do in the face of God's failure to create a better human nature?

VI

Awareness of the social order and involvement in it are but two sides of the same coin. The basic pattern of awareness which we summed up in the preceding pages has, therefore, its counterpart in people's involvement in their society.

The confusion of universal and historically unique dimensions of society, the experience of society as a sum of individuals and the denial of 'system' bound collective forces all combine to make collective forces reappear with a vengeance. There is an overwhelming sense that the individual cannot do anything, that only 'collectively' one might be able to do something—if only that collectivity offered some possibilites of relationship.

But this is exactly the nature of the collective, of the mass: one is either free from it or one is immersed in it; but one cannot relate to it without being swallowed by it. Many people of the Commonwealth are in this dilemma: they have a sense of freedom but they are also very much afraid of losing their freedom. To break out of their isolation, to overcome the threat to their free self-development, they would have to be creatively related to others—in community rather than collectively. But they lack this experience of a power of relatedness just as they lack the power of true self-realization.

We come here to the focal point of people's awareness of their society and their involvement in it. The confusion between universal and historically unique dimensions has its counterpart in a confusion of what truly belongs to oneself as an individually unique expression of a human universal and what is the historically unique self which is merely a reflection of the values of one's culture. Hence a widespread feeling of powerlessness which is not primarily a feeling of lack of power in the decision-making process but of a lack of a sense of power to realize one's own potentialities in relatedness to others.

In this consists the alienation of the people of the Commonwealth: many of them are alienated from these universal powers which are the ground of their own potentialities as well as of their society.

In this consists their apathy: in so far as they are alienated from the universal ground of their Being, they experience destructive rather than creative tensions, have a sense of powerlessness and are unable to act.

These processes are well illustrated by people's attitude towards socialism.

To the extent to which it is seen primarily as an ethical ideal socialism has retained a dynamic, involving quality because it is still imbued by the experience of a universal element. When this universal is seen as a goal to work towards it brings about a creative tension. About a third of the people who are socialists are in this group. But for the majority, particularly among the workers, socialism has lost its universal power of a movement expressing the ethical aspirations of man—of all men. Many workers are primarily socialists because of their ill-feelings about capitalism or rather capitalists. Socialism gives no longer a vision of a new world. For many of them socialism is the receptacle of unresolved conflicts and of 'anti' feelings. It does not foster active involvement in the creation of a world in which destructive tensions are replaced by constructive tensions.

Some workers gain some sense of release by being more anti-communist than other groups but such a projection of unresolved conflicts does not help very much either. Many workers feel therefore more powerless, more caught in the system and more cynical than other groups. They see capitalism more in terms of money and are more ready to dissolve it into individual behaviour—thus supporting more effectively the existing order while creating more inner conflicts. They espouse competition as a universal good and are ready to close their eyes to competition on the labour market though it affects them most acutely. They are likely to be even more cynical about human nature than other people of the Commonwealth and to equate human nature with selfishness. On the other hand they have a deeper sense for the need of community and are more aware of the humanly destructive aspects of the present society—also as regards competition. They are, therefore, even more stunted in the expression of their ethical impulse and have to bear stronger inner tensions than many other people in the Commonwealth.

VII

The meaning of the basic pattern of awareness and participation briefly outlined here will become clearer as we look at it in the light of the characteristics of a secular capitalistic society.

Three peculiarities of such a society are relevant here: sovereign individuals, anonymous markets and sovereign national states. They form two pairs of opposites (i) the individual versus the state and (ii) the individual versus markets.

Ultimate sovereignty in a democratic society rests with the people. This is clearly expressed in their sense of freedom and their positive experience of democracy. If this were the whole story the state would be experienced as a communal extension of the person and not as an opposite to the individual. But the widespread feeling of political impotence often overshadows the experience of democratic freedom.

There is little if any overt animosity to the government and the overwhelming majority of the people feel that the government should take an active part in the economic affairs of the country. But the underlying feeling which gives rise to this demand does not stem from a sense of delegating communal tasks to the government as the representative body of the people. The underlying feeling is a sense of confronting socio-economic forces so much beyond one's control that 'only the government' can do something about them. The government is not called on to do a job because of a democratic relatedness to communal instruments of power but because people feel overwhelmed by a collectivity. Hence there is a strong ambivalence towards government action and a great sensitivity towards bureaucratization and centralization of power. This ambivalence affects the attitude towards nationalization. But it has a much more general effect: it alienates the individual from the state, which appears as an impersonal power—as red tape. The sovereign individual is thus brought in opposition to the sovereign nation state which becomes the embodiment of collective forces threatening individual freedom.

This process cannot be adequately understood if we look at politics as a separate sphere of life. The political realm constitutes the framework and the culmination of the social order and the state is the symbol of society and of the basic forces controlling the social order. In a capitalist society these are the market forces. They are the underlying reason for the state becoming a collective opposite to the individual.

The powerlessness of the individual in regard to the market does not need much explanation. Markets are ruled by the anonymous forces of supply and demand following the law of the great numbers—the universal law of probability. This law, or in the language of Adam Smith, the unseen hand, controls the markets. It is true that during recent years human hands have played a more and more active part but usually as manipulators of market forces, not as hands endowed by their Creator with a truly creative potential. Furthermore, the experience of this change has been too short to have decisively influenced people's awareness of their society. As a result the sovereign individual stands in opposition to the anonymous market forces.

Since the market often remains in the sphere of the anonymous and the unconscious, the sovereign individual is often quite unconscious of his dependency upon the forces ruling the markets. He is more conscious of the personification of these anonymous forces in the bureaucratic machinery of the state, or the bureaucracy of big business. The bureaucracy of the trade unions is also becoming suspect. Indeed all power is suspect because it is experienced as manipulative power, and because the ultimate source of power is felt to lie beyond the control of the sovereign individual. The glad hand is suspected to be a mere personification of the unseen hand, that is of uncontrollable and essentially non-human forces.

These are some major reasons why so many of the people of the Commonwealth see politics as unprincipled, as devoid of values and ideals. As the manipulators of market forces politicians are indeed ill-equipped to 'deal' with ideas, values and principles. In so far as their actions remain within the framework of markets, the law of great numbers rules with supreme indifference—irrespective of which party is in power. The official rationalization for such a situation is that politics is 'the art of the possible' whereas in actual fact politics thus limited degenerates into the art of avoiding the realization of the possible, that is of the potential contained in the universal realm.

A world characterized by the dual pair of opposites—sovereign individuals *v.* the sovereign state and sovereign individuals *v.* the market—is a de-humanized world no matter how affluent it may ever become. Being inhuman it is also a world which is essentially unethical.

The people of the Commonwealth experience human values and principles—for example in their attitude towards 'markets and men'. But equally if not more strongly do they experience the supreme disregard of values by the market. They have enough of a sense of universal ethics left to consider Christianity opposed to certain aspects of capitalism. But the majority of them are unable to express this ethical impulse in a constructive way and hence their ethical impulse remains thwarted.

Only exceptionally do people act as *interrelated* people who are aware of the implications of their actions on others. They usually act only as sovereign individuals exercising whatever power the market allows them to have. When confronted with a difficult ethical problem, many people of the Commonwealth were unable to think in terms of an interrelatedness, of an ethical concern with one's neighbour.

This situation leads to inhibiting, destructive conflicts. The temptation to find an escape from these conflicts and an outlet for one's stored-up energies in the competitive game is ever-present. But it is futile and offers no way out. The vicious circle is thus complete. The sovereign individual has become powerless without losing the title of sovereignty. As in Sartre's play *No Exit* many of the people of the Commonwealth have a social existence from which they know 'no way out'. They are caught in a pair of opposites which leads to loss of community and loss of true individuality.

VIII

The experience of and involvement in society are decisive for the meaning which work has in the life of the people. The particular pattern which we summed up has the following consequences:

(i) The lack of differentiation between universal and historically unique dimensions has a tendency to cut people off from the elemental universal aspects of life and render it more difficult to experience work as participation in a life process. The awareness of work as a creative activity becomes stunted. People become separated from 'matter', from the material and the whole feminine side of life.

(ii) The experience of overwhelming market forces and of the power of capital subordinates work as a human activity to uncontrollable inhuman forces. This inhibits a sense of purpose and makes a genuine service orientation more difficult.

(iii) Both factors mentioned combine to make it more difficult to experience work as part of a life in which the person realizes himself in true relatedness to others.

(iv) The thwarting of the ethical impulse deprives work of a deeper ethical meaning. Indeed, the process in which historically unique aspects of reality are given universal meaning and in which the level of ethical awareness is reduced, brings about a strange split in consciousness. It is as if 'life and death'—the most universal and elemental aspects of life—were different 'for the likes of us' and for the others.

(v) The possibility to make money without working has a strong influence in depriving work of an ethical content. Not the creative purpose of work but the speculative possibilities of gambling set the tone in our society. The possibility of unearned gains which must ultimately be paid for by work subordinates the ethics of work to the 'morality' of the Stock Exchange.

(vi) The a-morality of the political game makes it more difficult to build democracy in industry. The political institutions of the country are the model of democracy but people are alienated from them and consider politics unprincipled, devoid of ideals and values. Democracy in industry must therefore, be built up in spite of the meaning which political democracy has, not because of it.

(vii) Generally speaking, alienation and apathy in regard to the social order reinforce powerfully the alienation and apathy inherent in the inadequate relatedness of people to things, to the work process, to the people, to the organization and the purpose of work.

Chapter 24
Work and ultimate reality

I

The rise of capitalism was intimately related to what has been called the 'Protestant Ethic'. The core of this ethic is the idea of a calling, of a vocation to which man is called by God; equally important is the idea that success measured in profits may be understood as a sign of having been chosen to do God's work on earth—and receiving in addition an everlasting reward. Without raising the question of cause and effect we may say that capitalism would not have been possible if there had not been a devout group of people who experienced a close connection between their work and their God.

This is a specific historical example of a universal link between work and ultimate reality. Work is a realm of human activity which is embedded, so to speak, in the social order. The latter, in turn, is embedded in a universal human order which has its roots in an eternal realm outside time and space.[1]

We have already anticipated the significance of an ultimate reality by making the distinction between what is universal and what is historically unique the guiding thread throughout our discussion. Since the universal is rooted in a deeper realm, people's experience of ultimate reality is, as the word says, the ultimately decisive factor in their experience of their work and life.

II

A living experience of ultimate reality reinforces the experience of the universal dimensions of work and society. An inadequate experience reinforces the confusion of universal and historically unique elements with all the consequences indicated in

[1] See my paper on 'Evolution of Consciousness and the Sociology of Knowledge', Fifth World Congress of Sociology, Washington, Sept. 1962.

the preceding chapter. The people of the Commonwealth's experience of work and society leave two possibilities open as regards their experience of ultimate reality. Either they have a strong experience of an ultimate in life and somehow this experience cannot manifest itself in work and society. Or, their experience of an ultimate is as confused as is their experience of the strategic elements determining society.

A thorough investigation of this problem which will be part of the material to be published separately shows that the latter rather than the former situation is typical. We can only sum up here some conclusions and give some illustrations.

An important link between people's experience of an ultimate reality and of society is their experience of the Kingdom of God. For about a third of the people the Kingdom had a purely transcendental meaning. For another third the Kingdom did not mean anything. For others it was a spiritual state, a state of consciousness. For less than a third the Kingdom had both a transcendental and a 'worldly' meaning. Among this group we found an awareness of the Kingdom of God as 'presence' of an eternal reality which was directly relevant to man's social existence and his interpersonal relationships; we found people with a living awareness of the universal as a power in work and society.

Practically all the people were aware of an ultimate, a spiritual power permeating life and the universe. Many, however—between one half and two thirds—did not clearly experience this power. It did not enter their life in any central way. On the whole there was more of an awareness of the 'God beyond the God of Theism' or of God as spirit than there was of a Christian God in the traditional sense of the word.[2] Only for a few was God a living reality.

We can distinguish five approximately equal groups: those for whom God was an impersonal life-force, spirit or mind; those for whom God was the Creator, a Supreme Being; those who experienced God as a creative power dwelling in life and man; those who conceived God in the traditional Christian

[2] By tradition we mean the tradition of the last century rather than of the last two thousand years.

way; and a group who did not know what to say or who did not believe in the existence of God.

The quest for an ultimate meaning of life—and the difficulties of finding such meaning within the traditional framework—is evident in people's experience of various dimensions of ultimate reality. It becomes particularly apparent in their experience of Jesus of Nazareth. Only a minority emphasized His Divinity. Most people insisted on His humanity. For them He is primarily the Son of Man rather than the Son of God—assuming the latter had any meaning to them at all. For about two thirds Jesus' death on the Cross and His resurrection as the Christ had no meaning. He is simply a man who lived and died 2000 years ago. The more deeply we probed the personal meaning of Jesus as the Christ, as the 'new reality', the smaller was the proportion of those for whom He is a living Presence.

A basic reason for this situation lies in people's experience of time.

III

We may experience time as a movement, as a flow which passes by just as the hands on the dial of a watch pass by. An hour is 'just an hour', it is just like any other hour. The more removed it is from the present, the less vivid is our experience of such time. The present measured and experienced in terms of clock time shrinks to a fine dividing line between the past and the future. The sentence which I have just written belongs already to the past and the next sentence I will write belongs to the future. The present virtually vanishes from such an experience.

There is a very different experience of time, where its flow is 'arrested'. We all have moments where, like Faust, we would like to say to the moment 'remain, thou art so beautiful'. Some experiences in our lives are many years past but they are much closer to us than experiences which we had only yesterday. There are moments which seem to contain the fullness of life. Such experiences are best symbolized by a circle, by the round, since time no longer moves.[3] Indeed no movement of time can obliterate our deepest experiences because we have touched something timeless. The present, instead of shrinking to a hair's breadth, has widened to the infinite. We have become aware of an eternal Presence.

A few of the people of the Commonwealth did experience such an eternal Presence—in God, in Christ, in the Kingdom. But the vast majority did not. Not only did they not experience it but they scarcely knew that it existed. Only exceptionally were people aware of a difference between what is 'eternal' and 'everlasting'. For most of them eternity meant an endless movement of clock-time. This is the decisive factor in their experience of ultimate reality.

To speak about Jesus as the Christ means to speak about the mystery of the unity of man and God. Most of the people of the Commonwealth do not experience such a mystery. They are simply confused about the reality of Jesus the Christ. Hence the quite logical question: how can a man who died 2000 years ago have died for our sins? Or, in a less traditional language: how can a historical person be an eternal reality, how can He contain the divine imperative? The truth is that for the majority of the people of the Commonwealth He does not consititue an eternal reality, He does not contain the divine imperative.

IV

There are various reasons for this situation, only a few of which can be mentioned here. The people of the Commonwealth—like most of us in Western industrial countries—are the children of a rationalistic intellectual culture which is spiritually underdeveloped. People attempt to 'define' God rather than see Him with an inner eye, experience Him. They want 'factual knowledge'. They can, therefore, not grasp the eternal life which means 'to know Thee who alone are truly God and Jesus Christ whom Thou hast sent'. We are all, furthermore, the chil-

[3] The understanding of time as a circle is very articulate in the East. See F. S. C. Northrop, *The Meeting of East and West*, an inquiry concerning world understanding, New York 1946.

dren of a culture decisively influenced by capitalism. Rationalistic technological market values which make time empty are the real god of such a culture. Compared with the existential reality of this god, the proclamation of 'the good news' of the Gospel becomes mere preaching, particularly since the majority of the people experience a conflict between Christianity and capitalism.

The outward manifestation of this situation is the loss of meaning of 'the Church' for the majority of the people of the Commonwealth, though the number of regular churchgoers is higher than in Great Britain as a whole.[4] Somewhat more than one third of the people called themselves regular churchgoers, the remainder were divided between 'nominal' churchgoers and those who never went to church. Among the regular churchgoers we found some who experience primarily a vertical man-God relationship rather than a 'horizontal' experience of a gathered community. Most of the nominal churchgoers just drifted away without much apparent reason. For some the forced services in the armed Services was the last straw. Others consider the Church to be hypocritical, not practising what it preaches.

The inward manifestation showed itself in two major factors: The Church itself has often been caught in the confusion of what is universal, rooted in an eternal reality and what is historically unique. Hence its difficulties in activating the springs of the eternal and helping its incarnation in people's social existence. The Church often contributes to the absence of an experience of an eternal timeless reality and a reduction—or should we say imprisonment—of the eternal in a mechanical time without end. The traditional conception of everlasting life is but one example of a denial of the early Christian conception of eternal life.

But most important in this context is the failure of the churches to give to the true Christian conception of the nature of man any living meaning in our society. It may be said that this is due to the existence of a secular-capitalist society which is not open to the Christian message. This, however, is far too

[4] See p. 61 n. As regards church affiliation see pp. 60–61.

easy a way out. The fault rather lies in the inability of the Church to give to the universal conception of man as revealed in Christ a form which is relevant to man's social existence. Only a few people in the Church have been awakened and begin to bring the good news into the world of work. But the Church is as yet unable to speak in Truth because it is still existentially too involved with a system which breeds alienation and apathy.

It is true that for the majority of the people of the Commonwealth to be religious stands for a way of life, not for a creed. It is also true that the traditional criteria of what is religious have lost their meaning. But it would be as wrong to call the people of the Commonwealth irreligious as it would be to call them inhuman. Indeed there is a deep longing for a deeper meaning of life, a quest for relatedness to an ultimate reality. Religion is not rejected because 'secular man' does not need it. To the extent to which it is rejected people demand a wholeness which a 'religion' limited to a sphere of life cannot give. This will become apparant as we explore the way in which the people of the Commonwealth experienced the relationship of religion to their work.

V

The question whether religion has anything to do with work touches fundamental problems and opens manifold objective possibilities of choice.[5] The world of work may be seen as a world separate from the realm of ultimate values. Or there may be a conscious expression of an ultimate commitment in man's work. In the first case there is no awareness of the unity of life. The organization of work is seen to follow laws of its own, unrelated to the lawfulness of ultimate reality. An example of the second case is the activity of a person who experiences his work as a service to God.

Within this range we can discern a number of intersecting

[5] The actual question asked: 'Do you feel that religion has anything to do with the way you do your work?' points to the actual work but the reference to the way work is done elicits a general attitude towards work and the answers give a good idea of the way in which the people of the Commonwealth experience the relationship between their work and their religion.

planes of awareness which are defined by the problems of means and ends, freedom and necessity, the Way and the Purpose. The experience of a vocation or calling is also relevant here.

People may be aware of themselves as means or as ends in the work process; they may also be aware of the product of their work as a means or as an end; and/or they may be aware of the organization of work as a network of interrelationships in which people and things are ends and means.

They may, furthermore, experience a purpose in their work which relates them to life and gives them a feeling of freedom. Or they may feel that what happens in the sphere of work imposes a necessity which violates their true vocation.

The dimension of time also enters the possibilities of choice. Work may be related to a view of life which is time-bound in its specific historical expression. In this case the ethic of work, no matter how deep its roots, is bound to be a passing one. Or work may be seen in relation to a universal, an ultimate value. Under these conditions, the ethical meaning of work is both strong and flexible. Ever new forms expressing a universal meaning in different ways will emerge. The experience of time as monotonous, boring, or filled with life also relates work to an ultimate experience of life.

In this chapter we will examine the basic experience of religion in relation to work. In the following chapter we will explore some implications with regard to people's sense of freedom, their experience of time, etc.

VI

About two thirds of the people of the Commonwealth felt that religion has something to do with the way they do their work. The remaining third felt it has nothing to do with their work.[6]

[6] Asked: 'Does religion have anything to do with the way you do your work?' 19 out of 30 people answered in the affirmative (4 because work is part of life and life has a religious basis; 3 because of a person's attitude towards work and towards people; 4 because of a person's attitude to work; 5 because of a person's attitude towards people; 3 for various reasons). 11 answered in

A number of people saw work related to a religiously grounded life: 'Yes, it is the direct connection with the world. All work is an expression of our relations with others. Your work is how you think and what you feel in your calling, your obedience to God.' Here is a comprehensive experience of work as a vocation, a calling in which the relationship of God to the world of work is expressed directly and intimately—your thinking and feeling are moulded by it.

For another person religion 'makes all the difference, Christianity makes all the difference in your everyday work. In a nutshell, to take a word out of the Bible, you do everything unto the Lord, treating your fellow-workers, doing everything above board, doing everything to the glory of God . . . every little detail in your daily work. (It means) being honest, do unto others as you want them to do unto you, treat your fellow-worker as a human being not just as a cog.'

This person's life has been deeply shaped by a religious experience. He works and meets other people in a way which made some of his fellow workers mention him as an example of a religious person when they did not know how to put in words what it means to them to be 'religious'.

'Religion must have something to do with the way I work because as a Christian one believes in the Christian faith—it helps you to see a purpose in your life and in your work.' This person touched upon a central link between work and life; the purpose of man's activity. This is the only time when 'purpose' was mentioned explicitly though even here it was mentioned as a 'must' rather than as an experienced reality.

Another dimension of an ultimate in life was expressed in these words: 'I don't think one gets enough time to concentrate and meditate on the orientation of your work in religious terms. A great deal of effort is rather unsatisfactory. One's attitude is affected by one's desire to follow one's religious beliefs but the living out of it is often lacking. I think it is one of the failures of civilization, of the society we are building up, there isn't time

---

the negative (7 because religion has nothing to do with work; 2 because it is not possible to be religious at work and 2 for no specific reason).

during the day; or maybe this is an excuse, there isn't time during the day to examine the events in spiritual values.'

Other people's experiences were akin to those to whom we have listened so far but they had a somewhat narrower frame of reference. 'Yes, your religion or your faith has an influence on *everything* you do, because it's how you work and treat people—it's all in the faith.' Or: 'Definitely. I think it is in fact part of your character to do a job honestly if you have a religious background. It must affect work.' When his wife said that religion 'affects your attitude to other people' he agreed, saying 'definitely to be fair and just to other people and realize that they have difficulties just as you. Religion helps you to understand other people.'

A good deal of uncertainty was expressed by a person who felt that 'being a Christian is more the way you live than the way you work. Religion has something to do with work, but it's difficult to say how it does—you try to have pride in your work—something you would be willing to let anyone know or see—trying to carry out your ideas or principles through your work . . . You get hard workers who are not religious—but if they know you are religious and you are slacking they think the two don't tie up. Their attitude to their fellow-worker *should* be one of comradeship—being helpful—trying to assist them as much as possible.' In another context he said, 'I feel that religion has a certain influence on your general attitude when you are at work rather than to work. Even if people aren't religious they would work hard—they are paid to do it. Living out Christianity means going much further than that.'

This person first implied that religion and work are separate spheres but ended up with an assertion that Christianity goes 'much further' than a particular attitude to work. The 'further', however, remains more of a quest than an experienced reality. Yet the two main points made: (i) that religion affects the attitude towards work and (ii) towards people at work recur frequently.

'Religion must make one more conscientious . . . I don't know—unless it would give you a quiet mind. If you are an integrated person or a better integrated person you thereby increase your capacity to work.' This modern version of the 'Protestant Ethic' finds an echo in the following response about the influence of religion on work: 'I think so—indirectly—inasmuch as I try to be honest. If I did get lazy it jerked me... when the pay packet comes on Friday I sometimes feel guilty.'

More sceptical was a person who didn't 'know whether religion is tied up with being conscientious or not... No, I can't answer it, because I am not too religious.' Another person felt that this was not a religious but an ethical issue. 'It is important to be completely honest and to have complete integrity'. Asked whether work has anything to do with socialism (since he had previously indicated that socialism is, in a way, his religion) he said: 'definitely; if you believe that all men depend on one another'. Here is a recognition that work is done in community and an inkling of a problem of interpersonal relationships when people share a divided work process. Not too many of the people who consider themselves 'religious' were aware of this basic problem.

For a number of people the attitude towards other people is the main link between religion and work: 'To work for each other, to help one another, to do the best for the community at large' expressed a religious attitude in work. 'I feel that my general attitude towards people—I think that the underlying principles of the Bible govern my attitude.' Or: 'Religion has something to do with every minute of your life. It makes you more tolerant. You got to be charitable.' 'If you try and treat everyone as a human being you can say that was sort of religious.'

Most of the people who spoke to us so far talked about the work process or about people, rather than about the social order. Only one person referred to an 'employee'—in talking about religion and work. 'Religion is only remotely related to the way of work... You feel that if you have had a religious training... you have a moral obligation towards your employees.' He then mentioned the parable of the vineyard.

Questioned about this parable he spoke about the problem of promotion from within versus taking in people from the outside: 'Yes, I think the situation is more acute at Scott Bader in this respect. You have the feeling that the later you came to

Scott Bader the better you do. People who came most recently do best. If you accept the Christian teaching completely, you would tend to judge this situation in terms of the parable of the vineyard. You would say I undertook to do a certain job for a certain reward. In the parable of the vineyard the people who came in at eight o'clock in the morning undertook to work until ten o'clock for a penny. The people who came in the afternoon still got a penny. The people who came in the morning had a bad deal. On the other hand nobody has to do more than they agreed to. They made a contract and they should abide by it.'

He had mixed feelings about certain aspects of the work situation but attempted to justify it in terms of a fairly literal interpretation of the parable of the vineyard combined with 'contractual' thinking typical of capitalism.

For a few people faith relates religion to work: 'You could have a problem. If you've got any faith you can overcome it . . . I read something a parson said, "It's a marvel what can be accomplished even by raising your eyes to heaven."' More sceptical was a person who mentioned 'faith in life' but added 'I'm quite willing to believe that someone without religion could do it as well.'

One person felt religion may have a bad influence on work. 'Religion to me means a way of life which I endeavour to stick to.' He contrasted religion thus understood with the established religions which make people believe in life after death. This 'is a jolly good psychological tool to put people on the lines to doing the best things for the community.'

VII

Many among those who felt that religion had something to do with work were inarticulate and vague. Those who did not see any relationship between religion and work were brief and clearest:

'I don't think that my kind of work can be influenced by my religious outlook and belief.' 'No, none at all . . . I never go to church and have my views set against it. You have to work to get yourself a better place in society.' Or: 'No, I don't think it has . . . it's got nothing to do with your job—has it?' For him work has become a job because it has lost meaning and become a mere means—to 'make' a living. He has no sense of participation in nature, in things or in life. 'Making' means to make money.

'No, regardless what your religion is, you still work the same —unless you refuse to work Sundays owing to your religion.' Work on Sunday is mentioned here as a peripheral reference to a religion reserved for one day in the week. Not unrelated to such a conception of religion is the feeling that 'religion doesn't play a part in the running of any firm in industry. It evidently doesn't because there are not many people who attend these Monday meetings.'[7]

Some people felt that work and religion are simply incompatible. They have 'very little' to do with each other. 'It would be nice if you could, but if you did carry out your religion at work I think you would be put on . . . They would not expect you to grumble—you would have to be really good.' Or: 'No because when I work I work by the sweat of my brow. And I am inclined to blaspheme occasionally. When you work you don't think of religion. You do the job. You don't turn round and say to God: "Please help me to do this". You are on your own when you do your work.'

VIII

The summary picture shows a wide range from the experience of a calling and obedience to God to the feeling that work and God have nothing to do with each other. The extremes of the range mark distinct occupational differences. The remnants of the 'Protestant Ethic' are found among people with executive positions. Some workers experience God in their work—even strongly—but for the majority the link between religion and work is much more tenuous, if not completely broken.

[7] On some Mondays a group of people interested in religion held meetings in the Commonwealth Hall. These meetings took place intermittently. They were begun in 1963 and were attended by about half a dozen people.

Denominational differences, on the other hand, are not pronounced.

These findings seem to contradict our finding that for the workers 'to be religious' is more related to life and action than it is for other occupational groups.[8] One might expect that those people who have emphasized the 'existential' meaning of religion also feel that religion has something to do with the way they work. But the opposite is the case. In the factory where we had the greatest concentration of 'existential' answers we also find the greatest concentration of 'No's' to the question of the relevance of religion for work.

Major reasons lie in the following pattern of awareness: (i) religion is seen as more relevant to 'life' than to work, (ii) work is separated from life in terms of an inner meaning and purpose, (iii) work is seen as taking place within a sphere to which religion is in fact not applied.

These factors are interrelated. They explain why people who give the most existential meaning to religion also are most emphatic about its absence in the sphere of work. They miss religious values and an ultimate meaning but they are quite unaware that it *could* possibly be there: 'When you work, you are on your own.' Work is experienced as something soulless, something without deeper purpose. People in the factory thus highlight again a general trend. The separation of the spheres of life and the relegation of industry into a sphere cut off from the universe of ethics and values destroys the wholeness of life and alienates people from the ground of their being. The confusion of universal and historically unique dimensions reinforces this alienation. And the Church sanctions it in so far as it accepts the society as it is. A common theme which appears again and again in people's responses is a feeling of unresolvedness, a feeling that something 'should be' there which in fact is not; an inability to find something that people are looking for—a feeling of separation of spheres of life which are somehow felt to belong together.

[8] Asked: 'If you say a man is religious what do you mean?' 8 out of 30 people understood religion as a way of life, 6 as reading the Bible or going to Church, 6 as having faith or believing in God, 10 gave other reasons.

People have an urge to put some meaning, some values, some guiding principles into the world of work.[9] There is a deep longing for purpose, for community and for true self-fulfilment though not many people are aware of it as a longing for God. Nor are they necessarily aware of 'an absence' of God. But they would not have answered the questions about work and God as they did if there was not something in their soul crying out for Him. They would have reacted more clearly affirming or more vehemently denying the relevance of religion. They would have been neither as uneasy, nor as vague, nor as much trying to find a relationship where it was so difficult to find one.

God is not dead. God always IS. But in industry today His presence can only be sensed in His absence.

9 When asked: 'How do you feel after the day's work?' followed by the query 'Satisfied?' there was evidence of a strong urge to give meaning to work. There is also evidence of a strong need for inner freedom.

Part V

Conclusions

Chapter 25
Potentialities and realities

I

Our exploration of the deeper meaning of work showed a wide gulf between the world created by a century of capitalism and the world which the Commonwealth wants to bring into being. Can this gap be closed? Are we dealing with abstract ideas or with actual possibilities which may be realized?

These are the questions to which we shall turn our attention in this final section. In attempting to answer them we must deal with two related problems: What is the nature of the challenge which the Commonwealth offers us today? What are the implications for a new social order?

We shall deal with the first two questions in this chapter and with the last two in the following two chapters.

II

Three reasons support the view that the Commonwealth opened potentialities which we can realize provided we deal adequately with the problems of their realization:

(i) A number of people are already on the way of realizing the existing potentialities, (ii) All potentialities need time for their realization and (iii) we find ourselves at a stage in the development of human consciousness in which completely new possibilities of realization are coming into being.

In the preceding section dealing with the meaning of work we have, on the whole, stressed general trends rather than individual situations. We must, therefore, emphasize that there are people in all groups whose attitudes do not fit the predominant views. Some people are meaningfully related to their work, their society and an ultimate reality.

As we might expect, the Founders of the Commonwealth have attitudes quite different from the main stream of capitalism. Ernest and Godric Bader have a sense of purpose and they have hope. They have no illusion of being more than a drop in a vast sea but out of a deeper awareness of the eternal ground of all life, they have a sense of relatedness to a power greater than they are—a power which in some often mysterious way will ultimately win. They have a clear idea of what is historically unique and what is universal. They have an image of a better world. Socialism is an ethical ideal for them. Religion is central and encompasses the whole of life; the resurrection holds the key to the Kingdom.

There are other people with similar values. Each person is different and there is a great richness of views and experiences among the people of the Commonwealth. Potentialities of development too have a very personal dimension. But there are clear indications that the potentialities which the Commonwealth wants to develop have already taken root in people.

To assess the potentialities actually opened by the Commonwealth we have systematically examined the spontaneous references to the Commonwealth made in the course of our interview-conversations.

When people are not being asked any questions about the Commonwealth in a conversation which deals with quite different themes, yet the Commonwealth is mentioned, we may presume that the references to the Commonwealth indicates a potentiality of development. Even if only one person has developed a new awareness because of the Commonwealth this awareness could also be developed by other people provided certain conditions are fulfilled. In this sense it is a potential reality.[1]

The Commonwealth was mentioned spontaneously about sixty times by about twenty people. This means that almost two thirds of the people mentioned the Commonwealth, each of them referring to it about three times. Most frequently people saw a new human dimension and purpose in the

[1] It is true that the person may have wanted to please the interviewer or is an 'exceptional' person. This poses problems which cannot be discussed here. Suffice it to say that the examples given in this chapter come from a cross-section of people and not from any exceptional group or person.

organization of work created by the Commonwealth. They were also aware of the Commonwealth as a model for a new social order. Last but not least they experienced the Commonwealth as an expression of a new understanding of the nature of man.[2]

People's spontaneous reactions as well as the new views and experiences which the Commonwealth has brought about in some people show that the gap between the inherited reality of capitalism and the demands made by the Commonwealth has already been bridged by some people who have realized at least certain aspects of the new consciousness which the Commonwealth demands. However these bridges are still in the nature of precarious threads linking the old with the new. Is it possible to build solid bridges between the old world and the new? Can they be used as bridgeheads for all people to move into the new world?

We will answer these questions as fundamental problems, not in terms of the actual possibilities that Scott Bader will be the vanguard of the new movement. The latter poses many problems which do not belong here. Suffice it to say that Scott Bader must deal with the fundamental problems which we are discussing in this section if it does not want to go the way of Boimondau.[3]

III

A potentiality belongs to the future because it takes time, it needs growth and development to become a reality. But it also belongs to the present because it exists now, at this very moment of time, as a germ which may take root and grow into a new reality provided only it is properly nourished and culti-

[2] Among a total of 55 spontaneous responses 32 referred to work (of these 13 referred to human dimensions in work, 6 to common ownership, 6 to the purpose of work, 3 to the value and power structure, 2 to security and 2 to the willingness to resolve problems without destructive conflicts arising); 11 responses referred to the social order, 8 to human nature and 4 to the Commonwealth as a topic of conversation.

[3] By this I mean that a democratic organization is preserved without a new awareness developing which is in agreement with the Constitution of the Commonwealth.

vated. Whatever IS tomorrow exists today as a potentiality of BECOMING. Whatever IS today consists of the realized potentialities of yesterday and the potentialities inherent in the present—the eternal now.

To understand the problems of developing the potentialities opened by the Commonwealth we best visualize the latter as an organized organism.[4] It is an organism since it consists of people who are organically or communally related to each other; it is an organization because it functions within a framework of consciously determined means-end relationships. As an organized organism it partakes of the following stages of development: (i) the preparatory period, (ii) the birth of the idea and its embodiment in some form of organization (the Constitution of 1950) (iii) experience and experiment with a new reality (1950–1963) (iv) establishment of an organization tested by experience and experiment (Constitution of 1963), (v) unfolding of its potentialities, (vi) maturation and continuous transformation and / or (vii) decline and death.

These stages of development mark a complex process of growth. Certain potentialities of development are evenly distributed in time. We can make a new beginning at any time. But the kind of beginning we can make, the quality of the potential which we may realize depends upon the specific stage of development at which we find ourselves. The potential reality of a child is different from that of an adolescent or from a person in the second half of life. So are the potentialities of organized organisms at different stages of their development. We cannot expect a very young Commonwealth to have realized potentialities which belong to a later stage of development.

At the time of the main interview-conversations, on which this book is based, the Commonwealth was in transition from the third to the fourth stage: based on ten years of experience a new organization was about to be established. This stage of development is broadly characterized by two sometimes con-

[4] The concept of 'organization' is parallel to the concept of 'society' as used by Tönnies whereas the concept of 'organism' is parallel to Tönnies' concept of community. See Ferdinand Tönnies, *Community and Association*, Routledge & Kegan Paul, 1955.

flicting trends: the limitation of the extent to which a young organization can have realized its potentialities, and the vigour of youth. Given the relatively short time during which a radically new organization has been built up we can indeed speak about a vigorous development though there have been considerable differences in the participation of different groups in this development. Workers have undoubtedly participated less than other groups.[5]

After the adoption of the new Constitution in 1963 the Commonwealth has entered the fifth stage in which its potentialities may unfold. The extent to which its potentialities can be realized and the extent to which the gap between these potentialities and the existing realities can be bridged depends upon the level of mental health and the stage in the development of consciousness which we could possibly achieve.

There is indeed a wide gulf between the realities of capitalistic man and the potentialities of Commonwealth man. Even the metaphor 'capitalistic man' is misleading. Notwithstanding pious sentimentalities and pronouncements of the power élite, industry today does not have an image of man that deserves to be called human. We are dealing with a pre-human stage of realization. As well stated in 'Personnel Management', the rhesus monkey and not a human being is the standard of human relations 'skills'.[6] Cybernation proves this point. The tasks performed by people in industry today are of such a nature that the machine can do a better job! Men in indusry are mechanisms not beings of flesh, blood and spirit. Therefore the mechanization of sheer brain power shows them up as inferior mechanisms rather than as people who, being human, are more than machines.

The Rhetoric of democracy and the lip-service given to the dignity of man hide the sub-human conception of man which is still typical for industry today though the heyday of capitalism is long past.

[5] The extent to which this is true has been shown very clearly in the study made by Roger Hadley. See Appendix on Method, pp. 173–174.

[6] See *Personnel Management*, Vol. XLIII, No. 358, December 1961, p. 219. See also Chapter 27, note 4.

In sharp contrast to the sub-human mechanical conception of man stands the conception of man which is rooted in the Judeo-Christian world view. This conception is in essential agreement with the standards of mental health which are emerging today. They are human because they recognize the essence of man, his spiritual qualities, his quest for wholeness. These standards have to be realized if the Commonwealth is to realize its own potentialities of development.

IV

The implications of the new standards of mental health—which are a new form of the universal image of man underlying all great religions—can best be clarified as we examine the criteria for a healthy development of a person in the perspective of the development of human consciousness. In doing so we must keep in mind the inadequacy of purely historical evidence to indicate the extent to which potentialities of development may be realized. What is possible today cannot be derived from what was possible yesterday. It can only be defined in terms of the potentialities of a new age whose dawn we are witnessing today.

The criteria for healthy development will be presented as part of a developmental scheme of man's growth which has been tested by a good deal of experience.[7] We shall indicate (i) major requirements for health, (ii) the extent to which the Commonwealth has recognized or realized them and (iii) the challenge which the Commonwealth poses as regards future developments.

The prime requirement of all healthy growth is trust. The Commonwealth has indeed established a basic atmosphere of trust. There is still mistrust and considerable fear. But they are remnants of the old order and often have a projective quality.

A sense of autonomy rooted in the ability of a give and take

[7] The basic scheme as presented here has been developed by Erik Erikson. See Erik H. Erikson, 'Growth and Crisis of the Healthy Personality', in *Symposium on the Healthy Personality*, Editor M. J. E. Senn, M.O., the Josiah Macy, Jr. Foundation, 1950, pp. 91ff.

is another requirement. In this respect the Commonwealth itself is in a stage of transition. Inasmuch as it still has elements of the old pyramidal structure, genuine give and take is not possible. To the extent to which people move in a five-dimensional universe of circles or rather spheres the preconditions for a give and take have been fulfilled.

A third condition is the ability to develop initiative, to exercise a healthy self-assertion and a *true* 'competitve' spirit. Here too the Commonwealth is in a transitional stage. Being an island in a society in which a deep sense of powerlessness makes genuine initiative difficult, in which self-assertion has degenerated into ego-centricity and competition into a struggle to outdo others, it has to fight against great odds.

The three conditions of health mentioned so far—which also correspond to the first three stages of man's development—determine the *basic* security and the 'internal' power structure. As we have seen the people of the Commonwealth experience a high degree of security. But this is only half of the story. The other half is contained in the question: is it compensatory security or is it security which becomes the basis for creative development?

If trust, autonomy and initiative cannot be developed properly, the need for unilateral control, for power *over* other people arises. Basically this need is a compensation for a sense of inferiority. It has, therefore, a compensatory quality and leads to the need for compensatory security. The security which a person reaches through proper development of trust, autonomy and initiative is of a very different quality. It is an inner certainty which has its correlate in power exercised as influence in relation to people, not as control over people.

Being the children of an industrial society for which power is the right to command and to give orders, the people of the Commonwealth have only begun to experience new modes of power. Living in a world which separates 'the material' from 'the spiritual' and confuses the universal with the historically unique, they cannot help being confused about the meaning of power. Power still has a tendency to be attached to a position and to show itself in a desire for self-aggrandizement, in a striving for status and prestige. Much of their security remains, therefore, compensatory.

Speaking about the advantages of the Commonwealth a person commented: 'You are insured twenty-four hours a day.' Insurance against certain unforeseeable risks is a necessary and important thing. But the desire to feel insured for twenty-four hours a day makes 'material' security a substitute for the security of a meaningful life. It is an expression of profound insecurity, reminiscent of the comments made by workers in the United States about the way they feel when they think about death. Many, after having said that they were not afraid, mentioned that they had taken out life insurance. Again a very worthwhile deed but hardly a meaningful answer to the problem of death. It is a compensation to avoid the encounter with an ultimate situation—an extreme illustration of a compensatory security. In Britain none of the people of the Commonwealth responded in the same way when asked about their feelings about death.[8] This fact, if generally true, would indicate that the process of dehumanization has not yet reached the same proportions as it has in the United States.

But the fundamental problem of a false separation of the spheres of life and a search for a deeper meaning and purpose of life exists in both countries. This situation deeply affects the experience of security, and helps to explain the mixture of uneasiness and of cynicism of some people in regard to the most clearly established function of the Commonwealth—the security of the provision of basic needs in health and sickness. 'It is really only a sick-benefit club, isn't it?'

This is another illustration of the odds against which the Commonwealth is struggling to realize a new conception of power and to give to people the kind of security which can be the basis for a genuine development. The changes in the power structure which have been accomplished so far have at least neutralized the game of power which is so central in industry and there are clear indications that people object to the old

[8] In the series of questions on religious consciousness people were asked: 'Do you ever think about death?' and 'How do you feel when you think about death?' I undertook the comparable American study in Austin, Minn.

forms of power. In its basic approach the Commonwealth stands therefore, for a genuine security based on trust, autonomy and initiative.

V

Based on these three requirements, 'industry' in the sense of being industrious, of developing basic skills, is necessary for health.[9] The sense of industry thus understood is related to the sense of identity, of knowing who one is, what one's own peculiar abilities and potentialities are—another requirement for health.

In illustrating the lack of a sense of identity, Erikson refers to 'The death of the Salesman' in which Biff says 'I just can't take hold, Mom, I can't take hold of some kind of a life.'[10] How many people in industry are in this position? Though extreme cases are exceptional in the Commonwealth, a sense of industry and identity has difficulties in developing. This is particularly true if we think of a genuine creative expression.[11]

The problem can again be well illustrated by reference to the problem of security—in this case the experience of financial security versus a wider sense of security.

Financial security may be experienced as part of a sense of security which allows a person to concentrate his or her effort on the achievement of those values and purposes which have personal significance. It is true that in going one's way towards these goals and values one may find that 'there is no such thing as security in this world'—as one of the people of the Commonwealth said. But in saying this this person moved into a realm of ultimate experience. The truth of his insight must, therefore, not be misused to question the desirability of financial security as part of a sense of security. People who complain about other people's desire for financial security are usually people who themselves enjoy a high degree of such security.

The desire for financial security becomes problematic only

[9] See Erikson, *op. cit.*, p. 132.

[10] *Ibid.*, p. 137.

[11] From this point on, I do not follow any more Erikson in terms of sequence of stages.

if people have a craving for financial security because they lack a real sense of security. In such situations the desire for security is a compensation for lack of meaning and purpose in life. There are quite a few people at Scott Bader for whom this is true. Not many of the people of the Commonwealth are imbued by a clear sense of meaning and purpose in their work and life. Work as we have seen, is only exceptionally experienced as an important part of a meaningful life. But the Commonwealth offers opportunities for development beyond the financial security given. Some people are already moving to meet these opportunities.[12] The Commonwealth poses a challenge to make security the basis for growth and development instead of allowing it to be merely a compensation for lack of deeper meaning.

VI

The ability to relate to other people is a prime requirement of health. In this sphere of life the Commonwealth offers a fundamental challenge by demanding a widening of consciousness to a communal awareness of other people.

Shrinkage of consciousness is a typical attribute of the sovereign individual who can only see half of the real world. To understand this situation we may visualize our daily world of experience as consisting of an intricate pattern of small red dots symbolizing people and connecting green lines symbolizing the interrelationships between people. The consciousness of egocentric man has shrunk to such an extent that he has become blind to the colour green, indicating a loss of the sense of community. This tendency came clearly to the surface in people's attitude towards the transfer of the ten per cent. Founder Shares and towards common versus part-ownership.

Common ownership means that there is something truly in-

[12] Over half of those who mentioned security and sick leave also mentioned other aspects of the Commonwealth—such as participation and service—when asked what the advantages of the Commonwealth are. Twelve people mentioned either participation or service or a general advantage other than sense of belonging, understanding, and freedom of expression.

divisible, something that exists only as a unit, something that can only be shared by participation in this unit and not by dividing it into individual segments. Take, for example, the factory at Scott Bader. It is an intricate network of reactors, machines, implements of all kinds, storage equipment, boilers, etc. This equipment is connected by wires and pipes, and controlled by many instruments and by chemical and physical processes. Could we possibly divide the factory among the people who work at Scott Bader? Which part would we give to whom? Who would get the boilers? the reactors? the transformers? the pipes and lines connecting them? the instruments through which the chemical processes are controlled?

To raise these questions is enough to show their meaninglessness. Yet many people find it easier to think in terms of owning a part rather than in terms of common ownership. They experience themselves as red dots, as inflated little egos, who would like to divide the world into little bits since it is much too big to be swallowed whole. Owning 'a part' of the company is congenial to this red-dot-centred-consciousness because whatever transcends the ego is divided into shares and dividends and thus used to inflate the ego.

The existence of such a shrunken consciousness is greatly facilitated by the transformation of use into exchange value. Once we transform the indivisible 'plant' of machines into pieces of paper called titles for ownership with a monetary value we can divide it indefinitely. We can print as many shares as we want. There is no end to the fragmentation of human experience once man is sufficiently alienated from his true self to live primarily in a world of exchange value.

Consciousness dominated by exchange value is a perverted consciousness because it implies a confusion between means and ends. Money, essentially a means, becomes an end, it becomes the central factor in the consciousness of man. This aspect of modern industrial societies (which Marx called 'the fetishism of commodities' and which influences strongly the consciousness of Western industrial man) is a decisive factor in making us unable to see the green lines which create unity and indivisibility between red dots—be they people or machines and equipment. Sharing in something that is indivisible or holding something in common is impossible for a red-dot-centred individualistic consciousness, because it presupposes a living experience of relatedness, of an organic totality of dots and lines.

As always in life we must pay a price for denying an aspect of reality. The price of red-dot-centredness is meaninglessness. No man is an island, no man can exist independently from others, particularly in modern industrial society. Every attempt to isolate one's consciousness from the facts of interdependence by 'owning' (and hence 'controlling') a bit must fail. No amount of 'ownership' of exchange value can substitute for the genuine experience of the interrelatedness and interdependence of the person and the community.

By its emphasis on use-value, its demand for a communal consciousness based on common ownership, the Commonwealth poses a fundamental challenge to realize the requirement of a genuine human relatedness.

VII

True relatedness to people and creative expression in work are only possible through relatedness to the ground of one's being. Such a relatedness is the last and most comprehensive requirement for healthy growth. It is a fundamental requirement for wholeness.

The deepest sense of security is rooted in an experience of this universal ground which expresses itself as an experience of one's own true self in conjunction with the experience of a universal power. This security implies true freedom, that is power to realize one's true potentialities. It is in sharp contrast to the shrunken consciousness in which the little self becomes the centre of the universe, in which people are unable to distinguish between their true and their little self, between their own peculiar potentialities and such manifestations of one's little self as status and prestige.

True freedom in a deeper sense of the word has only exceptionally been realized by the people of the Commonwealth. For many people freedom is equal to non-interference.[13] They have an awareness of something universal and of an ultimate, but this awareness has rarely become central and operative in their lives. Free time has, therefore, a tendency 'to drag' rather than being a positive experience. While working time has a tendency to be a regulating, restricting factor—not a fulfilling element.[14] Some of the most sensitive people experienced work as 'life regulated by time' and hence as something 'from which you would like to break out'. The lack of freedom experienced in connection with work is enhanced for those whose choice of work has been dictated by outer circumstances rather than by an inner calling. The confusion of universal and historically specific dimensions of life and the loss of an experience of the eternal are decisive for this situation.

In this respect the Commonwealth poses the greatest challenge. It implies a concept of mental health which makes the quest for a clearer, more objective and more encompassing view of life central. This requirement for a new clarity and wholeness sums up all the previous requirement mentioned above.

The Commonwealth wants to make Christianity—to use the words of Ragaz, who inspired Ernest Bader—real dynamite. Ultimately it is a witness to the spirit of Christ in the midst of a world which is only nominally Christian. It is one of the few ongoing experiments in industry which challenges us to realize the spirit of truth in a world which has lost the sense of the eternal.

[13] When asked: 'Do you have enough freedom to do your job your own way to satisfy you?', the large majority answered in the affirmative, but freedom to them means essentially non-interference. The expectation of freely using one's abilities is limited. Asked: 'What abilities do you have that you want to use but can't use on your job?', the majority indicated that they had none. This is no indication of any objectively valid lack of potentialities but of a low level of expectations as to the possible meaning of work.

[14] Time which is not filled with activity tends to become time which 'drags'. This is clearly shown by people's answers to the question: 'When you are at work does the time generally pass slowly or quickly?' 'When does it pass slowly and when quickly?'

VIII

The way we experience and see the world expresses itself so vividly in the way in which we participate in work and society that we may speak about an outer and an inner participation or involvement. All outer activity is the result of an inner involvement and all inner activity has its expression in a gesture or a more complex behavioural pattern.[15]

The experience and perception of life briefly outlined in the preceding section (and summed up in some universal standards of mental health) finds therefore expression in corresponding modes of participation in work. What are the realities and potentialities which the Commonwealth has opened in this respect?

During the first decade of its existence the Commonwealth has opened channels for participation far beyond what is usually known in industry. The result is a most varied pattern ranging from practically no involvement to lives very much centred around the Commonwealth. Manifold factors influence the way and extent to which people availed themselves of the new opportunities for participation.

(i) The general personality orientation plays an important role.[16] People have a tendency to move in the direction indicated by the type of person they are and the specific potentialities they have. A person with strongly developed feelings for people and an intuitive understanding of immediate life situations will seek satisfaction within the work community or in contact with people in the local community. A person with a well developed capacity for technical or for abstract thought will find in the organizational aspects of work and in technical development his most meaningful relationships.

(ii) Equally important but more complex is the specific per-

[15] About the significance of gestures and their relationship to human universals see Stuart Hampshire, *Thought and Action*, London 1960, pp. 54ff.

[16] By personality orientation I mean basic personality types such as introversion, extraversion, feeling, thinking etc. types. We are dealing here with basic orientations of a person rather than with stages of development of a person.

sonality development, that is, the development of people's emotional, intellectual, aesthetic and other potentialities, particularly their ability for a mature give and take and a mature response to the manifold problems arising in a work situation. The degree of inner security and the need for power over others versus power through influence are decisive in this respect. Participation in the organs of the Commonwealth fosters power through influence and presupposes, therefore, a good deal of inner security.

(iii) Cultural forces shaping people's attitudes are of great significance. The nature and the level of expectations indicates major cultural forces. On the whole the level of expectation is low, particularly with regard to the possible meaning of work. There is little expectation that either work or life are meaningful ventures. The only clearly established expectation is of a constantly rising standard of living (accompanied by attempts to keep up with the Jones). Energy is thus channelled away from the wider goals and objectives of the Commonwealth. This tendency is reinforced by the acceptance of the world 'as it is' and the—usually indirect and unconscious—sanctioning of the historically given by the power of the universal. Even a confusion without sanctioning of 'what is' has an inhibiting influence on participation.

The result of these three factors may be summed up in the following pattern of participation: there has been more involvement in the concrete aspects of work—people, the work environment, etc.—than in the organized aspects—the goals of the organization, the new structure of values and power. Participation in a Commonwealth movement concerned with a new social order beyond the gates of the firm has been exceptional.

The Commonwealth demands a development of participation along the lines initiated during the first decade but moving considerably beyond what has been achieved. Having had considerable success in neutralizing the negative forces inherent in the traditional organization of work, the Commonwealth has only begun to transform destructive into creative tensions. This transformation gives us the key to the future.

The Commonwealth has created a new field of forces which has a tendency to release energy for participation because it potentially resolves some of the destructive tensions inherent in the traditional organization of work. If this resolution goes far enough, constructive tensions replace destructive ones. The people of the Commonwealth form a wide range as regards the extent to which this release of energy and transformation of tensions has actually taken place. At one extreme of the range are those who did not benefit from the new potentialities. In some cases, when the new goals were too removed, there may even have been a hardening of destructive tensions manifesting itself in cynicism. At the other extreme the Commonwealth has given a new zest for life. In between are varied and manifold patterns resulting from a number of factors. Education, the position in the firm, the kind of work done combine with the factors mentioned above in determining the extent to which constructive tensions arise.

The most creative tensions arise out of an awareness of universal forces and an attempt to mould a given situation in the light of the universal. This demands a vision of a new order and/or a vision of human potentialities. The realization of the basic values of the Commonwealth will ultimately depend upon its ability to bring to life such a vision. It is not necessary for everybody to have a definite notion about a new social order. But it is necessary to have an inner vision of human potentialities for growth and development and of relatedness to a human community. It is necessary to have some kind of experience of a true self as distinguished from a little (or false) self.

To put the problem into sharp relief we distinguish between three models of participation:

(i) Participation out of habit or out of conformity. We go to work because this makes us appear respectable citizens rather than beatniks. We follow all kinds of practices and rules without questioning their value and meaning. We may even go to meetings to be looked upon as good members of the Commonwealth. This mode of participation is marginal in terms of the responsible participation which the Commonwealth wants to foster.

(ii) Participation satisfying the needs of our little self: we gain respect, we are liked by the boss, we gain power over others. We work hard to get a promotion, we shine in the new car we get as executives. This kind of participation is a response to a human situation, but it is an inadequate response since it is based on a false perception of ourselves as the centre of the world. As a matter of fact the world does not turn around us —not even around the most powerful of us.

(iii) Participation satisfying the needs of our true self: we strive to develop our abilities and share the fruits of such development with other people while learning from them and growing with them; we gain respect for our achievements without demanding it, we gain true power and influence which does not aim to control others; our work is creative because it expresses an inner meaning and purpose; we go to meetings because we are involved in the problem at hand and have taken the responsibility of contributing to its solution.

As we combine the three models of participation with the three areas in which people may participate—the various concrete and organizational dimensions of work and the world beyond the factory gates we get a clearer understanding of the potentialities of participation.

We may participate in different areas with different parts of our being—that means at different depth dimensions. Participation through habit, through satisfaction of our little self and through satisfaction of our true self may coexist. We may for example do our work out of habit, strive hard to be liked by others and at the same time develop some genuine ability peculiar to ourselves.

We may also participate quite unequally in different areas. We may be related to the people who form the community of work with our true self while the organization itself is pretty much outside our awareness. Or we may be absorbed in an attempt to change society without much contact with people.

The challenge of the Commonwealth is to realize the third mode of participation—a genuine creative participation—which expresses the universal concept of mental health outlined above. Through creative participation we enter the realm of religious experience, since we are involved with our true self and thus are most deeply related to the human situation and to God. We follow our calling—our vocation. In this sense participation in terms of our true self results from man's response to that of God in him.

Chapter 26

The new and the old consciousness

I

To understand the deeper meaning of the challenge presented by the Commonwealth and to see its potentialities in a proper perspective we must explore the Commonwealth conception of man and society in the light of the evolution of human consciousness.

Potentialities of development are defined by man's essential nature. If we assume human nature to be essentially selfish or see it in terms of a given historical situation, potentialities of development are circumscribed by this selfishness or by the limitations of a passing and unique situation. Only in exceptional circumstances can we expect these limitations to be overcome. If we combine an understanding of history with an awareness of human universals we know that human nature cannot be defined in terms of the peculiarity of a specific period in history but must be understood in terms of an evolutionary process in which universal potentialities may find ever new, more personal and more truly communal expressions.[1]

The concept of mental health outlined in the preceding chapter is part and parcel of a new stage in the development of human consciousness. The Commonwealth, boldly anticipating its realization, is at the cutting edge of experimenting with this new understanding of man and society. It implies new modes of seeing the world and of participating in its development, as well as new ways of feeling, thought and aesthetic experience.

[1] The knowledge of such a process must not be confused with 19th and 20th century belief in progress. It does not exclude the rise and decline of cultures, indeed it implies that any society which is cut off from its creative universal ground is bound to decline.

To grasp the deeper significance of these new ways we must compare them with the old ways which dominate the present industrial and social scene. Such a comparison must be based on an understanding of the salient characteristics of the structure of human consciousness, particularly (i) the nature of the opposites (or complementaries), (ii) the nature and the degree of differentiation and (iii) the way and the level at which the divided parts are integrated into larger wholes.

When an epoch in the history of man is coming to an end and a new era is beginning, fundamental changes in all three aspects of consciousness are taking place. We must therefore explore (i) how the opposites or complementaries on which the Commonwealth is founded differ from those typical for work and society today, (ii) how the Commonwealth demands different modes of differentiation of work and of the whole pattern of relationships forming society, and (iii) how the Commonwealth leads to different forms of integrating various parts into a new whole.

II

The Commonwealth attempts to overcome the old opposites of sovereign individuals versus the sovereign state and versus markets. It aims to foster the development of the potentialities of people who stand in a complementary relationship to the human community of which they are part. It thus attempts to find a new freedom for the people.

Community in this newly developing mode of consciousness must be understood in a new—synthetic—way and must not be identified with the group, the organization or a wider entity as such. It means interrelatedness and interdependency. Community thus understood does not exist apart from the person but is a complementary aspect of the consciousness of people who are aware of their relationships and interrelatedness with others.

To develop this kind of communal relationships poses a dual problem (*a*) of determining the rights of the person and his obligation to other people, and (*b*) of the degree of autonomy and of mutual responsibility of people. The communal bond relates man to man by giving a certain degree of freedom to the person and making freedom interdependent with the freedom of other persons. It is a bond which delineates the areas (*a*) of individual-personal freedom and autonomy as well as those (*b*) of common concern and action. The Commonwealth is aiming to develop such a community of autonomous persons who are able to give out of the fullness of their hearts, people who are aware that they can develop their own potentialities only in relatedness to others.

Such a conception of persons living in community implies a radical transformation in the conception of 'self', 'selfish' and 'true self'. The old opposites are selfishness (often identified with 'the material') versus 'selflessness' (often identified with 'the spiritual' and service given to others). The new opposites are the development of a person's true self (which leads to true relatedness to others) versus development of a person's little or false self (which cuts the individual off his own true self and from other people while making him a prey of uncontrolled collective forces). In the new consciousness the material is recognized as an expression of the spiritual, not as an opposite.

The old consciousness made the experience of freedom precarious. This was a result of the disorder of society rather than of an overt denial of the value of freedom. Indeed modern industrial society is rooted in the recognition of the value of the individual. Without activating the universal power of the autonomy of the individual, capitalism could never have arisen. But the attempt to realize this universal principle of freedom within an organization of society based on the two opposites of individuals versus the state and individuals versus markets has only made it possible to free man from old dependencies (expressed in the development of a self-reliant individual) but not to develop true autonomy and personal meaning. This has led to a crisis which threatens the basic values and principles of modern society: the freedom of the individual is threatened by collective forces and jeopardized by meaninglessness and lack of purpose.

The Commonwealth is both the child of this crisis and the

promise of its resolution. It attempts to develop a communal consciousness which overcomes the traditional opposites of employer—employee, an opposition which reflects in the industrial sphere the presently prevailing structure of opposites implying a purely formal concept of freedom of contract devoid of any positive conception of freedom. This opposition between employer and employee permeates the whole organization of work and manifests itself in such psychological subtleties as the distinction between 'we' and 'they' as well as in the intricacies of a cost accounting system which reduces some people to variable costs and thus formalizes their existence as mere objects.

The Commonwealth shows new ways by accepting the complementary principles of democratic integration in industry and common ownership. It recognizes the communal character of the means of production which are created in common and used in common and it attempts to build true freedom of the person on the basis of a new relationship between the person and the organization.

A conflict between the goals of the organization and the aspirations and needs of the people is typical for industry today. Tensions between people and the organization may arise because the demands of the people are without proper balance or because the goals of the organization violate people's true needs and aspirations. Both causes for tension exist. The goals of most industrial enterprises are in conflict with man's true nature and freedom; and the licence with which the managerial task is defined in the typical company is bound to evoke unbalanced demands among the opposite numbers.[2]

Everything in the realm of human experience has its limitations, its inner balance. Freedom has too. Freedom without

[2] Hence all the money spent on 'human relations skills' which—as presently used—are primarily an attempt to reduce tension sufficiently so as to avoid the necessity of fundamental changes in organization. No matter how successful these attempts may be, they are unlikely to lead to true freedom. At best these skills if applied within the present basic structure of work may implement a freedom defined as the opposite of regimentation. This is progress as compared with traditional authority but it cannot solve the destructive human conflicts inherent in present-day industry. The quest for freedom

limits loses its true ethical quality, and becomes sheer licence no matter how it is rationalized, even if it is rationalized as managerial prerogatives.

The Commonwealth has created a new structure within which true freedom and new creative tensions may develop because the adjustment of the goals of the people and of the organization follows a new dynamics. The manifold opportunities for participation and the new balance of power embodied in the Constitution of 1963 make it possible to express personal aspirations within the organization and to mould the organization in agreement with one's true needs and aspirations.

As a result the Commonwealth has in principle—that is in beginning and in power—overcome the conflicts which arise when employer and employees are opposites. It has not 'resolved' the basic problems of work because they are universal problems. They are not due to capitalism—or any other ism. But the Commonwealth deals with these universal problems in a different way. Typical for the Commonwealth is the creation of a framework within which creative tension can replace destructive conflicts.

This becomes only possible as the existing opposites are overcome and a corresponding reorganization of the whole structure of work takes place. Within the present structure of opposites only false compromises are possible. Individual ownership of pieces of paper in combination with the existing value and power structure of corporate enterprise exclude the development of true values even if some form of collusion (sometimes called co-operation) takes place between employer and employees. Creative development is impossible as long as the central value of the enterprise is a concept of productivity defined in terms of technological-market chances, and as long as the power structure is defined in terms of a two-dimensional concept of subordination and superordination. The Commonwealth makes a creative development of true values possible

---

remains, therefore, an escape: escape from the meaninglessness of work into the diversion of leisure and escape from the boredom of empty time into working activity. Unfortunately no true freedom can be found in this way. Only the rat-race can be made all-encompassing.

because it substitutes for the present opposites new polarities and new opposites.

It is true that there remain conflicts between different values as decisions about the universal problems of work have to be made. Ideas about the way in which the common product should be distributed, for example, may differ greatly, and in some ways irreconcilably. But as people's awareness of their interrelatedness with other people deepens, the range within which different value positions can be creatively adjudicated widens. If this is not possible and no agreement on fundamental values can be reached, new communities expressing different values would have to be developed. The Commonwealth is in no way a monolithic model for industry. Rather it is a new form which opens new ways and possibilities. This is of particular importance as far as the ethical basis of industry is concerned.

The sharpening of an ethical awareness which is an important goal of the Commonwealth revives a dichotomy which has been slowly but surely submerged in the morass of present-day industry; namely the opposition between ethics and lack of ethics. Granted that the sovereign individual has ethical standards: he would neither steal nor cheat. But this is a primitive ethics, at best it has a tribal character. It is not the ethics of a human community. In industry today supply, demand and market conditions determine whether people have work, how they perform their work and what products they produce. Success, not personally meaningful values, determines goodness. What 'works' is accepted, not what has intrinsic value. Exchange value dominates, not use value. Affluence is trumps, not the development of true persons living in true community.

As contrasted to these false values—and false evaluation of means and ends—the Commonwealth attempts to create an order within which ethics can again become operative. It is concerned with true manhood and womanhood, not with the false personalization of a marketing-orientation.[3] It is also concerned with humanity as a whole. A true person is conscious of being part of mankind as a whole as well as of his or her own culture. The primacy of an awareness of our common humanity

[3] See Erich Fromm, *Man for Himself*, New York 1947, pp. 67ff.

has a particular importance today because for the first time in history we witness the development of a cosmic *human* consciousness distinguished from a 'Western' or 'Eastern' mode of consciousness.

As a form of organizing work the Commonwealth is as important for the spiritually underdeveloped Western countries as for the technologically underdeveloped Eastern countries. It shows a new way to man.

III

The realization that the traditional opposites have lost their original meaning and have become false opposites implies the realization that the divisions existing in the present mode of consciousness and the corresponding forms of social organization have become equally false. Today we witness a lack of necessary divisions and differentiations as well as divisions along lines which are destructive of true human development.

Besides the lack of a differentiation between true and false Being and Becoming there is an equally fundamental lack of differentiation between what is universal, rooted in the eternal ground of all Being and all Becoming and what is historically unique. We have seen that the lack of such a differentiation is rooted in the predominant awareness of ultimate reality and makes the perception of society a false one; it is a major factor leading to alienation and apathy and it impedes the experience of a deeper meaning of work. Instead of distinguishing the historically unique aspects of competition, markets, profits, wages, etc., from the universal aspects, most people confuse them. This confusion enhances the hold which the present social institutions have on people and intensifies their anxiety about radical change. Ultimately this confusion cuts people off from the universal ground of their own true Being and impedes the potentialities for true Becoming.

The Commonwealth has created an organization of work which attacks this confusion at a strategic point: the basic conception of wages and profits. It restores the universal meaning of profits as the surplus resulting from the work of all members of the community of work and abolishes the traditional historically unique meaning of wages. Wages cease to be income arising out of an exchange relationship to the firm and become a share in joint earnings.[4]

These changes in the basic organization of work create a new existential situation in which an awareness of universal and of historically unique aspects of work and society can develop more readily. As this happens, the implication of the Commonwealth for new possibilities of dividing work will become more apparent.

The forces determining the presently predominant division of work can best be understood in analogy to the growth of cancerous cells which divide and subdivide themselves without limit or without inner balance. Work tasks are being divided into the minutest movements—completely unrelated to a human need for balance, proportion, wholeness and integration. As a result man becomes fragmented and his soul becomes dissociated. The result is the truncated consciousness typical of modern industrial man.

Instead of contributing to the mental health of whole people, industry today makes the dubious contribution of allowing people to 'act out' their neurosis as divided beings. Industrial man is caught in the destructive conflicts created by a differentiation of work unrelated to human needs for growth and development. The Commonwealth opens the way for a very different understanding of mental health and demands much greater maturity from people than does life in an 'ordinary

[4] In the literature on wages and profits there is little explicit reference to the universal meaning of wages and profits. Some of the neo-classical economic writers distinguished between 'monetary' and 'real' terms. What they called 'real' referred indeed to the universal functions of wages and profits. An outstanding example is Taussig's *Theory of Wages*. But they contributed more to the confusion of thought rather than to any clarification because they applied their conclusions derived from reasoning in 'real' terms *as if* they would explain historically specific phenomena as such. Only Henry George made a systematic distinction (in his book *Progress and Poverty*) and Karl Marx's attack on capitalism is ultimately based on Aristotle's concept of the true nature of things (See Karl Marx, *Das Kapital*). In espousing an Aristotelean conception Marx has in fact created a common ground with Christianity, at least to the tradition of St. Thomas Aquinas.

company'. In particular it makes it more difficult to use the power of a position as a vehicle for acting out one's own unresolved anxieties, feelings of powerlessness and lack of fulfilment.

IV

A mode of consciousness and the corresponding forms of social organization are like patterns or configurations consisting of parts which are related to each other and unified in a whole. Inadequacies in the way in which consciousness and the spheres of life are differentiated are, therefore, inevitably reflected in inadequacies of integration.[5]

Living in modern industrial society tends to split human consciousness and to reduce man's awareness of himself to a small dot unrelated to the human community. The result is a shrunken inadequately integrated consciousness which in the extreme becomes schizophrenic. This limits the meaning of work and enhances the impact of an inhumanly divided work process ruled by technological market considerations. It also makes it more difficult to see the product as a link with a wider human community.

This situation is all the more significant since technology and markets have already created a world-wide human community. We are interdependent on a world-wide scale. But while technical developments and the division of labour between country and country have created a basis for a consciousness of a human community, Western industrialism has led to the shrunken consciousness of an isolated sovereign individual.

It is a tragic comment on our time that such a consciousness could be called by one of the people of the Commonwealth a 'scientific' consciousness. Though not scientific in the true

[5] There are manifold relationships between differentiation and integration of consciousness. The less differentiation, the lower the level of integration. There is a relationship between the nature and degree of differentiation of consciousness and the nature of projections and the extent to which they occur. As a genarel rule we may say that whatever is undifferentiated is projected in some form. For further discussion of this point see my paper on 'The Evolution of Consciousness and the Sociology of Knowledge'. See above p. 309 n.

meaning of the word 'science', it expresses the kind of 'scientism' which results from the predominance of technical considerations and the absence of a service orientation in the organization of industry. The shrinkage of consciousness just noted in conjunction with the central orientation of industry towards the principle of efficiency makes this so-called 'scientific' attitude possible. In its extreme form this attitude leads to what Ladriere called 'the nihilism of the technician'[6]—the consciousness of 'the technological idiot', who functions only as a fragmented individual unrelated to man and the universe of human values.

The Commonwealth aims to overcome this lack of integration by creating 'organized organisms'. Being organized they are the result of a conscious effort to integrate the activities of different people; being 'organisms' they are natural bodies regulated by the need for proportions and harmony. They are small enough to form a framework for meaningful participation and at the same time they are genuine links to a wider human community.

The deliberate attempt to control the size of the firm must be seen in this light. It is an assertion of the ultimate supremacy of human considerations in organizing work, not of 'smallness' as such. Basically it is an attempt to create a five dimensional universe of intercommunicating circles or spheres, forming an integrative framework within which true human values can develop. Each person has the opportunity to participate in a circle which is commensurate with his capacity for understanding while opening the way to a holistic and hence more wholesome experience of work. Split-off activities are thus 'rounded off' and the person is related to a wider community.

There is an explicit recognition in the new Constitution that such a development requires a tension between 'mere conventions' and the universal aspects of man's true nature. This does not mean that every convention is false. But to follow conventions merely because they are traditionally accepted subordinates the universal to the historically unique. It substitutes a

[6] See *Christians in a Technological Era*, Edited by Hugh C. White, Jr., New York 1964, p. 65.

rigid form for a living awareness of the universal ground of life. The new consciousness will be based on such a living awareness manifesting itself in ever renewed ethical and aesthetic forms.

In an industrial world which has lost a sense of the beautiful as well as a sense of the ethically good, the renewed awareness of aesthetic values deserves special emphasis. In the new order aesthetic values will be again part of the daily life of man. They will be recognized as the visual expression of the world which man is in the process of creating and as visual symbols of the new mode of consciousness. In this sense the Commonwealth Hall is already the symbol of an organization of work fostering the development of whole people and of a social order honouring God by recognizing the true humanity of His creation.

V

The new consciousness is in sharp contrast to the false consciousness typical of present-day industrial society. The new ways imply a new conception of what is normal or healthy and hence a fundamental re-orientation of the whole structure of consciousness.

A key to the understanding of this re-orientation lies in an understanding of the nature of projections typical for the existing organization of industry. The traditional power and value structure of industry rests on a projection of inner potentialities for responsible participation on 'the head' of an organization—'the governor', to use a British term. Projection is an inevitable psychological process unless we have reached a stage of non-involvement that Eastern philosophers portray as an ideal of relatedness to the world. But the kinds of projection which occur in Western industrial societies are not inevitable aspects of human nature. Rather they are a result of the emotional illiteracy which is typical of the present stage in the evolution of human consciousness and of the organization of industry. The Commonwealth marks a decisive step beyond this stage by creating a structure of power and channels of participation which demand that this projection be 'taken back' and that man become aware of the potentialities of the true powers within himself.

To take back such an all-pervading projection implies fundamental changes in the structure of human consciousness. It implies a freeing of potentialities which the truncated and stunted consciousness of modern industrial man has great difficulty in comprehending. The spiritual potentialities of man which may eventually be freed within a Commonwealth organization of work are therefore as much beyond the 'normal' consciousness of our time as our technological achievements were beyond the consciousness of medieval man.

Today we are still caught in forms of thought which can best be understood as modern forms of animism. The concept of animism is often used by anthropologists with reference to so-called primitive cultures. It is a process in which 'inanimate' objects are animated: trees are felt to have souls and to be inhabited by ghosts and nature seems a hiding place for good or for evil spirits. Present-day animism manifests itself in the ideology of efficiency and in the philosophy of marketable exchange value determined by the forces of supply and demand. Modern industrial man 'animates' the inanimate market forces with directive power beyond the control of man.

The animism of industrial man has a particular quality because it relates to exchange value rather than to use-value. It is true that exchange as well as use-value is a genuine and important aspect of the social order. But the exclusive emphasis on exchange value implies a particular danger of alienation because exchange value is an abstraction from the inherent qualities of a product, of a thing. Whereas the animism typical of earlier stages in the evolution of consciousness has often expressed an essential quality of the 'thing' which was animated, the animimism of modern industrial man is more likely to conflict with the essential quality (or use-value) of a thing.

The call to members of the Commonwealth to re-orient their lives beyond the confines of work and to be concerned with community is fundamentally a call to take back the projections which pervade people's perception of society. The rejection of the stock-exchange in particular is a rejection of social institutions expressing an animistic-projective mode of consciousness. The policy in regard to the sale of the product for war purposes is also important in this connection because it shifts the central emphasis from exchange to use-value. When this shift has been realized and animistic projections have been taken back we will be able to see man and society in a new light. The present world of industry will be as strange to the new man of tomorrow as the world of slavery is to us today. We will cease to rationalize the violation of human values typical of industry and be aware that ultimate values must be realized in daily life to be more than words. In so doing we will have moved a step further in man's quest to realize his true nature—to live as persons in community.

Chapter 27

Towards a new social order

I

A new consciousness and a new social order are interrelated. To overcome the false consciousness of industrial man and to counteract the rationalistic manipulative attitudes which are an important aspect of it, the new social order must have a new centre and a new configuration based on reason, understood as a synthesis of thought and feeling.

Two principles must guide the development of the new order: (i) man must become the centre of the organization of work and hence its ultimate end and (ii) money must become a means in the organization of the economy as a whole rather than being an end in itself.[1]

If consistently applied these principles would bring about changes so radical in the sense of going to the roots of things that none of the existing 'isms' can give us an adequate idea of the new order. The presently existing opposites would be overcome by a holistic conception of productiveness as the new centre and of service as the new goal of the organization. Markets would become links connecting people and the products of their work rather than dominating men and human values. With the resources of modern technology people would produce what they need for self-realization as persons living in community, rather than being waste-makers and victims of hidden persuaders buying things which must be sold to keep the economy running. Unemployment as known under capitalism could not exist since money would be a means and not an end in itself.

[1] We speak here about means and ends as embodied in the organization of industry, not about the means and ends of individual people. Money, for example, is an end as long as considerations of finance or profit are ultimate determinants of whether production takes place and what is being produced. no matter what role it plays in the value systems of any individual.

Equally fundamental changes would take place in the physical layout and in the nature of the community. Just as the organization of work would have a new centre so the community in which people live and work would have a new centre. Facilities for cultural and recreational activities and for worship would replace the business district as the centre of the community. Places of work, the home and these centres would be in an organic interrelationship fostering the development of whole people living in relatedness to others.

We cannot elaborate here the basic structure of this new order.[2] But we must examine the question of the significance of such a relatively small firm as Scott Bader as a model and first step in creating the new order.

II

Many people who hear about the Scott Bader Commonwealth become intrigued; something is stirred in them and they know in their heart that something significant is going on. They also sense that more demands are made on people than industry does in general: the Commonwealth demands more maturity, it calls for personal change besides change of organization and it requires the ability to give up false power, status and values to realize true relationships.

It is understandable that many people attempt to avoid growing-up—it is often a painful process. 'The gate is wide that leads to perdition, there is plenty of room on the road, and many go that way; but the gate that leads to life is small and the road is narrow, and those who find it are few.' Many rationalizations may be found to avoid taking the narrow road. It is always easy to find some fault in all that is human. Those who are blinded by the neon-lights shining on the wide road and who confuse the emotional illiteracy which is now considered 'normal' with true standards of sanity can always point to the Commonwealth experiment as something strange off the beaten track. Or people can find peculiar circumstances why it would work in Wollaston but not in their home towns.

[2] See my paper on 'Work in the Social Order of Tomorrow'.

When these rationalizations and arguments are spent there remains a last-ditch rationalization—often presented as an appeal to 'facts'—namely the idea that the Commonwealth is all right for small firms, for the little fry among the giants of industry but not for big business. It is considered a benevolent but ineffectual sideshow which is rather enjoyable to look at while the forces now determining industry are in the process of transforming the industrial jungle into the well organized world of cybernated machinery oiled with the brotherly love of cloth-monkeys.[3] But for the big firms which really count and which the new technology will make dominant, the principles of the Commonwealth are said not to apply. Meaningful participation is held possible in a small firm but not in a big industry.

The truth and the fallacy of this argument deserves careful consideration.

It is undoubtedly true that the kind of participation which allows people to develop their emotional, intellectual, intuitive and aesthetic potentialities requires small groups; it can only take place within a small circle of people. Indeed the Commonwealth itself is much too big to form the basic unit for meaningful participation thus understood. The Commonwealth must be seen as a wider circle or sphere consisting of many smaller circles or spheres which touch each other, intersect and cut across each other in a five-dimensional space.

It is also true that new problems arise as the organization becomes larger and more nuclear circles or spheres—as we shall call the small groups within which meaningful participa-

[3] I am referring here to the experiments made in the United States with cloth-monkeys who have the main physical qualities of a real monkey mother—like physique, warmth, etc. Newly born monkeys seemed as much attracted to these cloth monkeys as they are to a live mother, but when these cloth-monkeys grew up they were uninterested in their environment, and they did not mate with each other. The journal of the British Institute of Personnel Management had an editorial on 'The Cloth-Mother' discussing a talk given at the 1961 National Conference of the Institute. The speaker, Professor Drever, Head of the Faculty of Arts at Edinburgh University, compared the personnel manager to 'Joe, the Rhesus Monkey' who offers 'the shadow for the substance' and thus makes people the children of a cloth-mother. See 'The Cloth-Mother' in *Personnel Management*, Vol. XLIII No. 358, December 1961, p. 219.

tion can take place—come into being. But it does not follow that firms larger than Scott Bader will find only increased difficulties in creating meaningful ways of participating. Compensating advantages may exist and larger size may give increased scope for the development of people's potentialities.[4] It is, therefore, a matter of weighing the advantages and the disadvantages of different sizes rather than making generalized—and unsubstantiated—claims about the relationships between the size of the organization and the possibilities for participation.

The real test for the possibility of realizing the basic principles of the Commonwealth is men's power to build a truly human order, not the question of size as such. It is undoubtedly true that in an industrial civilization which Coomeraswamy has well characterized as 'neither human nor sane nor Christian'[5] the Commonwealth principles can be realized only in a limited way. Those who allege that size is incompatible with the realization of Commonwealth principles really say that the present disorder of society is incompatible with the realization of human values and the development of new forms of humanly meaningful participation. The Commonwealth is indeed incompatible with an economy over which man has lost control, which creates giants irrespective of any reasonable human considerations, even irrespective of the universal needs and demands of technological developments.[6]

[4] Even within its own limitations, the argument that participation is only possible in small firms is false because participation in the decision-making process may be easier in a larger firm than it is in a small one. Once we give up completely unrealistic concepts of 'worker's participation' in management in the sense of a worker participating in the technical day-to-day decision-making process outside his own competence, there is no reason why participation based on development of abilities, knowledge and experience would be less in a larger firm. A larger firm, for example, because it can afford more opportunities to more people may retain talents which a smaller firm can retain only to a more limited extent.

[5] See A. K. Coomeraswamy, *The Bugbear of Literacy*, London, Dennis Dobson, 1949, p. 1. quoted by A. K. Saran, 'India', *Contemporary Sociology*, Philosophical Library, New York, p. 1015.

[6] There are various technological developments which favour small rather than large firms. Electricity is an example. Even the most recent tech-

At present size is not primarily the result of the desire to use the 'best' methods of production. Most of the giants of industry consist of smaller production units which are combined for financial-power reasons. Technology, furthermore, can be used to make smaller production units viable and not only to make bigger production units bigger. Automation and cybernation reduce the number of people working in a given production unit. They also open up new possibilities for increasing the efficiency of smaller units.

Once we have understood that technology is not the basic factor determining size we get a new basis for examining the relationships between meaningful participation and the size of an organization. We shall then realize that meaningful participation demands a network of nuclear circles or spheres which must be organically related to each other and to larger units. This requires an organization of work determined by consciously chosen criteria of human development (including technical considerations) rather than by unconscious and uncontrollable market forces. Only a logic debased by emotional illiteracy and absence of ethical considerations could reject the Commonwealth principles *because* they are incompatible with the trend towards concentration. The truth is that the forces now determining our economy—including the forces making for increased concentration—are the reflection of a power and value structure which is incompatible with the true nature and destiny of man.

The first task in dealing with the problem of size is, therefore, to build a social order in which man can consciously control the size of the work units. The recognition of the need for limits in size expressed in the Commonwealth's effort to limit its size to reasonable proportions is of great importance in this context. Ultimately it is a demand that men take dominion of the earth rather than playing the role of the sorcerer's appren-

---

nological developments such as the computer and atomic energy may be used to foster small firms if they are made subject to public control and not left to competition among so-called private enterprises. I am indebted to R. Theobald for a deeper insight into some of the problems of modern technology.

tice who can no longer control the powers which he brought into existence. This is the prime requisite in building up a new order in which man can responsibly participate.

III

The transformation of the existing disorder of society into a social order which is based on human, sane or Christian values requires the formation of a 'Commonwealth' movement. This movement must foster a radical transformation of human consciousness and the corresponding forms of social organization. It must be based on the principle of non-violence—of Truth and Love—and implement a new dynamics of personal change interrelated with organizational change. As a movement it must rely on the development of creative tensions rather than exploit destructive conflicts.

We cannot discuss here in any detail the nature of such a movement and the problems of transformation. Suffice it to conclude with a few comments on the role of the people, of management, of unions and of the Church in this transformation.

Every person sensitive to the human situation of our time has a responsibility to become an agent of transformation for the new order. The people of the Commonwealth have a special responsibility if they want to become the core of a movement. They must systematically develop and evaluate what has been begun and enable other people to learn from their experience.

Management, being in a position of power, has a special responsibility to take the initiative in transforming the value and power structure and thus to do homage to a true function of management: to have a wide vision and to initiate new ideas.

Unions have a decisive role to play in the transformation of industry. If they want to gain more than countervailing power they must use their strength to build up a new organization of work. If they do not take the initiative in creating a new order, changes in their functions will be imposed on them since the Commonwealth changes the function of unions. At the same time the Commonwealth movement needs the help of unions to create a new social order within which it can properly develop.

And the Church or the churches? What role have they to play?

The true Church which is the mystical body of Christ or the body of mankind united in oneness does not 'play a role' but expresses the reality of true Being and Becoming. In its ultimate dimensions the Commonwealth is rooted in this reality. We would, therefore, expect that church which is the human expression of the true Church to be a major help to a Commonwealth movement. There is indeed a deep affinity between the Commonwealth and the new religious communities and movements—such as the Iona Community, the Community of Taize, the Seminar for Church Service in Industrial Society in Mainz-Kastel, the work of Abbe Pierre, the industrial missions and similar movements. But the Church as a whole is far from having grasped its role in the ongoing transformation of human consciousness and the corresponding forms of social organization.

The demand that service be the guiding criterion in men's relationship to each other has been a universal religious demand and is a central theme in the Judeo-Christian social witness. But few people take this demand seriously because it is made as a demand on the individual rather than as a demand on the organization of work. To be taken seriously service must be incorporated into the value and power structure of industry. This poses a challenge so far not answered.

The Church has a special responsibility to create a living awareness of the universal which is rooted in the eternal ground of all Being and Becoming and to make the 'new man' a dynamic reality and power for change. This task demands a willingness to be guided by the living spirit rather than by the dead letter of the law. It demands a willingness to be 'honest to God' in regard to the present disorder of society and the necessity of a new social order to come.

A church whose servants command such honesty will be intimately related to the 'Commonwealth' movement because such a church will articulate the vision of the Kingdom of God which men are striving to incarnate in their lives.

Epilogue

'Ultimately', Max Weber said, 'every social system is to be evaluated in terms of the type of person to whom it gives the greatest chance to become dominant—through inner selection of values and through selection of people with certain values.'[1] Our ultimate evaluation of the Commonwealth must therefore be in terms of our agreement or disagreement with the fundamental values it aims to realize, the ideal of persons living in community.

This ideal may be formulated in different ways. But its actual realization always depends upon its incorporation in human consciousness and the social order. The founder of the Commonwealth recognized that in an industrial civilization ideals can only become a reality if they are related to the organization of industry. The Commonwealth endeavours therefore to create a social order in which man truly related to himself, his neighbour and his God has a chance to develop. The Commonwealth thus challenges the disorder of society with a new order, the illness of industry with a concept of health rooted in the wholeness and holiness of man.

Can the Commonwealth possibly succeed in this challenge?

The first question which arises in this connection is: How well has the Commonwealth done so far?

The Commonwealth ideal as formulated in the new Constitution is far ahead of the presently prevailing mode of consciousness of most of the members of the Commonwealth. By and large the Commonwealth consists of people who are more strongly shaped by the present disorder of society than by the forces which the new order wants to activate. This is a decisive factor in any attempt to evaluate what has been achieved so far. We must evaluate the first twelve years of the Commonwealth as an attempt to create a new world view and a new social order

[1] See Max Weber, 'Der Sinn der 'Wertfreiheit' der soziologischen und ökonomischen Wissenschaften' in *Gesammelte Aufsätze zur Wissenschaftslehre*, Tübingen 1922, p. 479.

with people who were formed by a very different world view and society.

We may ask: How successful was Ernest Bader, coming into a new country with a few pounds in his pocket, first building up a thriving business in a very competitive field and then transforming this business into an outstanding experiment to give back to man the dignity which he lost in the disorder of industry? How successful was he in articulating a new vision of a human order and in realizing this vision in his own life?

How successful were the people of Wollaston in responding to the best in him and to the best in themselves? How successful were they in understanding what he really means, he whose way of life is different from theirs, who came as a missionary among people not too anxious to be converted? How quickly did they succeed in growing out of the heritage of their past? How well did they succeed in overcoming the anxieties, insecurities, and the cynicism which their working experience and life had created in them?

The reader may answer these questions for himself on the basis of the material presented to him. But he must realize that these are questions similar to the question: How well have I done, how successful was I in doing what I wanted to do, in being the kind of person I want to be? How well have I implemented decisions which I made ten years ago? Perhaps I would do it differently today, but after all, I have now the experience of the last ten years. What was achieved in Wollaston during the first twelve years of the Commonwealth was achieved without any previous experience, with a knowledge which was necessarily fragmentary, and without much help. Whoever feels that the questions raised above must be answered critically must therefore give meaning to his judgment by doing better himself. Or at least by saying how to do better.

It is as valid to say that what has been accomplished is miraculous as to find fault with it. But whatever our judgment may be we must not miss the essential point, namely that the Commonwealth came into being, that it exists and that it is developing.

The fact of its existence and of its potentialities of development is decisive. Already during the first twelve years of existence Wollaston has attracted people from all over the world. Not because they knew of its fame, not because they knew of its successes—but simply because they heard of its existence. Because somebody somewhere in the darkness of our age had the courage and the convictions to kindle a light. Because they heard a voice crying in the wilderness of the industrial jungle that man is more than a hand, a brain, an expert, a self-centred automat; that man is more than a role-playing animal performing certain functions. They heard and understood that if we really believe in the dignity of man, in that of God in everyman, then we must practise it in industry. In this lies the fundamental challenge of the Commonwealth to the world of today.

The Commonwealth shows us what we know deep down, that we have come to the end of an era and that we are witnessing the beginning of a new age. We are witnessing such fundamental changes in human consciousness that the past loses its significance as a guide to the future. This is why the question of the past success of the Commonwealth is irrelevant for any evaluation of its future. We stand at the dawn of a new epoch whose potentialities can only be assessed by an intuition of man's destiny—not by a knowledge of his past performance.

Seen in this light, not only the question as to the past success of the Commonwealth becomes incidental. But even the question as to the ultimate success of the Commonwealth takes on a new meaning. As Bernard Canter said so beautifully: 'there are sparks which kindle a fire even if they themselves go out.'[2] In a religious sense the Commonwealth is such a spark. Whether it will be a part of the flame of the new order depends on every one of us. It is a responsibility in which we are all involved.

The Commonwealth stands for an idea whose hour has come. And an idea whose hour has come is invincible. Individual sparks may go out. Battles may be lost. Whole cultures

[2] See *The Friend*, A Quaker Weekly Journal, Volume 120, No. 9, March 2, 1962. Bernard Canter said in an editorial on 'The Trial of the Six': 'Great fires have been lit from little candles that themselves were snuffed out.' *Ibid.*, p. 251.

may vanish, and God in His majesty may decide that He can do without the churches as presently constituted. But the fire of Truth will be triumphant. A new world view and a new social order is beginning to emerge—call it Christian, call it human, call it sane, call it non-violent. What really matters is our involvement in it. Our basic choice is whether we are actors or being acted upon, whether we attempt to heighten the darkness or herald the dawn of the new age, whether we are already dead without knowing it or whether we participate in shortening the agony of a dying world and bring to fruition the potential of the new age.

As far as industry is concerned, the Commonwealth stands at the gateway to the new social order.

Appendix
On Method

The methodology of social research depends upon the world view of which it is a part. The research project on which this book is based expresses an attempt to develop an integrative framework which will eventually encompass major dimensions of the social sciences and of theology. The basic framework of such an approach has, so far, only been elaborated in fragments, ('*Some Contributions of Dynamic Psychology to the Sociology of knowledge*' Transactions of the Fourth World Congress of Sociology, Milan and Stresa, September 1959 volume IV, 1959 pp. 67–83; and '*The Evolution of Human Consciousness and the Sociology of Knowledge,*' paper delivered at the Fifth World Congress of Sociology, Washington, September 1962, published in *Ideologie*, Soziologische Texte, edited by Kurt Lenk, Hermann Luchterhand Verlag, 2. Auflage 1964 pp. 297–317; '*The human problems of work*' and '*Religious consciousness and the social order*' unpublished.)

These papers define the ontological and epistemological presuppositions of this research project. Based on these presuppositions the concept of human universals has been developed and is being subject to experimental testing. The conceptual framework for the experimental research is centred on the problem of universal standards of mental health. Such standards express values which have variously been called 'democratic,' 'human,' and/or 'non-violent'. These standards have been conceptualized in different ways but their common characteristic is their focus of attention on man's inherent struggle for 'wholeness', for a balanced, integrative development of his various potentialities and purposes within a creative relationship to a broadly conceived human community.

The basic conceptual framework within which the validity and implications of such a concept of mental health are being tested conceives of man as existing in a social reality or as part of a social process in which cultural and broadly human forces interpenetrate. These forces crystallize in structures or patterns of value and power: personality structures on the one hand and social structures on the other hand. These two structures (and processes) are dynamically inter-related. They are defined in terms of a pattern of values and power relationships (or field of forces) which 'correspond' to criteria for mental health.

Attention is focused on those aspects of the dynamic interplay of personality and social processes and structures which are expressed in modes of consciousness of and participation in certain aspects of work and society. Both perception and participation are conceived in broad terms. Perception is understood as a process of selection of certain elements of 'objective reality', a term denoting all known aspects of a given phenomenon, not only those of which any particular person or group of persons may be conscious. Among the factors determining the selective process are (i) the degree and nature of projections and idealizations, (ii) the awareness of human universals (iii) the development of rational versus autistic ('wishful') thinking and (iv) the inter-relationship between these elements. The 'personality structure' conceived as interacting with the 'social structure' mediates this process. Perception may thus be considered a type of 'inner involvement' and participation a type of 'outer involvement.'

The research project concentrates on the examination of the following hypotheses:

(i) Modes and consciousness and perception of work and of the social process are interrelated with modes of participation in the corresponding aspects of the work and social processes in such a way that initial changes in one of these interrelated phenomena must be followed by changes in the other to lead to lasting modifications in personality and social structures and processes.

(ii) In order to be lasting, not only must changes take place interdependently in perception and participation, but there must also be interdependent modifications of perception and participation pertaining to different dimensions of the work and social processes. In particular

(a) there must be interrelated changes in the immediate work environment, in the organization of work and in the broader social processes.

(b) changes of each of these dimensions have equal significance in the sense that they affect different aspects of the personality which are dynamically interrelated and must, therefore, all be developed to achieve unity and wholeness.

(iii) Perception and participation in the immediate-concrete network of social relationships are of particular significance for an ethical involvement in the social process. They are interrelated with perception and participation of broader, organized aspects of social processes and structures such as the conception of society and corresponding political activities.

(iv) Differences in the rates of change of modes of consciousness and modes of participation as well as differences in rates of change of different dimensions of work and society express themselves in tensions, anxieties, tendencies toward lower degrees of differentiation and levels of integration.

To test these hypotheses an action-research design has been developed. Since such a design is unusual, a few words about the basic differences between the traditional approach and the approach on which this project is based may be helpful.

The fundamental principles on which action-research as understood here is based may be summed up in the following propositions:

(i) There is an objective universal truth. We can gain a partial understanding of this truth through categories which make it possible to grasp certain aspects of reality. These fundamental categories have universal as well as historically unique dimensions. They differ basically from the traditional categories now prevalent in the social sciences which belong to a mode of consciousness violating the unity of human existence and threatening the creative development of man. The traditional categories are based on falsely defined opposites, such as 'subjective' and objective'—'thought' and 'action' —'facts' and 'values', to mention only a few of the most fundamental categories underlying much of present-day social research. They are also based on a spurious conception of time, namely 'instantaneous clock-time' and an inadequate conception of space as linear-perspective space.

(ii) Action-research as understood here replaces opposites with polarities which form part of a synthetic view of life. Objectivity, for example, demands both 'distance' and 'involvement'; what 'is' exists not only in the realized potentialities of yesterday but also in the potentialities of today which may be realized in the future; all 'thought' has an action dimension and can best be verified through experimental action; 'the subjective' is a unique combination of objective elements. Time is not only 'clock time' but also '*durée*' in Bergson's sense and space does not only separate 'subject' and 'object' but unites also all Being.

(iii) Action-research tries to make its own value implications as explicit as possible and to achieve objectively through the greatest possible consciousness about values rather than through a false pretence of 'freedom' from value judgements. (See my article 'Max Weber's Postulates of "Freedom" from Value Judgements' in *The American Journal of Sociology*, July 1944). Ideally it uses a team of people with different personal values and different philosophies of life.

(iv) Action-research has a 'diagnostic' and a 'therapeutic' phase. In the diagnostic phase an attempt is made to understand the situation as it 'is', that means both in terms of realized and unrealized potentialities, of 'Being' or 'Becoming'. The therapeutic phase consists of change experiments made with a view to realizing as yet unrealized potentialities. Action-research thus makes explicit its fundamental values rather than unconsciously accepting existing values. (See: 'Action-research—A Scientific Approach?' *Philosophy of Science*, January 1955. See also 'Action-research and Industrial Relations' *Proceedings*. Second Annual Meeting, Industrial Relations Research Association, 1949.)

(v) 'Participant observation' and 'interview-conversations' are best suited for an action-research approach. They allow a mutual involvement and facilitate a holistic understanding of people as human beings. (See 'Getting Individuals to Give Information to the Outsider', *Journal of Social Issues*, vol. VIII No. 3, 1953.)

(vi) Sampling procedures are determined by both diagnostic and therapeutic requirements. From a diagnostic point of view ordinary sampling procedures are applicable. From a therapeutic point of view stratified samples including key people initiating change or being affected by change are necessary. We used two types of samples: (a) a random sample consisting of 42 people. If large numbers are involved interviews of the people in such a sample cannot go beyond a certain degree of intensity. Even if everybody selected were willing to give freely of his or her time, the amount of material collected would be so voluminous that it could not be interpreted unless unusual resources for research were available. Interviews of people in the random sample were, therefore, limited to one hour. (b) A quota sample consisting of 30 people. Each of these people participated in interview-conversations lasting from 10-20 hours (average about 10 hours). The quota sample was chosen with a view of combining the diagnostic and the therapeutic requirements. It gave a 'representative' cross-section of the 'universe' and included key people. (The random sample, for example, did not include anybody from the Board of Directors. But a knowledge of the attitudes and ideas of key people on the Board is essential if changes are to be undertaken.)

The validity of such a sample cannot be exclusively determined by the ordinary statistical procedures. It is based on the premise that essential features of a whole 'culture' or 'subculture' are reflected in the personality structure of the average or typical representative of the 'culture' or 'subculture'. The validity of the sample therefore depends not only upon a statistically adequate selection of the total number in the universe but also on the validity of the choice of an 'average typical' group. 10 per cent. must be considered a rule of thumb figure rather than a generally valid figure.

In June 1959, when this research project began, 207 people worked at Scott Bader. Of these 19 were excluded because they worked in the London office (4 people) or were representatives usually away from Wollaston (8 people) or because they were in special occupations (5 in the gardens, 2 in the house). Three people were excluded because no age data were available for them. The 'universe of people' consisted, therefore, of 185 people.

These people were divided in the following groups: (a) according to status following the designations actually used in the firm: workers, clerks, junior managers, technicians, managers, executives; (b) according to their main functions: people using primarily chemical reactors, mechanical tools and implements other than office equipment, clerks, people using chemical equipment in the laboratories, junior managers in the factory, junior and senior managers in the laboratory or office, executives. They were, furthermore, divided according to (c) sex, (d) age and (e) place of work.

The criteria for selection of any of the 185 people were as follows: (aa) from each of the main groups just mentioned at least 10 per cent. had to be selected. The actual selection of people followed near-random procedures similar to those used in a previous research project. (See *Towards A Democratic Work Process*. The Hormel—U.P.W.A. Experience, Harper, New York, 1953, 229 pp.). (bb) In addition to the representative selection of a minimum of 10 per cent. specific people were added because they had a key position from the point of view of change.

The combined quota sample may be summed up as follows:

QUOTA SAMPLE BY SEX

	n	QS	QS% / n
Females	27	4	15%
Males	158	26	16%
	185	30	16%

QUOTA SAMPLE BY AGE

Age group	n	QS	QS% / n
61–	4	1	25%
51–60	28	5	18%
41–50	28	3	11%
31–40	59	12	20%
21–30	48	7	15%
–20	18	2	11%
	185	30	16%

QUOTA SAMPLE BY WORK PLACE

	n	QS	QS% / n
Factory	109	15	14%
Laboratories	48	8	17%
Office	28	7	25%
	185	30	16%

QUOTA SAMPLE BY STATUS

	n	QS	QS% / n
Executives	7	4	57%
Managers	13	3	23%
Technicians	35	5	14%
Junior Managers	14	4	29%
Clerks	24	3	13%
Workers	92	11	12%
	185	30	16%

(vii) The interview-schedule which was used for the interview-conversations consisted of over 300 questions pertaining to the following aspects of life: (a) participation in different aspects of work, relationships to fellow workers and to various organizational aspects such as the company and the union, the experience and meaning of work; (b) work in the perspective of off-work activities, particularly leisure; (c) perception of society and politics; (d) meaning of life and consciousness of ultimate reality.

The method of interpreting the interview-conversations was as follows: First, each interview-conversation was studied with a view of understanding the person as a whole and to get an idea of the general configuration or pattern of his or her basic attitudes to the main areas just mentioned. This pattern was then diagrammed and the underlying dynamics was examined. This first step may be considered as an attempt 'to be' the person and to understand the forces affecting a person's 'becoming'.

The second step consisted in the interpretation of the answers of all 30 people to each of the key questions. Whereas in the first phase the meaning of the answers to all questions given by one and the same person were examined, we analysed in the second phase the responses of all 30 people to specific questions. Criteria for this analysis were 'all known' aspects of 'objective reality'. For key questions we indicated the major criteria and the reader can judge for himself whether the selection is adequate. This part of the analysis may be considered an attempt to locate a particular human being within a range of humanly possible 'beings'.

Data were 'fed back' to 5 groups of people, each consisting of about 10 people. Some members of these groups had taken part in interview—conversations, others not. These groups met over a period of about a year. The group discussions were of great help in throwing further light on the interpretations and results of our inquiry.

Note on comparison of the quota and the random sample

In addition to a representative cross-section, the quota sample includes, as already mentioned, people who had key positions with reference to problems of change. This sample is, therefore, bound to give a different perspective on the problems of work and community. These differences are well illustrated by the following comparative data:

In a study of participation based on the random sample Roger Hadley used four criteria for participation: (1) speaking at General Meetings, (2) obtaining information from representatives, (3) standing for election, (4) initiating proposals through one of the participative organs. Four categories of participation were developed: high, moderate, low and non-participation. About a fifth of the managers, technicians, junior managers and clerical workers were either high or moderate participants; all the factory workers were low participants or non-participants.

In a study of high participants based on all available information about criteria (1) (3) and (4) for *all* members of the firm, twelve high participants were identified: 4 managers, 5 technicians, 2 junior managers and 1 clerical worker. No factory workers were among the high participants. There were three high participants in the random sample compared with eight in the quota sample. If the high participants had been distributed proportionately in both samples, two would have been found in either case. The greater representation of high participants in the quota sample was also expressed in the greater representation of office holders in the Commonwealth. Two members of the random sample had been Commonwealth Directors compared with four members of the quota sample. Seven members of the random sample had served on the Community Council compared with eleven in the quota sample. (See p. 91.)

The implication of these differences in composition of the two samples is that the quota sample considerably over-represents the more active and informed section of the employees and under-represents the less involved and less well-informed. This is illustrated by the following comparisons:

Knowledge of the powers and functions of the Community Council. In the random sample separate questions were asked on the functions and powers of the Community Council. Interviewees were divided into three categories: (1) working knowledge—those with a sufficient understanding of the main powers and functions of the Council to use it for the purposes intended in the Constitution; (2) partial knowledge—those with knowledge of at least one of the more important powers of functions but ignorant of others, (3) little or no knowledge—those with knowledge of minor powers or functions only, or no knowledge at all. The percentages in each category in the random sample were (1) working knowledge, 26%, (2) partial knowledge, 36%, (3) little or no knowledge, 38%. (As regards the quota sample, see p. 99.)

Knowledge of the powers and functions of the General Council. Similar categories of knowledge to those used for the Community Council were used in the analysis of the replies to the questions on the General Council. The percentage in each category was (1) working knowledge, 12%, (2) partial knowledge, 62%, (3) little or no knowledge, 26%. (As regards the quota sample see p. 103.)

Departmental Committees. From 1951–1959 there is little firm evidence of the frequency of Departmental Committee meetings or on the topics discussed. According to members who had been with the firm during this period the Committees ceased to function within one or two years after the inception of the Commonwealth. In most departments they were not even elected to choose the departmental representative on the General Council, the representative being chosen instead by the direct vote of all those in the department. The General Council expressed repeatedly concern at the inactivity of the Departmental Committees and on two occasions made attempts to revive them. (See General Council Minutes, 14th Meeting, September, 1953, and 43rd Meeting, May, 1958.) However, when the field work began at the end of 1959 the Committees were still inactive. (See p. 105.)

Attitudes to the transfer of the Founders' Shares to the Commonwealth. 21% of the people in the random sample thought the Founders' Shares should be transferred to the Commonwealth immediately. A further 31% thought they should be transferred ultimately but not immediately. 19% were opposed to their transfer at any time. 10% could not make up their minds on the issue and the remaining 19% had no idea to what the question referred. (See p. 140 for quota sample.)

Index of Names

Index